LOOKING AT ASKAM

1850s - 1930s

KEVIN ALEXANDER

I DEDICATE THIS BOOK TO THE MEMORY OF ASKAM FOLK THAT HAVE BEEN AND GONE, FOLK WE FONDLY REMEMBER AND THOSE THAT ARE SADLY FORGOTTEN.

Published by Kevin Alexander

Copyright © 2025 by Kevin Alexander

All rights reserved. No part of this book may be reproduced in any manner whatsoever without written permission except in the case of brief quotations embodied in critical articles and reviews.

Printed by www.Ingramspark.com

A catalogue record for this book is available from the British Library.

Proofread by the Author; Apologies for any mistakes!

Queries to: alexanderbook21@gmail.com

Front cover; A view of Askam from the Golf Course. (Cumbria Archive Centre, Barrow. 3531, BDB 86/1/871. Sankey Collection)

CONTENTS

INTRODUCTION	PAGE 1
THE BEFORE	2
THE BIRTH OF ASKAM	8
BUILDING ASKAM	13
LOTS ROAD	33
1871 CENSUS – ASKAMS FIRST SETTLERS	42
ASKAM RAILWAY STATION	56
ASKAM CO-OP	69
THE WATER FOUNTAIN	74
BRICK MAKING	79
HOW BLACKS POND GOT ITS NAME	97
THE RUGBY	100
THE IRONWORKS	132
THE PIER	191
THE MINES	202
SCHOOL	232
ASKAM BAND	241
PUBS, HOTELS AND OFF-LICENCES	247
DIRECTORIES	258
ACKNOWLEDGEMENTS & BIBLIOGRAPHY	298

INTRODUCTION

I have been interested in the history of Askam from an early age, I remember my teacher Mrs. Warwick, of Askam School once showed us maps and plans and explained the history to us. We did a walk around the village looking at the buildings and compared them with old photographs and maps, we also walked on the shore to look at the Red Hills, Blacks Pond, the Pier and Slaggy; all playgrounds for me and my mates!

I would say that sparked my interest in local history, learning about the origins of the places where I spent a lot of my time, the place where I was brought up, or even "Dragged up off the shore," that was the saying I used to hear once over about Askam folk. I had always known my family had lived here since the village was first begun, many generations of Alexander's choosing Askam as their home and place of work, and with that we have a shared history with other Askam families. Our families came here to make a life for themselves living on the sandy windswept marsh, in small, mainly red brick terraced houses and we were predominantly working-class folk earning a wage in the mines or the ironworks.

It's this shared history of our community that I would like to bring to life in this book. I would like the reader with old ties to the village the chance to at least find some mention of their family amongst these following pages, and on the other hand I would like the reader, whatever their connection to Askam, be it new or old, the opportunity to bring answers to questions, possibly debunk a few myths here and there, or even simply to bring to light things you never knew about Askam. Using original newspaper articles from the 1850s to the 1930s. (I might dip into later decades here and there too, but I'll try to keep within the time frame).

I hope to offer the reader with as much information as was supplied at the time as opposed to just a brief mention of an event like you see in a more typical history book. However, I have tried to supply many interesting articles about a chosen subject, a bit of meat on the bone if you will! I of course cannot list everything, and I have selected as many as I deemed sufficient to that subject, as in all honesty many of the subjects covered could have separate books written about them too with all the content I have come across!

Overall, I hope the reader finds the book an interesting read and something to pick up in the future as a reference book to Askam's early history.

Kindest regards, Kevin Alexander.

THE BEFORE

Well, let's imagine what the spot we now call Askam-in-Furness looked like, once over in ancient times it would have been under water at high tide and then a sandy shore when it ebbed. A larger sized Duddon Estuary existed than what we see today, in fact the very name of the impressive landmass we call Dunnerholme rock suggests it was once surrounded by the sea, its name can be traced back to that of Scandinavian origin, meaning Dunner Island, or even Duddon Island, Dunner being the ancient word for the Duddon.

And so, over the years with the help of the westerly winds and the tides, huge deposits of golden sand have built up along this stretch of the Furness Peninsula, creating dunes and marsh land beneath the small farming village of Ireleth, a process that is continuing down on the shore to this day.

This created what became known as Ireleth Marsh, this large extensive area of new land had formed in the Duddon Estuary, in a part owned by the Duke of Buccleuch, (they still own below the high-water mark today). This new land had been used as a common by the Ireleth farmers, but realising this the Duke started to enclose and reclaim it, he allotted parcels of this land known as allotments to them as tenants, and quite often would sell on the land soon after, these were effectively large fields, pretty much the same as the flat marshy fields between here and Kirkby today. These allotments contained many acres of open ground as opposed to the modern namesake full of greenhouses and sheds and plastic that you might be imagining.

In 1831, the very last piece of this land was reclaimed, allotted, and subsequently sold on to defray the cost of hedging and fencing it to Ireleth landowner, Jane Towers. This area of the marsh was sold on again to another Ireleth landowner/farmer, John Chapman and divided into two lots, giving rise to the name of this land as Chapman's Lot, or even, the Lots, as it is known today. The Duke of Buccleuch however kept hold of some land which became part of his Marsh Grange Estate, this land was at the northern end of the turnpike road also known as the Sands Road, Millom Road, Marsh Road, Marsh Lane and the one it kept; Duddon Road.

Ireleth Marsh picked up yet another name; Ireleth Gates, this was because the Furness Railway opened its line from Kirkby to Barrow in 1846, dissecting the fields of the marsh and Duddon Road. Bringing the need for railway gates at the crossing; hence Ireleth Gates. Another road known as Drain Road or Sandy Lane connected here at the crossing and led in a southernly direction towards Chapmans Lot, at the time it was described as a "Narrow, dirty lane" where the fine main road we now know as Duke Street was constructed in 1876.

So, by the 1850s the area was known by all three names, Ireleth Marsh, Ireleth Gates and Chapman's Lot, and all the land was now in agricultural use, even though the Lots is described as a Rabbit warren in the 1850s ordnance survey map, farmer John Chapman was also growing many crops there including potatoes, wheat and oats.

My lad Doug walking amongst the marshland towards Kirkby, showing what we can imagine Ireleth Marsh was like before being developed. (Kevin Alexander Collection).

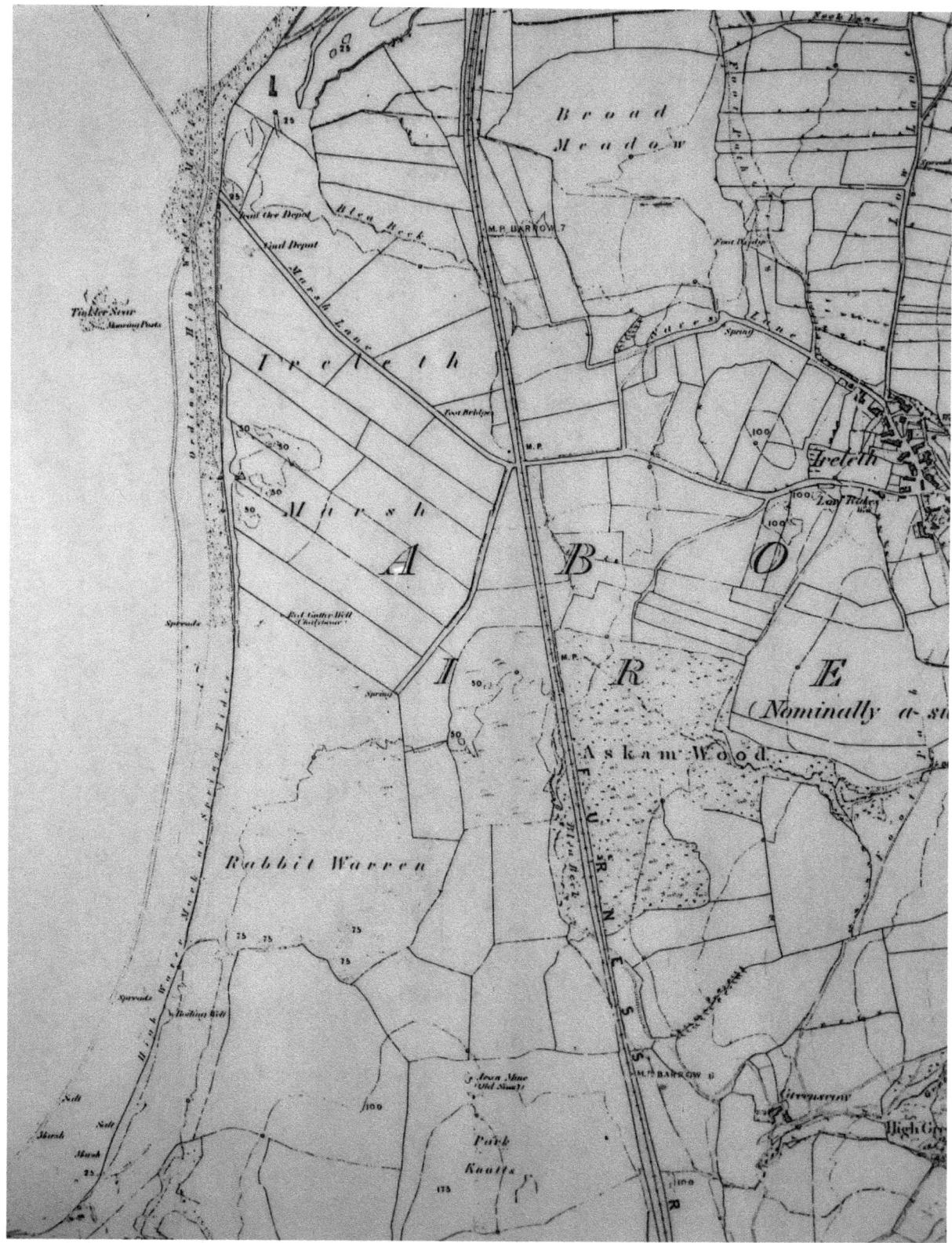

Ordnance survey map of the 1850s showing Ireleth Marsh as farmland. (Courtesy of Janice Cumming, Askam History Club)

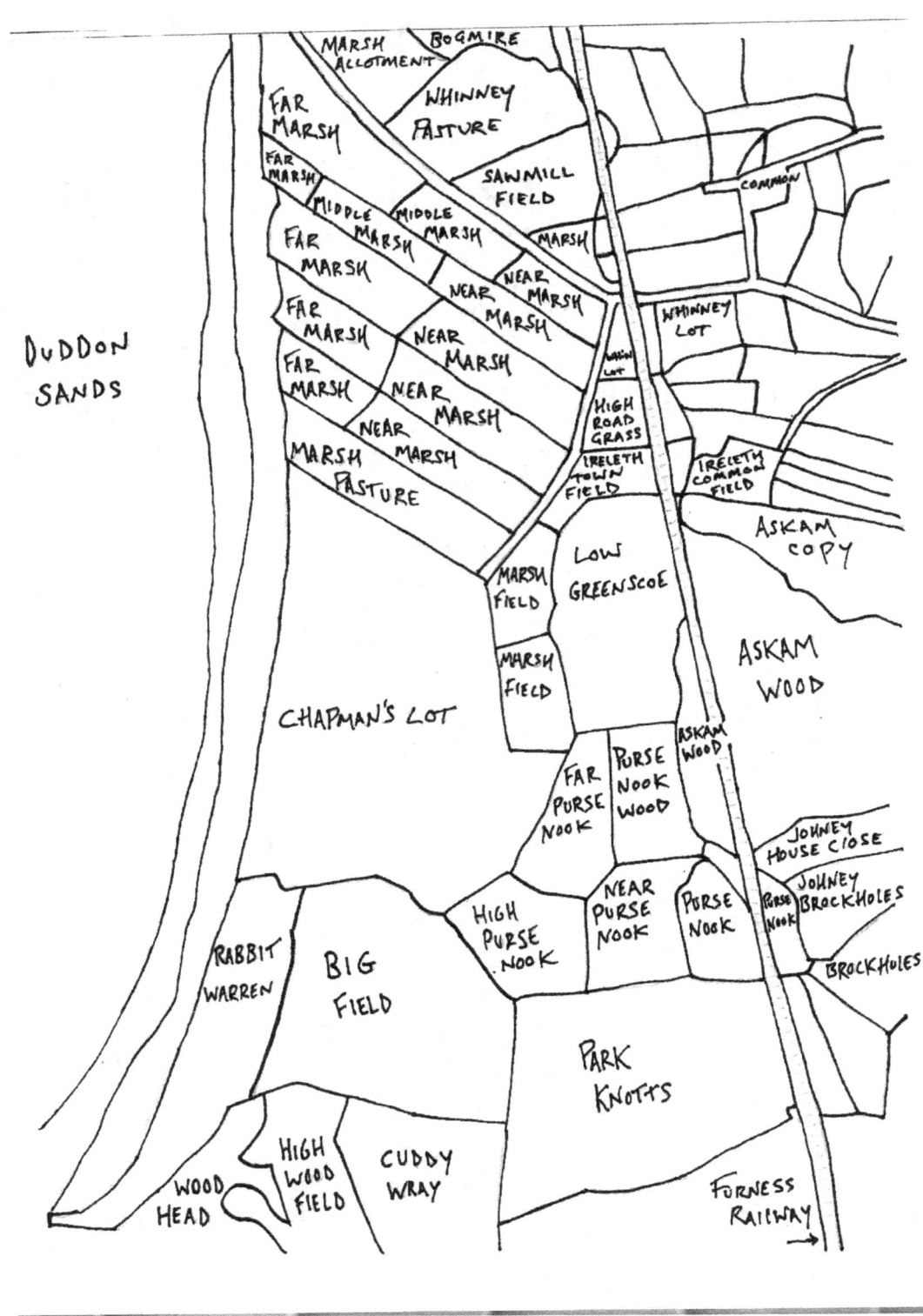

Ireleth Marsh field names. (Drawn and compiled by the author)

Whin or Whinney is the old local dialect for Gorse, along with Cuddy Wray (Donkey Corner) and Brockholes (Badger holes).

Barrow Herald & Furness Advertiser. 8th August 1863.

POTATOES AND OATS FOR SALE.

TO BE SOLD BY AUCTION,

Upon the premises, on SATURDAY, August 15th, 1863, at five o'clock in the evening,

FIVE Acres of excellent POTATOES, growing in an inclosure known by the name of "Chapman's Lot," situate near Ireleth, belonging to J. R. Chapman; also three acres of OATS, growing in an inclosure called Road Grass, belonging to Mr. John Kitchen.

403   JOHN SHAW, Auctioneer.

Barrow Herald. 19th September 1863.

GAME CASE. – James Gaskell was brought up charged with having, on the 13th inst., nets in his possession for entrapping game. – Mr. Park appeared for the prosecution, and Mr. Thompson for the defence. – Police-constable Broomhead stated that in consequence of information he received last Saturday night, he watched a certain place in Ireleth, until about one o'clock on Sunday morning, when defendant and two other men came, and he saw part of a net hanging from defendant's pocket, and he refused to turn it out.

Witness then took it out, and also a second one.

In the other side pocket, he had three nets and a snare. They appeared as if they had come out of wet grass. Wilson (one of the other men) said he claimed them. They had two dogs with them. They would be 500 yards from their homes. - This being the case, Mr. Thompson said he would have to ask the bench to put a construction on the second section of the act. There had been two cases decided, which had ended in favour of the applicants. It was plain and evident that the defendant had the nets upon him; but it was not proved what the nets had been used for.

His case was that Wilson had a game certificate, and it was not likely that a man who paid his duty regularly would go out a poaching, and that Wilson and the other men had been to Ireleth Marsh to watch for someone who had been in the habit of netting, and the nets now produced were what Wilson had found on a previous night, and had put them into a hole, and on the present occasion handed them over to Gaskell.

The case, he said, might be summed up in half a dozen words. It was, that a man of the name of Chapman, and Wilson had had a very serious quarrel about the game, and he had given the information to revenge himself. -Robert Wilson, of Ireleth, produced his game certificate, and stated that he farmed the rabbits on the allotments on Ireleth Marsh belonging to Mr. Hodgeson. Was out on the 13th with Gaskell and Hornby on the marsh. Was there about half-past four on Wednesday morning and found the nets produced. Put them into a rabbit hole out of sight. Took them out that night and gave them to Gaskell. Claimed the nets when Broomhead took them.

Gaskell had helped him to watch before. Neither a snare nor nets were set that night. Gaskell had his sheep dog with him. -Robert Hornby, of Ireleth, said he went with Wilson and Gaskell to the lots which Wilson farms. He fully corroborated the evidence given by Wilson. – The magistrates retired for a short time, and on returning the chairman said they were not quite satisfied, and would like to hear some more evidence. - James Chapman and Thomas Edmondson said they saw the three men together on the night in question. -Mr. Thompson submitted that the bench could not commit these men upon the evidence of the policeman.

They had also try the fact whether the men had used the nets for the purpose of illegally taking game- the act said "shall have used," but there was no evidence whatsoever to show that the nets had been used. -Fined £2, including costs. – Wilson and Hornby were charged with the same offence, and Mr. Thompson urged that as they had already convicted one man for the offence, they could not charge these two men with the same offence. The correct course, if he might suggest, would have been to have summoned them as principals. -The case was then proceeded with, and the same evidence was given as in the previous one.

Mr. Thompson raised two points. First, that in as much as Gaskell had been convicted of using the nets, separate summonses and separate information's having being taken out, the present defendant, Wilson, cannot be convicted on the present information for using the nets for the purpose of illegally taking game. Second point was, he submitted that the evidence was not sufficient in law – to entitle the magistrates to convict. He concluded by urging that as nothing had been found upon Wilson, it threw a considerable doubt upon the case, and he was fairly entitled to the benefit of that doubt.

The bench then retired, and on their return the chairman said they had decided to convict in the sum of £2, including costs. – In the case of Hornby, Mr. Thompson made an appeal to the bench, stating that they had already had two convictions, they might probably consider that the ends of justice were met, and would either dismiss the other case or mitigate the penalty considerably. -The chairman, in reply, said that as Mr. Thompson had conducted the cases so fairly towards the bench, and also towards his clients, that they decided to dismiss the other information.

THE BIRTH OF ASKAM

So, by the 1850s the area was known by the three names of Ireleth Marsh, Ireleth Gates and Chapman's Lot, so where did the name Askam come from? And who decided on the name for the settlement in the first place, or even the correct spelling?

The name Askam comes from a large woodland nearby, which was considerably a lot larger back then compared to now and was situated to the south of Ireleth Village and extended in a westerly direction towards the Lots. An amusing fact is that the wood was the northern most part of the Greenscoe Estate, which means technically Askam was once upon a time in Greenscoe as opposed to it being the other way around like it is now.

The name Askam itself is thought to be that of old English and is thought to mean the place of the ash trees, which makes sense with it being a woodland. The spelling has varied over the years which was quite common when a writer would make their own interpretation of the spelling, Askam, Ascombe and Askham being the main variations. You see in the local dialect when spoken, the "H" is dropped or rather in Queens English, letters are added to the original local words! The local dialect spelling "ASKAM" prevailed in this occasion over Queens English, which is quite rare, although some do interpret it with the "H" still and no doubt this will continue forever more. Examples where Queens English prevailed over local dialect include; Ulverston (Oosten), Barrow (Barra) and Roanhead (Ronhead).

We can credit one man and one man alone for the naming of the settlement as that of Askam, no doubt he chose the name after Askam Wood with it being the prominent large landmark close by, and probably as it sounded better than keeping a previous owners name (Chapman's Lot). His name was Edward Thomas Wakefield, an Irish barrister and landowner who lived most of his life in London and in the south of England.

On the 1st April 1865, Ireleth farmer and landowner Joseph Sharpe paid the Chapman family £1776. 8/7d 1/2p. (Roughley £186,917.04 in 2024 prices) for Chapman's Lot which was two parcels of land or allotments. Wakefield then paid £800 (£84,196.87) to Joseph Sharpe for the southernmost lot containing 26 acres, this marked the birth of Askam-in-Furness. For Wakefield had laid out a plan to build a town of his own design of that name. The town was to have a large square in its centre that was to be known as Wakefield Square containing a church and a covered market. Several streets were to surround the square, these were to be called Furness Place, Victoria Street, Albert Street, Florence Place, Stafford Street and Duddon Street, and the area containing the sand dunes was to be a large public park overlooked by Duddon Terrace containing the largest houses with great views of the Duddon sands. The town was also to have a school and to the south, land was reserved for future building.

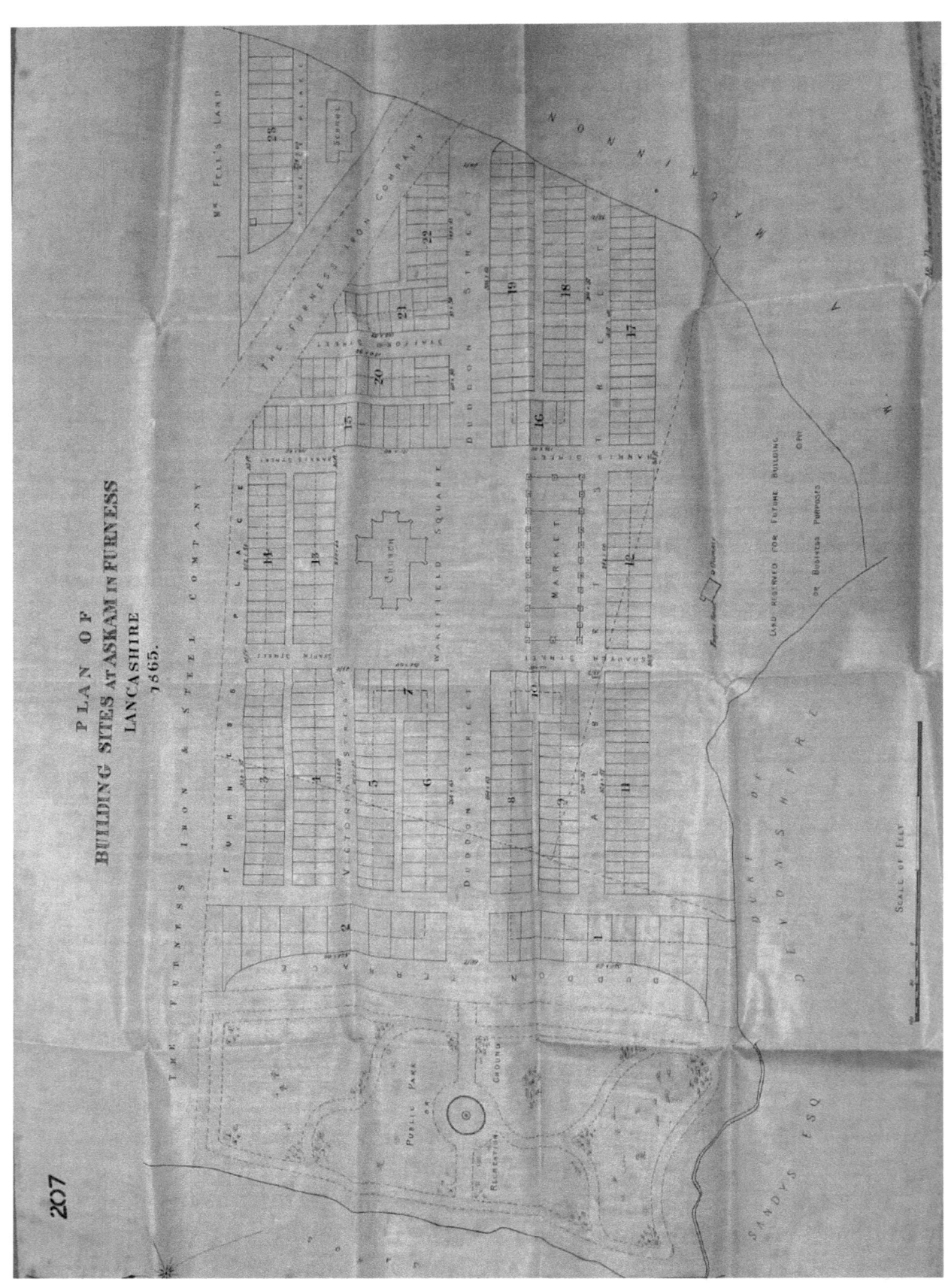

Plan of Edward Wakefield's town. (Cumbria Archive centre, Barrow BDBUC 40/3/16)

Barrow Herald, 12th August 1865.

Advertisement relating to the building plots on Wakefield's land as to his Plan of Askam-in-Furness (The Lots.)

TO BE SOLD BY PRIVATE TREATY,

A Number of very eligible BUILDING LOTS, portions of the surplus Land adjoining the Works of the Furness Iron and Steel Company, at Ireleth, in the county of Lancaster.

The above Lots offer every advantage to purchasers, the Site being an excellent one, in immediate proximity to the Works now erecting for the Iron and Steel Company, where the demand for Dwellinghouses for the reception of the Employes at the Works, and at the neighbouring Mines of Askham, Park, and Roanhead is practically unlimited.

Material advantages are offered to purchasers in reference to the conveyance of materials, and in the supply of Bricks, Lime, &c., at cost price, at the purchasers' option.

Plans of the premises and conditions of sale are deposited at the Office of S. H. Jackson, Esq., Solicitor, Brook Street, Ulverston, who is authorised to sell; and particulars of the Lots may be had, and Plans seen on application to Mr. Millar, at the Furness Iron and Steel Company's Works, Ireleth, or to Mr. William Gawith, Shipping Agent, Barrow.

Ulverston, July 18th, 1865.

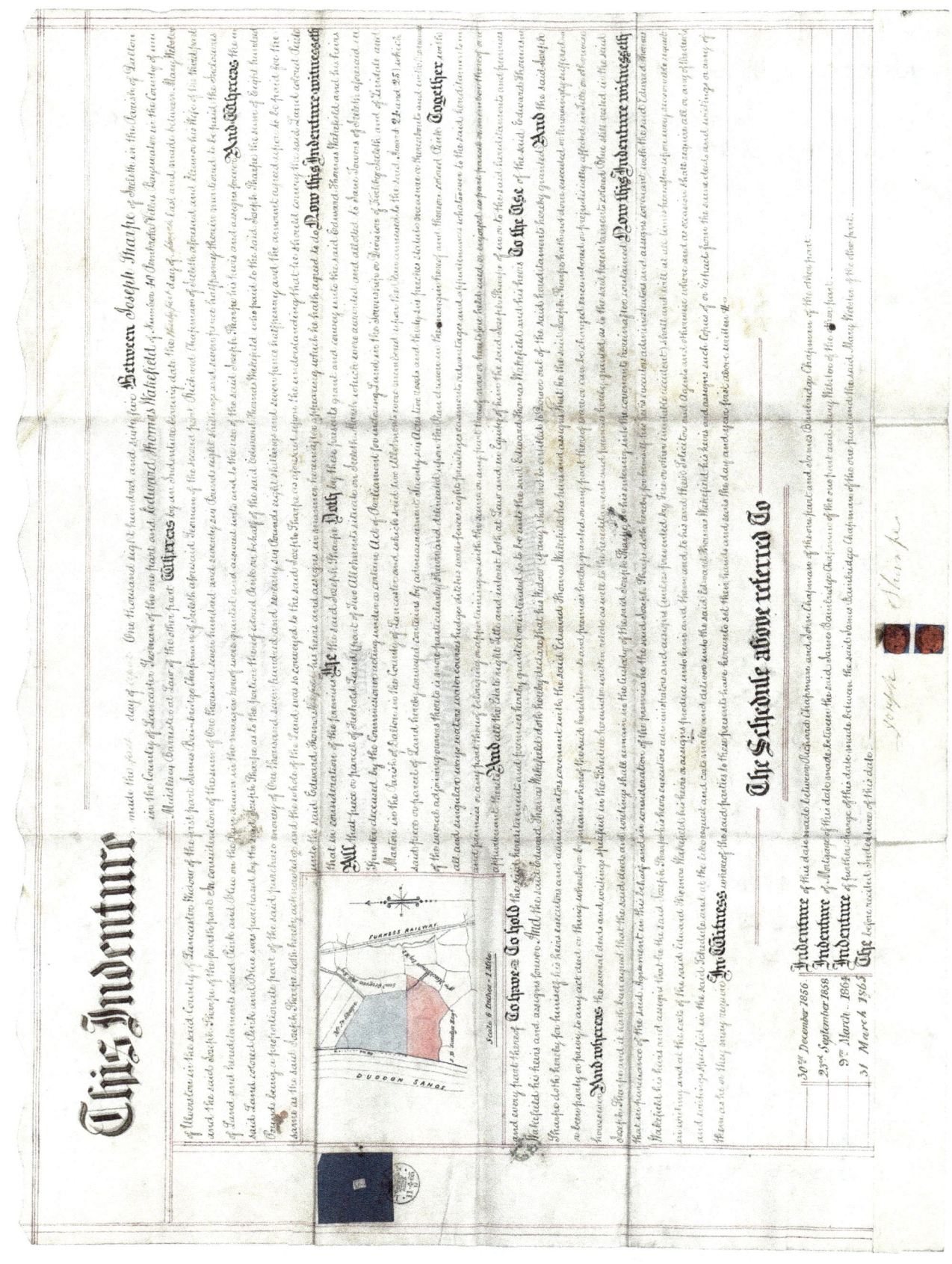

Askam's birth certificate! (Copy of Deed, Kevin Alexander collection)

Wakefield had confidence in his own town developing due the fact that on his newly bought land contained a known deposit of iron ore which had been discovered in 1863. Also, further to the south bordering his land the well-established mines of Park (1850) and Roanhead (1849) were already producing good quality ore, along with the extensive mines in the Dalton and Lindal areas. This undoubtedly spurred him and his associates to form the Furness Iron and Steel Company and invest and build an ironworks in the northern most part of Chapman's Lot to process this readily available resource.

So, with the sale of Chapman's Lot and the announcement of the building of the blast furnaces in April 1865, this created a boom in building, with the Ireleth land owners selling off plots of land for the building of cottages on their Ireleth Marsh fields. firstly, this was by Joseph Sharpe in May 1865 at his land to the north of the Ironworks site (where Sharp Street and Steel Street are situated) and then by Wakefield himself up on the Lots in July 1865. Streets and houses started popping up all over the spot after this. however, before any of that some houses already existed upon the marsh, in fact they can claim to be Askam's first and oldest buildings. Four cottages were built in 1855 and rented out by the Duke of Buccleuch on the 18th April 1855 to house agricultural workers on the marsh, they were; Addison Coward, Matthew Hunter, John Towers and Edward Walker being the first residents at Marsh Cottages, which later became Marsh Farm, these families could rightly claim to be the first to live in what we now call Askam.

Marsh Cottages now Marsh Farm. (Courtesy of Mark MacLean)

BUILDING ASKAM

BUILDING LAND AT IRELETH FOR SALE.

TO BE SOLD BY PRIVATE TREATY, A CLOSE OF LAND, in Building Sites, adjoining the site of the Blast Furnaces, now in course of erection on Ireleth Marsh; also adjoining to the sea shore, and to the road leading from the Furnaces and Askham mines to Ireleth.

This property is in the immediate vicinity of the projected Junction of the Whitehaven and Furness Railways, and affords the best sites in the neighbourhood for the erection of houses and shops, to meet the requirements of the present and prospective inhabitants. The land contains clay for building purposes.

Plans of the land may be seen, and all information obtained, at the residences of Mr. Sharpe, Ireleth; Mr. J. Threlfall, Market Street, Ulverstone; Mr. James Threlfall, Duke Street, Barrow; the Surveyor, W. Settle; or at the offices of Messrs. Woodburne and Poole, Ulverston and Barrow.

Ulverston, May 27th, 1865.

Barrow Herald, 12th August 1865.

Advertisement for the sale of Joseph Sharpe's land. (Marsh pasture on the field map and where Sharp Street and Steel Street are situated now.) The Railway bridge crossing the Duddon of course never happened.

As previously mentioned, a building boom began where a kind of a sandy desert once existed with streets being cut and bricks being tipped in all directions as the Ireleth landowners chose to profit from the ironworks development. Along with Wakefield on the Lots and Sharpe were Messrs. Ashworth and Robinson, Robert Ashburner, John Kitchen, Mr. Todd-Newcombe and John Chapman.

Individual builders bought plots of land and began building rows of red brick terraces to house the workers of the ironworks and the mines. These rows tended to be known by the builder's names at the time like Ashworth Row, King's Row, Huddleston Row (Furnace Place 1- 15) and Dutton Terrace. Joseph Threlfall of Ulverston and Benjamin Fish of Barrow did a fair amount of building along with Robert Banks who did a lot of building in Sharp and Steel Street and his houses were then leased by the iron company.

Street names that are unrecognizable to us like Madeley Street and Newcombe Street once existed. More unrecognizable named streets were further planned to be built to the north of the ironworks, these included a King Street, Ashburner Street and a Clipran Street. Also, a large housing estate was planned on land from John Street to Duddon Road by Builder Nicholas Mandall.

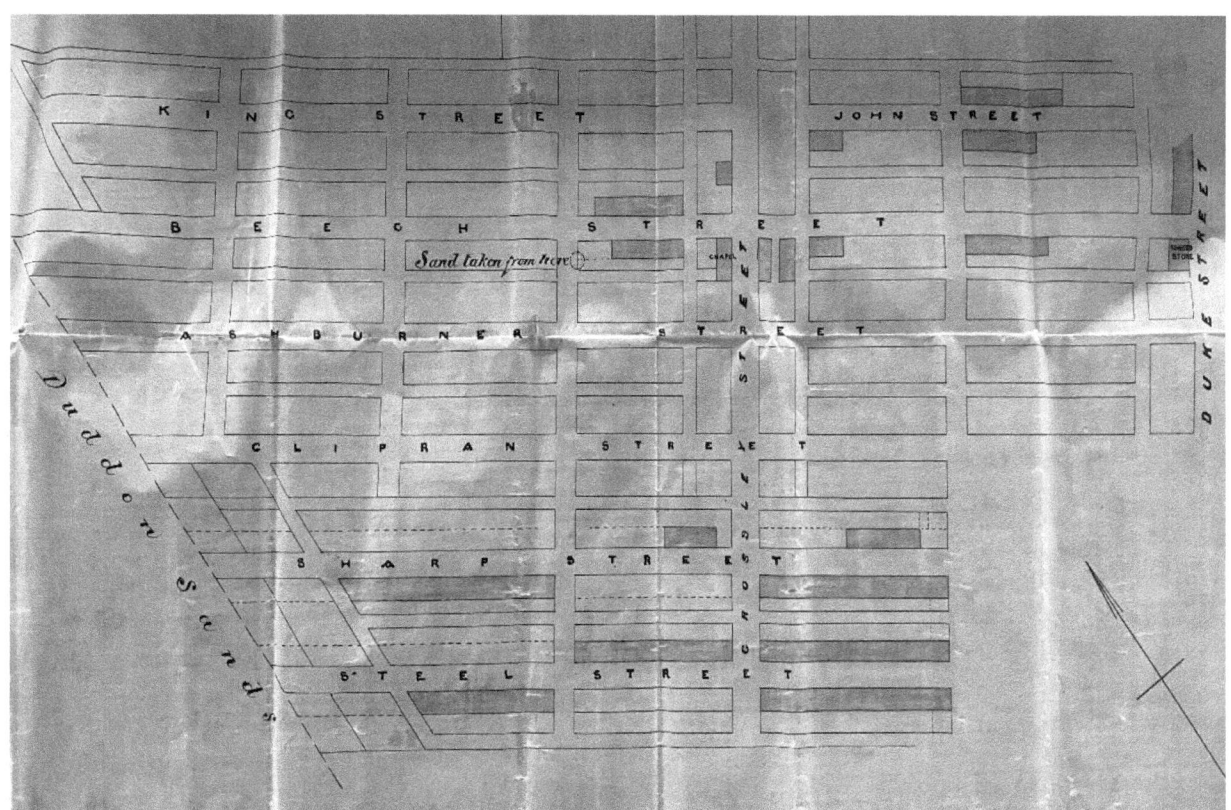

(Cumbria Archive Centre, Barrow, BDBUC 40/3/14)

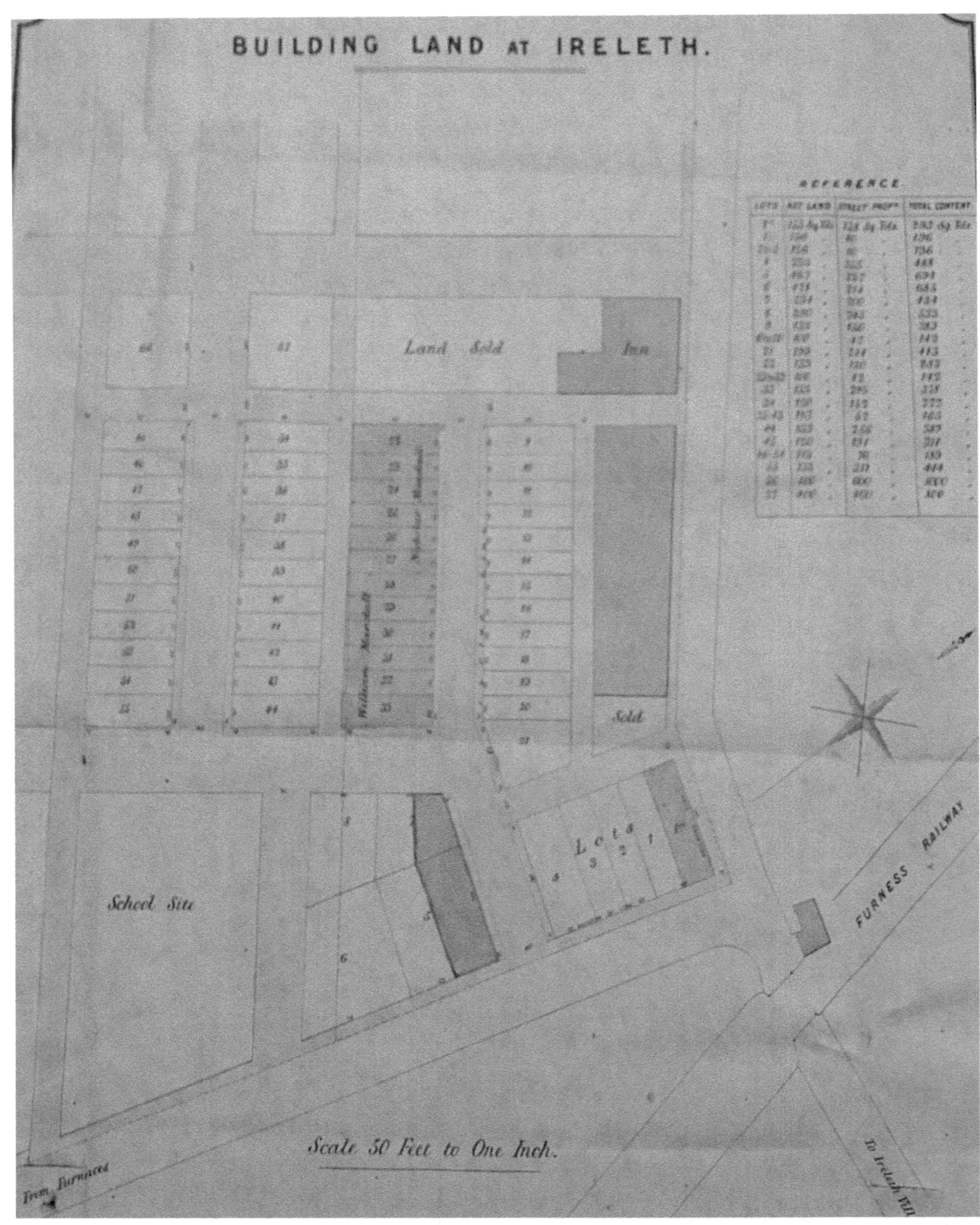

A plan showing part of the Mandall Estate, with William and Nicholas Mandall named and showing the buildings already built in grey. (Courtesy of Steve Alexander.)

Ulverston Mirror, 20th September 1873.

TO BE SOLD BY PRIVATE PREATY,

Two Shops and Dwelling HOUSES, nearly completed, situate between the Railway Station, and the Iron Works at Askam. Also Two SHOPS and Seven COTTAGES, in Stafford-street, Askam; and Four COTTAGES in Ashworth Field.

The above are in excellent situations, and well deserving attention.—Apply to NICHOLAS MANDALL, Builder, Askam.

Barrow Herald, 27th July 1889.

ACCIDENT.—An unfortunate accident befel a little girl named Standing, who resides with her parents in Sharp-street, on Thursday evening last. The girl, who is only eight years of age, was playing, with others, about some shops which are being erected. Hearing something overhead, as they were under the scaffolding, they looked up, and almost immediately a quantity of mortar fell on the girl's face. The pain caused by the hot lime in her eyes caused her to scream loudly. Besides others, Mr. J. K. Butcher came to her assistance. That gentleman, who is an Ambulance man, bound up her face, and took her to Dr. Challinor's surgery, where she was at once attended to. On Dr. Challinor's advice, she was, however, on Friday morning taken to the Eye Infirmary at Manchester, as the injury to the eye is very serious.

Ulverston Mirror, 6th August 1870.

IRELETH.

THE NUISANCES OF THE DISTRICT.—The nuisance authority—that is to say the Board of Guardians—are taking steps to improve the drainage of Ireleth Marsh. There are about three hundred houses built upon the marsh, none of which have hitherto been sewered, and with the exception of one street, there is no water supply in the Low Marsh. The guardians have already served notices on the occupiers and owners to sewer and provide other necessary accommodation.

Steel Street, looking towards the Shore. (Cumbria Archive Centre, Barrow. Album 12. 2021_2318. Sankey Collection)

Soulby's Ulverston Advertiser, 7th October 1875.

DALTON LOCAL BOARD MEETING.

The Rev. J Padley said he did not notice any reference in the report to Sandy Lane, (Duke Street) Askam, and he considered the Board ought to pass some resolution to put it in temporary repair.

Mr. Crossley thought the Board was bound to do so. They had broken up that street, which was as yet private property, having previously given notice; but they had not left the lane in so good a state as when the work was begun, and its condition now was very bad indeed. He had left a shoe in it on Saturday, and many other persons had suffered much inconvenience. He was told by a shopkeeper whose business had been seriously interfered with on account of the state of the lane.

Mr. Mandall enquired if the notices had been properly served, and the clerk replied that they had.

Mr. Askew moved that the report be adopted as read. He believed Sandy Lane was referred to in the Surveyor's report, and as Sandy Lane was private property, it would have to be put in proper order by the owners, or the Board would have to do so and charge them.

Mr. Crossley proposed that the Board see that Sandy Lane be put into the same condition it was in before it was interfered with for drainage purposes.

The Surveyor believed the contractors would have to do that.

Mr. Crossley strongly urged that the lane should be at once put in order, and pointed out at some length the great inconvenience arising from its remaining in its present state. He thought the contractors could hardly be expected to leave the road in quite so good a position as when they began the work there. As it was the road was in passable, and the shopkeepers had suffered, and he held that the Board should have the road repaired immediately.

Mr. Postlethwaite seconded the motion, and told of the difficulty many children had in attending school in consequence of the bad state of Sandy Lane.

The Rev. J Padley spoke as to the state of the lane before the drainage works were started, and as its present disgraceful condition, and said there was some talk of legal proceedings being taken against the Board if the lane was not attended to.

Mr. Hosking also spoke to the disgraceful state of the lane.

The Chairman thought the contractors should be written to.

Mr. Crossley was in favour of immediate action being taken, and suggested the carting of slag on the road, which might be put on very cheaply.

Mr. Askew said the action of the Board in this matter would be regarded as a precedent; and did not see that they had a right to put Sandy Lane into a better condition than they found it. He had been in that lane some time before the drainage works were commenced, and it was then in very bad state; but he would not object to the Board doing some little work at the lane, though he held the contractors were responsible to put it in as good order as they found it.

Mr. Mandall asked the members of the Board to go and see it, and said that a gentleman would give any member a glass of wine and dinner, who would go through the lane. (Laughter.) In taking a cart of coals along it, the stuff had gone through the bottom of the cart and mixed with the coals.

Mr. Crossley said the contractor had made the road level, but the top was of clay, whereas the top was previously of slag, 200 or 300 carts having being put on. He suggested that the Board have the requisite work done, and leave the question of the contractor's responsibility to be settled afterwards.

The Surveyor read that portion of the specifications bearing on the question, and the Clerk observed that the sewer constructed in Sandy Lane was for more than that street. It was agreed that the lane should be attended to, and notice given to the contractors.

It appears that Dalton Local Board took steps soon after this to make up the road. A Dalton Local Board Letter dated 7th February 1876 mentions "the new road now in the course of construction, called Duke Street at Askam," implies to me they decided to adopt the lane and improve it with it being the main thoroughfare through the settlement.

It seems there had been an ongoing theme in Askam with regards to the streets being made up and sewers built. The builders of the houses and shops on the whole tended not to bother at all in constructing them and the original landowners didn't think it was their responsibility either. And so the Dalton Local Board seemed to take up the responsibility themselves in the end. Although I must stress that the council didn't make up and adopt all the roads, as even to this day we still have many that are not finished and there doesn't seem to be any plans in the line for them to be finished any time soon.

One street that will never be finished and needs a mention is Crossley Street, a unique street in the fact that that it is broken up in three parts and scattered right across the village from Steel Street to Duddon Road and would have been roughly the same size as Duke Street in length if finished, it has a Rugby pitch in the middle and a mix of houses and open ground where a road surface would/should be. The reason for this was that the development of Askam was directly affected by the fortunes of the ironworks and when the ironworks was started there was the building boom with the builders laying out their planned streets and houses, and then when it wasn't doing so well the investment and building stopped. The land where Crossley Street was planned was subsequently sold on without any intention to carry on the street and by the 1930s it was known that the ironworks would never fire its furnaces again and Askam altogether was left in an unfinished state with open ground where the houses were once intended. Washing posts and pens took up much of this space with the odd bungalow appearing here and there. Building basically didn't start up in large scale again until the 1990s.

Sharp Street, looking West. (Cumbria Archive Centre, Barrow. BDB 86/1/384. Sankey Collection)

Duke street, looking towards the Ironworks. (Cumbria Archive Centre, Barrow. BDB 86/1/1154 Sankey Collection)

Duke Street, at Beach Street Juntion. (Kevin Alexander Collection)

View from the slagbank "slaggy" looking onto Duke Street. (Kevin Alexander Collection)

Another view looking across Askam to the hills. (Kevin Alexander Collection)

Duddon Road, Duke Street corner. (Cumbria Archive Centre, Barrow. 2146. BDB 86/1/383. Sankey Collection)

Duddon Road. (Cumbria Archive Centre, Barrow. 2147. BDB 86/1/384. Sankey Collection)

Beach Street. (Cumbria Archive Centre, Barrow. 2150. BDB 86/1/387. Sankey Collection)

Duke Street. (Cumbria Archive Centre, Barrow. 4229. BDB 86/1/1153. Sankey Collection)

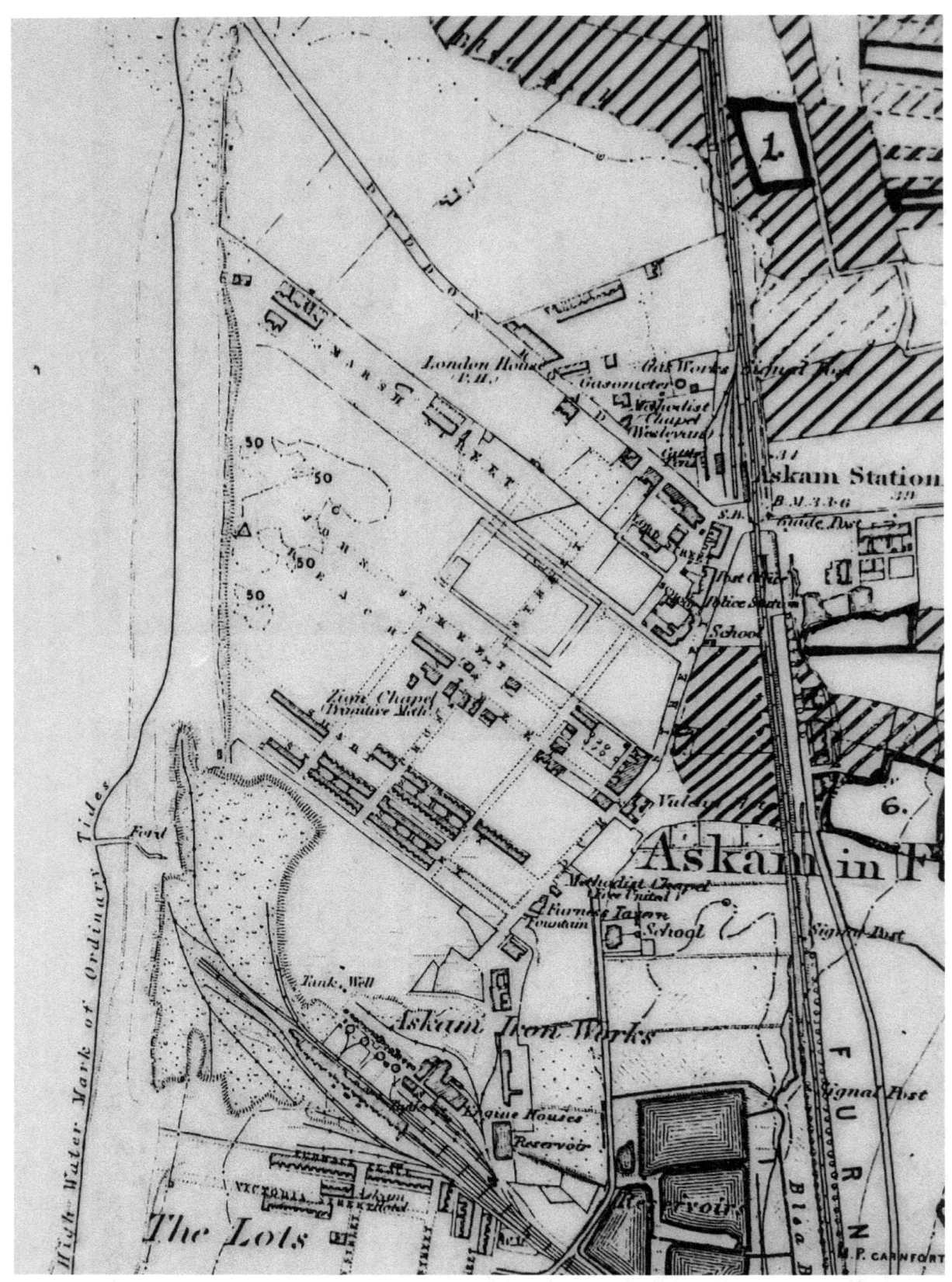

Ordnance Survey map from the 1890s showing the layout of the settlement.
(Courtesy of Janice Cumming, Askam History Club)

Soulby's Ulverston Advertiser, 27th August 1902.

ASKAM PRIVATE STREETS.

THE QUESTION OF MAKING ROADS ON THE LOTS.

The Dalton Urban District Council have decided that proper roads shall be made to a group of streets at Askam, known as the Lots. Consequently, they applied to the Local Government Board for sanction to borrow £1,250 to carry out the work. For the purpose of inquiring into the subject matter, Mr. A. A. G. Malet, M.inst.C.E, attended at the Board Room of the Millom and Askam Haematite Iron Company, on Wednesday afternoon.

Prior to holding the inquiry, the Inspector, accompanied by the officials of the Council, had visited the site of the proposed works. There were present, Mr. James Tyson (Clerk to the Council), Councillor J. Hamer, Councillor J. W. Lawn, Councillor M. Backhouse, Councillor J. K. Butcher, Mr. W. Richardson (Surveyor to the Dalton Council), Mr. T. Procter (sanitary inspector), Mr. W. Caine (assistant sanitary inspector), Mr. Moore (late assistant inspector, and now sanitary inspector of Maryport), Mr W. Settle (architect, Ulverston), Mr. Wakefield (E. T. Wakefield's son, London), Mr. Lomax (Ratcliffe, Manchester), Mr. John Noble, and Mr. Thomas Robinson (estate agent for Mrs Wakefield).

The Inspector asked if there was any opposition to the scheme.

Mr. Tyson said he had notice of objection from Mr. Wakefield only.

Mr. Wakefield intimated that he represented his mother, Mrs. Wakefield, the owner of the estate.

The Inspector: Do you oppose the scheme in toto, Mr. Wakefield?

Mr. Wakefield: Yes sir.

Mr. Lomax, who also opposed, said: You may charge what you like, you will not get paid. I cannot afford to pay. The property won't allow it. The income of both houses is only £9 4s. 0d. a year. There is no necessity for the scheme.

Councillor Hamer: You have no locus standi as regards the other property.

Mr. Lomax: If the scheme goes on it will raise the rents of the property, and the property will not allow it to be done.

Mr. Noble: I oppose as an owner. I think a slag road would be quite sufficient.

Mr. Tyson then gave some of the necessary particulars. He said the population of the Urban District at the last census was 13,020, and the accessible value £90,589. The total outstanding loans amounted to £6,687 14s. 0d. on December 31st last, made up of £4,560 under the Public Health Act, and £2,127 under the Local Government Act.

The Inspector: Does this represent the total sanction?

Mr. Tyson: I have no particulars with me, but I will forward you them.

The Inspector: The borrowing powers are represented by the amount sanctioned, not what is actually raised.

Proceeding, Mr. Tyson said the application affected the fronts of Wakefield-street, Victoria-street, Duddon-street, Harris-street extension, Stafford-street extension, Back Furness-street, Back Victoria-street (East and South), Back Harris-street, and Back Stafford-street. The total estimated cost was £1,282 11s. 8d., and the Council applied for a loan of £1,250 in respect of the works, to be repaid in a period of five years. Mr. W. Settle would produce the original plan, showing how the estate was laid out by Mr. Wakefield in 1865. The front of Furness Place was made by the Council sum time ago without having recourse to a loan. The cost was met out of revenue. The Council subsequently made a portion of Harris-street below Stafford-street. The cost had been repaid by the owners. Proceeding, Mr. Tyson said that district south of the iron works had been a source of considerable trouble for the last 30 years. Two or three years ago the Council endeavoured to get the whole of the owners to come to some amicable understanding to have the streets made.

Mr. Wakefield explained that the Council had written to Mrs. Wakefield intimating that she would not be charged anything except a piece of land which was her contribution.

Mr. Tyson said the offer was a conditional one, and that was in the preliminary stage. The Council were trying to get the whole of the owners to agree tom have the streets done, but they did not succeed, and the whole thing went over.

Mr. Wakefield: That may be your impression, but it certainly is not mine.

Mr. Lomax: As an owner I objected from beginning to end.

Mr. Tyson said the object of the Council was to make the streets passable, and in order that the people might travel more conveniently along them. He referred to the difficulty that vehicular traffic experienced in traversing the streets. The work of scavenging – a most important work- was greatly impeded, and rendered more expensive. Notices had been served upon the various owners but those present were the only ones who objected. There appeared to be an impression on the part of some of some of the owners that the work, or at any rate some portion of it ought to be done out of the rates. The Council had no power to spend money on private street improvements. He took it that the Inspector would be able to convoy to those present that the cost would fall on the owners in the ordinary way.

Mr. W. Settle (of the firm of Settle and Farmer, architects, Ulverston) produced a copy of the original plan of 1865. He assisted in laying out the estate for building purposes for the late Mr. Wakefield eight years before the establishment of the Local Board. All persons who purchased land then would be entitled to a right of way over the whole streets shown on the plan. The terms were freehold.

Mr. Richardson, surveyor to the Dalton Urban Council, said he had prepared the plans relating to making the streets. They were already well sewered, the sewer mains being laid some 30 years ago. There was no question in his opinion as to the necessity for making streets. One reason was on account of the difficulty of scavenging and the great inconvenience suffered by the various occupiers of houses in the streets. At present there were no proper means of communication, and if the scheme were carried out it would facilitate the scavenging by 50 per cent. Children experienced great difficulty in getting over the roads, and if a fire broke out in the Lots he doubted whether they could get the fire engine there; with considerable difficulty he had got the steam roller there. Considering the present state of the ironworks there was every probability of the other portions of the streets being built upon. Even if the native ore gave out, Askam was one of the most promising furnaces in the country, as it could be kept going with foreign ore. He did not think it would be Advisable to depart from the plan of the streets as laid before the Council. He had made the estimates on as cheap a basis as possible. The Surveyor then entered into a detailed explanation of the plans, as well as the sewerage system.

Answering Mr. Wakefield, Mr. Richardson said slag was all right for the foundation of a road, but he did not like it for the surface. Slag was very dangerous for traffic, and broke into holes and depressions. As regarded Duke Street, which had a slag surface, he did not know how long it had been made, but it was in a bad condition at the present time. His impression was that limestone would come in quite as cheap as slag.

Mr. Wakefield: Do you remember writing, as the Council's surveyor, to Mrs. Wakefield in 1899 to the effect that she would have to pay no portion of the cost of making the new roads?

Mr. Richardson: Yes; but that was a preliminary matter.

Mr. Wakefield: I should consider that in any ordinary business transaction it would be conclusive.

Mr. Lomax: Hear, hear, so would I.

Mr. Richardson: I wrote to Mrs. Wakefield saying the Council would do the road if she would give the land.

Mr. Tyson: The owners were not unanimous, and we had to fall back on the Public Health Act.

Further questioned, Mr. Richardson said the correspondence was entirely preliminary, and was entirely upset by the action of the owners who would not agree.

In answer to Mr. Lomax the Surveyor said they had to take up the slag surface in Duddon Road, and he would soon commence to remove that in Duke Street with the intention of constructing it again. He certainly thought a macadamised surface would not only last as long as the slag one, but would be better.

Councillor J. W. Lawn said they had experienced considerable difficulty with regard to the property, which was increased by the small value of it. The district was in a bad sanitary condition and the Council were bound to improve that. The great necessity for the streets was obvious, and he pointed out the tremendous advantage obtained by the people living in Furness Place as the result of a street being made there. It would not be fair to other parts of their districts, where the owners had paid, if they put the cost on the rates. If the streets were made the sand would not accumulate so quickly, and it could be more easily removed.

Councillor J. Hamer said he had been a member of the North Ward for 25 years, and during the whole of that time the improvement of streets was continually before them. The Lots were in a shameful condition. At one time Sharp-street and Steel-street were in as bad a state, but they had considerably improved them. The streets at the Lots were in a state of chaos.

The Inspector remarked that of course he could not answer for the Local Government Board, but he didn't think they would consider the application unless the Council took up the question of properly draining the streets. If the Council could give a guarantee that that would be properly dealt with it would probably save them the trouble of writing on the matter.

Councillor Hamer was of the opinion that the Surveyor might get out sections showing the drainage, and then they could see what the Board recommended on the matter.

Mr. Wakefield, in a short address, said his principal objection was that the estimated expense was out of all proportion to the value of the property. (Mr. Lomax: "Hear, hear.") They did not want a London street in an Irish bog, nor expensive streets in a district like that. He continued that if the streets were necessary much cheaper ones would do quite as well. He thought the Council had not taken every means possible to ascertain which would be the cheapest way of making the streets. So far he as he could gather there was only the opinion of the Council's surveyor, which was not corroborated.

He suggested that the roads be made of slag, joined with siftings on the surface, as this would prevent slipping, and would meet all requirements. He claimed that so far as he was concerned, he would get no benefit from the streets being made. They did not intend to build there anymore, and it was more likely there would be a large pit there.

Mr. Robinson said he had lived in the district between 30 and 40 years. He knew several slag roads, and he had noticed that they had stood equally as well, and in some cases better, than limestone.

The Inspector: But this is not the evidence of an expert.

Mr. Robinson: It is from observation.

Questioned by Mr. Tyson, witness said he was a miner, and had not worked on the making of roads, not even as a labourer.

Mr. Wakefield drew attention to the fact the houses did not pay for there up-keep. It was ridiculous to talk of so much expense in such a poor district.

Councillor Hamer said if the houses were made habitable they would get a better class of tenants. The surroundings made all the difference.

Mr. Wakefield replied that the tenants were as respectable as others in the district, and were of a class who could not pay high rents.

Mr. Hamer: The value of the property would be considerably enhanced if the streets were made and a good drainage system carried out.

Mr. Lomax argued that it was never intended that a street should be made of Duddon Road. The proper way was by a path near the ironworks.

Councillor Backhouse mentioned that when the level crossing was done away with Mrs. Wakefield gave a piece of land as her portion of the cost of building the bridge.

Mr. Lomax remarked that there was considerable depression in the district, and as an indication of it mentioned that at one time he got 5s. per week per house, but now he could only get 2s. 6d.

Councillor Hamer: that must have been in 1873.

Mr. Lomax (excitedly): If you want to buy the property you can have it very cheap. You are a councillor and of course councillors are very wise. Generally they are rag and bone dealers, and shop keepers. (Laughter.) Councillors are men of very wide experience. They know a great deal about roads, and they like to spend other people's money.

The Inspector: That is not the point at all.

Councillor Lawn: You are insulting the Council.

Mr. Lomax: I am not.

Councillor Lawn: Certainly you are.

Mr. Lomax: I am speaking about making these roads.

Councillor Lawn: You are speaking of the council personally.

Mr. Lomax: It seems to me to be more of a scavenging question than anything else. It will not be to the benefit of the ratepayers or the property owners. You can make the streets; I don't care a rap! You can take me where you like, I won't pay!

Councillor Hamer: We will take the houses.

Mr. Tyson: Would you like the streets to remain as they are?

Mr. Lomax: Yes, for what I care about it. I think it is a piece of ridiculous nonsense!

Councillor Backhouse pointed out that there was a provision in the deed of transfer that the streets should be made.

Mr. Lomax: What do you know about it.

Councillor Backhouse: I have lived on the estate 35 years, and know more about it than you do.

Mr. Lomax: You were born young. (Laughter.)

Councillor Backhouse said there were provision made in the deed of transfer that the streets should be made comfortable. Mr. Wakefield had done nothing of the kind. He had let the property go to the dogs. He blamed Mr. Wakefield for the whole thing not being done some years ago.

Mr. Lomax: Well, good afternoon, gentlemen. I have come a-many. I may come again to see you, but I won't be overridden. (Laughter.)

The inquiry then concluded.

In the end the Council went ahead and made up the streets on the Lots, even with the objections. An interesting note in the Inquiry is that Councillor Backhouse mentioned about a provision in the deed of transfer for the roads to be made up. I have read a document somewhere stating this also, but sods law would have it that I cannot find it or remember where I have seen it, I have even checked my deeds and did not spot it in amongst them, however I remember the basics to it and it was the responsibility of the builder of the properties to make up the street and not the Wakefield family. The result of this was a patchwork of surfaces leading to the poor state of the roads on the Lots, as no standard was set and the builder would use any spare brick or stone and rubble or even slag to make up the road and pavement, this surprisingly can still be seen in the pavements on Furnace place today as that road seems to be the only one where the pavement was not adopted by the council even though the road itself has been.

Soulby's Ulverston Advertiser, 30th March 1905

THE ASKAM DAMAGES CASE.

JUDGMENT FOR PLAINTIFFS.

In the King's bench on Monday, Mr. Justice Wills had before him the case of Brockbank's Trustees and the Urban District Council of Dalton-in-Furness, which was tried at the Lancaster Assizes before His Lordship and a special jury.

Mr. F. Sharpe was for plaintiffs, and Mr. W. Postlethwaite represented the defendant Council.

The plaintiffs were Mr. John J. Brockbank and Mr. Michael Birkett, executors of the late Joseph Brockbank who had owned a house and two cottages at Sea View, Askam-in-Furness. The action was brought to recover damages for injury to the property caused by the defendants having dug and deepened a sewer in Back Victoria-street in such a manner as to affect the foundations of the house and cause the walls to crack and give way and become ruinous.

Defendants denied liability, and pleaded that they had executed the work in pursuance of their statutory powers under the Public Health Act, 1875. Whilst denying liability, however, they brought into court £100 as sufficient to meet the damages. The jury at the trial found for plaintiffs, and the matter was referred to an arbitrator to assess the amount of damages on the case being called.

His Lordship said: I have not the arbitrator's report as to damages. I need not read it through, and I have nothing further to do except to give judgment for the sum he has found £192 3s.

Mr. Sharpe asked that the costs of Mr. E. M. Young, Barrow, and Mr. W. Sadler, Barrow be allowed. They were both expert witnesses, and had given skilled evidence as to the condition of the house affected by the digging of the ground.

His Lordship: Yes, I think that was necessary evidence.

Mr. Postlethwaite: The judgment, my lord, will be for £92 3s. beyond the £100 paid into court.

His Lordship: It is judgment for £192 3s. including the £100 paid into court.

Judgment was entered accordingly, with costs.

LOTS ROAD

I've done a separate chapter here for Lots Road even though it does fall under building, but it's quite an interesting subject in itself; well as far as a road gets interesting that is.

You see we take it for granted being able to go on Lots Road now to get in or out of Askam. But obviously once over it didn't exist, before it did all traffic had to go through Ireleth from either Dalton or Kirkby and over the level crossing and up Sandy Lane (Duke Street) to the ironworks. The only alternative was to travel along the shore from Kirkby or Roanhead and they weren't the most reliable routes with the tides and shifting sands, but that's all they had at the time. In 1872 it seems that Dalton Urban District Council created Dalton Road or Askam Road to the Dalton'ers reading this. The road went through the Greenscoe and Greenhaume Estates, owned by the MacKinnon family who had ties with the ironworks.

With the creation of Dalton Road, it gave a more direct route to Dalton and beyond. However, it is interesting to note that even though this road was in place the ironworks never made use of it until after a change of ownership in 1881, and sometime during this new ownership they built Ironworks Road with a bridge over the Furness Railway, connecting to Dalton Road, as can be seen in the following plan. Again, an exact date of this road's creation has been hard to find. In this plan you can see the level crossing they planned on going over the ironworks railway lines or "Tram lines," prior to the level crossing the public would use the lines to make way onto the Lots with passing through the Greenscoe mine.

Lots bridge incline showing the ironworks boundary fence. (Kevin Alexander Collection)

Further spiked fencing hidden amongst the hedging on Lots Road. (Kevin Alexander Collection)

The ironworks further extended Ironworks Road to Duke Street when they donated land to build the Victoria National Board School (Askam Village School) in 1887. They built the incline and Lots bridge over the ironworks railway lines at this point to improve access to the Lots. The entirety of the road was lined with spiked iron fences which the ironworks chose to surround their property with and this can be seen in the photographs in this book, this led to the nickname of "Spike Island" for the Lots as it was surrounded by spikes and the only ways to get there was over Lots bridge on Ironworks Road or under the bridge at Pier Gap on the shore.

You've probably thought but what about Lots Road? well this was originally the small road on the Lots incline for the Lots bridge, amusingly now it is an un-named dead-end road since the bridge was taken down in 1973, but prior to this Askam folk tended to call the entirety of Ironworks Road as Lots Road and it has stuck that way with Ironworks Road nearly being lost to history apart from a small information sign on the White bridge indicating the bridge is still called Ironworks Road Bridge to the railway authorities.

And the reason for the naming the bridge white bridge was that in 1938 Dalton Council widened and reinforced it with rebar and concrete, giving it a white sheen at the time which stood out in the landscape. It has since weathered to a grey colour, but the nickname still carries to this day. Confusingly it gets referred to as Lots bridge also, and this is the bridge referred to in the following articles with Lots bridge referred to as Lots tramway bridge.

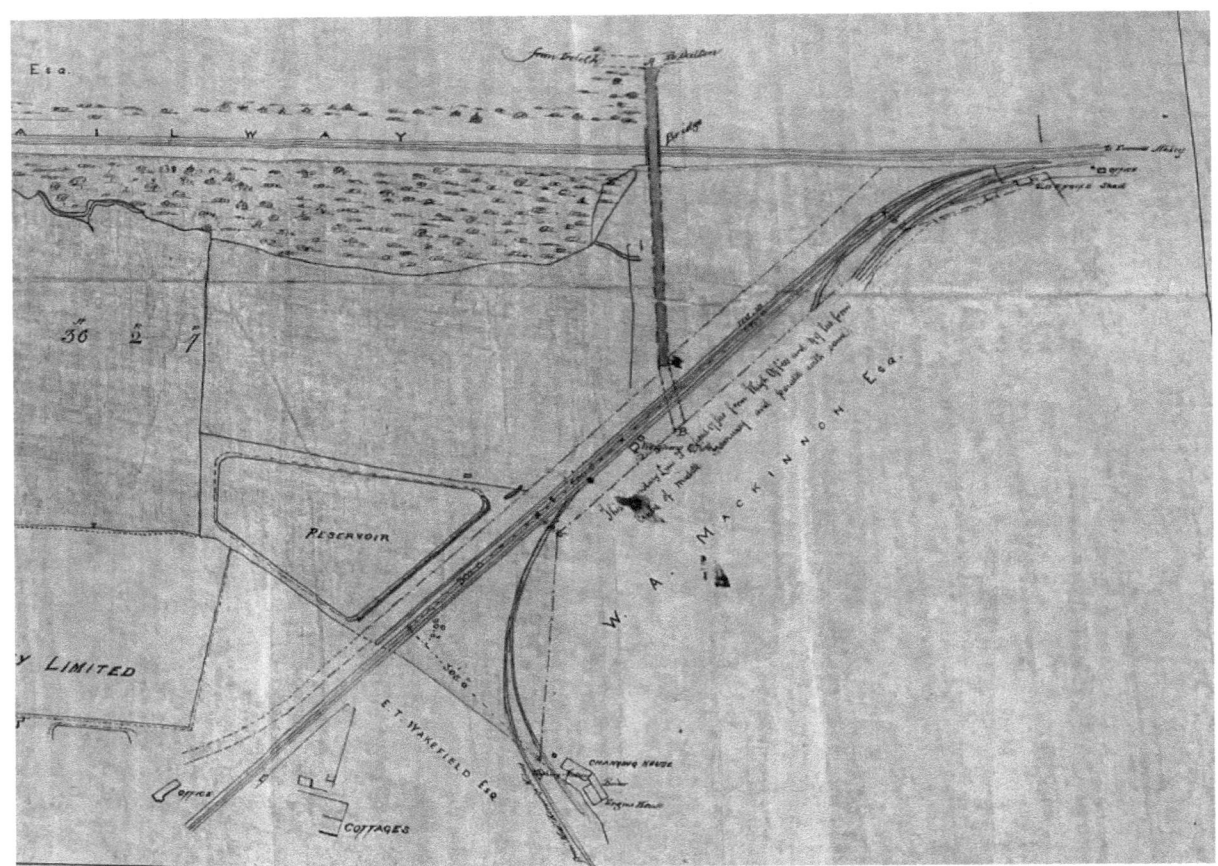

Lots Tramway level crossing plan showing Ironworks Road Bridge over the main line. Lots bridge, incline and road section where the school now is do not yet exist. Circa 1881. (Cumbria Archive Centre, Barrow. BDHJ/406/1/4)

Lots Bridge in 1973 before its demolition. (Courtesy of Jan and Pete Bigland)

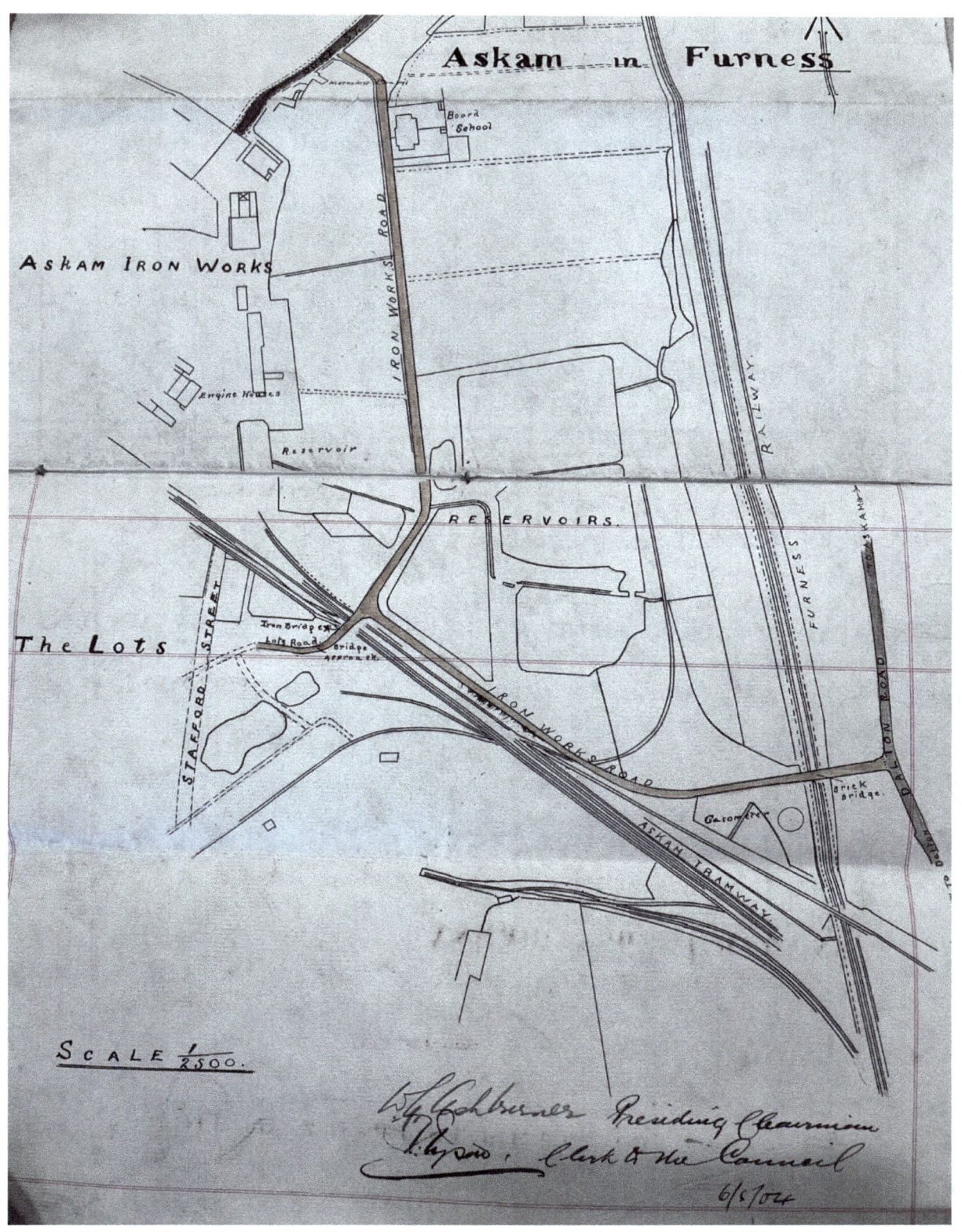

Plan showing Ironworks Road in 1904 when Dalton Urban District Council adopted the road. (Cumbria Archive Centre, Barrow. BDHJ/430/5/6)

Soulby's Advertiser, 28th January 1897.

THE LOTS' BRIDGE.

Councillor Jackson asked that the committee be requested to again open up the question of the Lots' Bridge. It was an unfortunate thing for the Lots that the Council could not see their way to take over the road and the bridge. There was practically no right of road to the Lots, and the people had to go through mud and mire to get there at all. When Mr. Taylor, the Local Government Board inspector, was at Askam, he showed clearly that there was a great nuisance there, and that was the large accummulation of sand. He wished the committee would consider the question of the Lots' Bridge because if the Council took it over, then they could look into the question of street making. The surveyor had already spoken highly of the bridge regarding its construction, and if the Council would but take it over the Lots people would then have a permanent road to their houses.

The Chairman pointed out that the business was not closed at all. There was a certain proposition offered by the Askam Company if the Council would take over the road and the bridge, and the Council accepted that offer minus the bridge. The negotiations were not closed by the Council, but the Askam Company declined to accept the terms of the Council as passed in the Council's resolution, and directed that future negotiations should be taken through their solicitor, Mr. Hart Jackson. All that Councillor Jackson need do was to move that the committee continue the negotiations and see if a satisfactory arrangement could not be come to.

Councillor Jackson moved that.

Councillor Butcher seconded, and said his reason for doing so was that now a matter had been cleared up. The Askam Company undertook in case of accident to the bridge through their engines or wagons running away, that they would put the bridge in good repair. That had cleared his mind. On January 4th the Company closed the bridge in order to assert their claims. No one, he felt assured, desired to dispute the Company's claim, but if the Company wanted to close the bridge it would make matters extremely inconvenient for the people on the Lots. He thought some amicable and satisfactory arrangement could be made with the Company if the negotiations were continued.

Councillor Walton said so far as the Highway Committee were concerned, they had not forgot about the bridge, because at their last meeting they had an informal conversation on the point, and they hoped that at the next meeting some arrangement might be come to, so that they could present to the Council a satisfactory solution towards the taking over of the road.

Councillor Cowan asked the Clerk whether the Askam Iron Works Company had power to close that road permanently?

The Chairman said that was a question which the Clerk would not like to answer straight off.

Councillor Edwards asked Councillor Jackson whether the Askam people had a right of way through the works.

Councillor Jackson replied that they had not.

Councillor Edwards understood that the company made the bridge for their own convenience and not for the convenience of the public.

Councillor Jackson said the bridge was made in order to accommodate the public, and to prevent the company being liable for accidents which might have occurred on the tramway. If the Council took over the road and bridge they could then ask the trustees of the late Mr. Wakefield to make the streets. The motion was carried.

Soulby's Advertiser, 12th May 1904.

AN AGREEMENT ADOPTED.

An adjourned meeting of the Council was held last night, when there attended Councillors W. G. Ashburner (in the chair), G. Donald, A. Jackson, J. Wharton, R. Baxendale, A. Cowan, W. Robinson, J. Polkinghorn, J. Edwards, J. E. McKelvey, T. M. Kay, and R. Holt.

HIGHWAYS AND LIGHTING COMMITEE.

Askam Iron Works-road: Read draft agreement prepared by the solicitors of the Millom and Askam Ironworks Co., Ltd., as to the taking over and repairing of this road, submitted through Mr Councillor Ashburner for the consideration of the committee, and as already read by the Council in General Purposes Committee. The Surveyor having reported thereon, the committee determined upon entering into the proposed agreement, subject to such a modification of its terms as they thought necessary. Resolved that the Clerk be directed to revise the draft agreement accordingly, and that Mr Councillor Ashburner be desired to arrange a further conference with the company's manager, Mr Mair) to reconsider the draft as amended.— The proposed amendments having been discussed with Mr Mair, and the latter intimating that the company were also willing to hand over to the Council that portion of the Lots-road leading, from its junction with the Iron Works-road, over the iron tramway bridge to the Lots, with such bridge and its approaches. Resolved that the draft agreement be amended so as to embrace such portion of the Lots-road and the iron tramway bridge and its approaches, that the draft be further amended as determined upon, and that the Clerk be directed to further revise the same accordingly, and submit the amended draft to the Company, through Mr Councillor Ashburner, for their solicitor's approval.

The report was adopted, on the motion of Councillor Robinson, seconded by Councillor Edwards.

GENERAL PURPOSES COMMITTEE.
THE ASKAM IRON WORKS-ROAD.

Askam Iron Works-road and Lots-road and bridge and approaches: Mr Councillor Ashburner reported having received the draft proposed agreement, from the solicitors of the Millom and Askam Hematite Iron Company, Limited, approved on behalf of the company. Read minutes of the proceedings of the foregoing meetings of the Highways Committee, also draft agreement as finally approved on behalf of the company.—Resolved that the Council enter into such agreement with the company for the taking over and maintaining of the roads and bridges and the approaches thereto, on the terms of the draft, as now finally approved.

Councillor Donald moved and Councillor Jackson seconded the approval of these minutes.

Councillor Holt asked if all the legal difficulties had been overcome?

Councillor Kay replied that the difficulties in regard to the company undertaking the cost had been settled.

In reply to Councillor Holt's enquiry whether the auditor would surcharge the Council, Councillor Kay said no expense would be incurred by the Council.

At the request of Councillor Cowan the agreement was read.

After further discussion Councillor Holt persisted with the question as to whether there would be a surcharge.

The Chairman: That bogey again.

Councillor Holt: Well, we are not all millionaires.

The Chairman: No, I should rather like to see a surcharge. This has been dangling before the Council for a long time. It is quite time we used our own discretion, I think—(hear, hear).

Councillor Holt: I want satisfaction, that is all.

The Clerk said the matter rested just as it did in April. He had nothing further to add and nothing to withdraw.

Councillor Holt: I shall vote against it, then.

The minutes were then adopted Councillor Holt only voting against.

Barrow News, 30th April 1938.

Lots Bridge.

Nearly two years after it was closed to road traffic through the danger of subsidence, Askam Lots-road Bridge over the railway, is in the hands of the contractors, who are erecting a structure over the line preliminary to dismantling the brickwork. It will be replaced by a concrete erection.

Barrow News, 22ND October 1938.

NEW RAILWAY BRIDGE

The new Lotts Road Railway Bridge, at Askam, which has just been completed.

1871 CENSUS – ASKAMS FIRST SETTLERS

IRELETH VILLAGE				
NAME	**SURNAME**	**AGE**	**OCCUPATION**	**PLACE OF BIRTH**
James	Downs	31	Furnace labourer	
Edward	Hodgeson	33	Iron miner	Cumberland
Henry	Wildman	29	Iron miner	Yorkshire
John	Jenkins	31	School teacher	
Richard	Rigg	34	Iron miner	Lancashire
William	Moody	50	Iron miner	Cumberland
Henry	Mellon	21	Mining engineer	Millom, Cumberland
Edward	Cole	35	Iron miner	Cumberland
Robert	Johnson	32	Iron miner	
George	Tyson	39	Iron miner	Cumberland
Robert	Pearson	70	Retired inn keeper	Dalton, Lancashire
Robert	Turner	36	Inn keeper	Dalton, Lancashire
Dorothy	Sharpe	21	Domestic servant	Dalton, Lancashire
Richard	Hughes	31	Iron miner	Northamptonshire
Joseph	Dixon	60	Labourer	Kirkby, Lancashire
John	Atkinson	47	Beerhouse keeper & Joiner	Colton, Lancashire
John	Dryer	25	Iron miner	Ireland
Elizabeth	Blackburn	78		Dalton, Lancashire
Daniel	File	37	Iron miner	Lancashire
Nicholas	Woodend	20	Iron miner	Lancashire
Henry	Brown	41	Iron miner	Cheshire
Ann	Kirkby	60		Millom, Cumberland
William	Dodgeson	10	Scholar	Millom, Cumberland
Mary	Beck	6	Scholar	Millom, Cumberland
Robert	Wilson	22	Miller	Sedburgh, Yorkshire
Robert	Swainson	50	Iron miner	Cartmel, Lancashire
Richard	Walker	31	Iron miner	Cartmel, Lancashire
Mary	Thompson	59		Kirkby, Lancashire
David	Sykes	16	Railway clerk	Barrow, Lancashire
Robert	Barton	34	Iron miner	Dalton, Lancashire
William	Fox	9	Scholar	Kirkby, Lancashire
John	Gawith	7	Scholar	Broughton, Lancashire
Mary	Walton	60	Lady	Hawkshead, Lancashire
John	Barnes	32	Iron miner	Colton, Lancashire
Margaret	Dixon	17	Domestic servant	Dalton, Lancashire
Ruth	Sharpe	32		Lancashire
Ann	Huddleston	12	Domestic servant	Dalton, Lancashire
George	Thompson	26	Iron miner	Cumberland
John	Rigg	24	Agricultural labourer	Lancashire
Samual	Brockbank	23	Iron miner	Aldingham, Lancashire

Micheal	Rigg	30	Labourer	Westmorland
William	Nicholson	25	Iron miner	Westmorland
James	Coulton	10	Scholar	Cumberland
Edward	Robinson	27	Iron miner	Scotforth, Lancashire
John	Pattinson	76	Agricultural labourer	Torver, Lancashire
Ann	Coward	14	Servant	Broughton, Lancashire
John	Hannah	30	Furnaceman	Ireland
Ellen	Hosking	59	Housekeeper	Ireland
James	Newby	54	Iron miner	Cartmel, Lancashire
Thomas	Swainson	29	Engine driver & Butcher	Cartmel, Lancashire
Thomas	Walker	29	Iron miner	Cartmel, Lancashire
Nicholas	Newby	81	Retired inn keeper	Dalton, Lancashire
Mary	Swainson	14	Scholar	Dalton, Lancashire
John	Newby	38	Iron miner	Dalton, Lancashire
Mary	Wilson	72		Dalton, Lancashire
Thomas	Pearson	28	Beerhouse keeper	Kendal, Westmorland
Ann	Spratt	15	General servant	Dalton, Lancashire
Robert	Philipson	41	Iron miner	Kendal, Westmorland
James	Kitchen	27	Labourer	Liverpool, Lancashire
George	Martin	26	Iron miner	Kirkby, Lancashire
Richard	Procter	34	Iron miner	Kirkby, Lancashire
Joseph	Dixon	28	Iron miner	Westmorland
Thomas	Dixon	43	Iron miner	Dalton, Lancashire
Thomas	Edmondson	42	Carter	Dalton, Lancashire
Joseph	Linde	28	Iron miner	Cockermouth, Cumberland
William	Kitchen	29	Iron miner	Dalton, Lancashire
John	Robinson	39	Farmer	Dalton, Lancashire
William	Fell	22	Labourer	Westmorland
Thomas	Robson	55	Servant	Westmorland
John	Robinson	23	Servant	Westmorland
Nancy	Metcalfe	16	General servant	Dalton, Lancashire
William	Nelson	51	Labourer	Kirkby Lonsdale, Westmorland
Bessie	Borwick	16	Dress maker	Westmorland
John	Kitchen	61	Retired grocer	Dalton, Lancashire
James	Hetherington	40	Iron miner	Dalton, Lancashire
Francis	Thompson	28	Iron miner	Aldingham, Lancashire
William	Long	51	Iron miner	Dalton, Lancashire
Alexander	Waters	39	Iron miner	Cumberland
John	Thompson	37	Iron miner	Lowick, Lancashire
Peter	Spencer	44	Inspector of waterworks	Derbyshire
John	Farrar	26	Mining agent	Devonshire
Thomas	Thompson	28	Iron miner	Lowick, Lancashire
Joseph	Sandham	28	Engine driver	Dalton, Lancashire
John	Knight	51	Engine driver	Cumberland
Robert	Mason	33	Iron miner	Westmorland
Eliza	Slater	20	General servant	Lancashire

Edward	Pool	54	Iron miner	Dalton, Lancashire
William	Kellet	13	Agricultural labourer	Ulverston, Lancashire
Joseph	Hornby	40	Iron miner	Cumberland
Thomas	Quayle	30	Iron miner	Isle of man
John	Huddleston	33	Butcher	Cumberland
Mary	Winder	6	Scholar	Kirkby, Lancashire
John	Sawrey	19	Assistant butcher	Kirkby, Lancashire
Martha	Clayton	15	General servant	Derbyshire
Agnes	Martin	44	Grocer	Egremont, Cumberland
James	Townson	28	Iron miner	Ambleside, Cumberland
John	Chapman	44	Yeoman	Dalton, Lancashire
Richard	Chorley	63	Agricultural labourer	Cumberland
Margaret	Brockbank	13	Scholar	Dalton, Lancashire
Thomas	Birkett	27	Iron miner	Ulverston, Lancashire
Samual	Mason	58	Landowner	Kirkby, Lancashire
	Baxter	43	Iron miner	Dalton, Lancashire
Richard	Robinson	43	Iron miner	Cartmel, Lancashire
John	Myers	49	Iron miner	Dalton, Lancashire
Andrew	Lowther	47	Farmer	Dalton, Lancashire
Jane	Harrison	17	General servant	Dalton, Lancashire
Benjamin	Clark	23	Iron miner	Warwickshire
James	Stephenson	22	Agricultural labourer	Dalton, Lancashire
William	Jackson	28	Iron miner	Baycliff, Lancashire
John	Cotton	14	Agricultural labourer	Kirkby, Lancashire
William	Wilson	27	Blacksmith	Oxenpark, Lancashire
Thomas	Clayton	41	Iron miner	Derbyshire
James	Chapman	46	Landowner	Dalton, Lancashire
Elizabeth	Cunningham	70	Farmer	Millom, Cumberland
John	Townson	7	Scholar	Dalton, Lancashire
Joseph	Sutcliffe	37	Iron miner	Burnley, Lancashire
Sarah	Wilson	70	Farmers wife	Broughton, Lancashire
William	Seward	22	Carter for ironworks	Hensingham, Cumberland
Isaac	Burney	57	Iron miner	Bootle, Cumberland
Edward	Jenkins	6	Scholar	Dalton, Lancashire
Henry	Dixon	38	Iron miner	Dalton, Lancashire
Robert	Fell	42	Iron miner	Ulverston, Lancashire
Thomas	Robinson	68	Iron miner	Ulverston, Lancashire
John	Coward	60	Engine driver	Scotland
Charles	Richards	50	Iron miner	Birmingham
Samual	Park	53	Iron miner	Dalton, Lancashire
Anne	Postlethwaite	4	Scholar	Dalton, Lancashire
Thomas	Wilson	51	Iron miner	Dalton, Lancashire
Thomas	Simpson	24	Engine driver	Bootle, Cumberland
Joseph	Williamson	19	Engine driver	Ulverston, Lancashire
John	Kitchen	36	Iron miner	Dalton, Lancashire
James	Padley	45	Curate of Ireleth	Lincoln

Harriet	Harrison	22		Stafford
Ann	Chapman	58	? Nurse	Lancashire
Mary	Repton	20	Cook & Domestic servant	Derbyshire
Mary	Bickerstaffe	18	Housemaid	Gleaston, Lancashire
Edward	Riley	31	Iron miner	Kirkby, Lancashire
Thomas	Riley	55	Carrier & grocer	Kirkby, Lancashire
George	Atkinson	45	Iron miner	Millom, Cumberland
John	Atkinson	23	Furnaceman	Colton, Lancashire
William	Brockbank	4	Scholar	Dalton, Lancashire
Thomas	Sproat	9	Scholar	Dalton, Lancashire
Thomas	Dickenson	40	Iron miner	Cartmel, Lancashire
Daniel	Holme	43	Inn keeper	Dalton, Lancashire
Margaret	Woodburn	71		Dalton, Lancashire
James	Atkinson	37	Agricultural labourer	Kirkby, Lancashire

IRELETH MARSH/ASKAM

NAME	SURNAME	AGE	OCCUPATION	PLACE OF BIRTH
James	Postlethwaite	32	Accountant	Salford, Lancashire
Rose	Jones	30	Domestic servant	Staffordshire
Nelson	Dalton	36	Clerk	Caton, Lancashire
James	Riley	31	Furnace manager	Halifax, Yorkshire
Kate	Molay	20	Domestic servant	Penrith, Cumberland
William	Turner	24	Horse keeper	Burton, Westmorland
Elizabeth	Strickland	20	Charwoman	Hale
Henry	Jackson	24	Labourer	Yorkshire
William	Herring	29	Station clerk	Lancashire
Robert	Butterfield	21	Railway porter	Broughton, Lancashire
George	Stephenson	55	Coal dealer	Kirkby, Lancashire
Joseph	Lancaster	34	Railway station manager	Halifax, Yorkshire
Thomas	Slater	49	Miner	Ireleth, Lancashire
John	Cooper	34	Miner	Cartmel, Lancashire
Abraham	Carlisle	3	Scholar	Dalton, Lancashire
John	Wright	49	Furnaceman	Derbyshire
Ellen	Houghton	13	Domestic servant	Southport, Lancashire
William	Derby	30	Blacksmith	Langdale, Westmorland
Roger	Martin	19	Labourer	Kirkby, Lancashire
John	Sherwin	43	Miner	Kirkby, Lancashire
John	Millanson	43	Miner	Kirkby, Lancashire
Addison	Coward	54	Beerhouse Keeper	Kirkby, Lancashire
Elizabeth	Morris	21	Servant	Kirkby, Lancashire
Thomas	Woodburn	45	Miner	Ulverston, Lancashire
Hannah	Smith	30	Inn keepers wife	Lancashire
Robert	Simpson	24	Waller	Lancashire
Betsy	Langhorn	65		Westmorland
John	Robinson	40	Miner	Lancashire

Andrew	Kirkwood	40	Miner	Scotland
Joseph	Woodend	28	Miner	Coniston, Lancashire
Henry	Wood	33	Miner	Glossop, Derbyshire
Martha	Grimshaw	13	Servant	Failsworth, Lancashire
Thomas	Gregory	26	Miner	Derbyshire
Joseph	Macleod	20	Bricklayer	Ireland
Jabbez	Hoffnor	49	Bricklayer	
James	Stockwell	40	Miner & Beer	Gloucestershire
Robert	Woodburn	15	Miner	Dalton, Lancashire
Mary	Heaton	76	Servant	Dalton, Lancashire
David	Kendall	32	Innkeeper	Hawkshead, Lancashire
Alice	Fawcett	20	Servant	Dalton, Lancashire
Mary	Park	61	Dress maker	Ulverston, Lancashire
William	Martin	29	Stonemason	Hawkshead, Lancashire
John	Slackley	29	Miner	Eskdale, Cumberland
William	Dobson	28	Miner	Millom, Cumberland
John	Farghar	25	Miner	Dalton, Lancashire
Joseph	Thompson Hall	32	Miner	Ambleside, Cumberland
Samual	Bell	42	Miner	Millom, Cumberland
John	Marr	59	Miner	Liverpool, Lancashire
John	Coward	45	Miner	Kirkby, Lancashire
Moses	Edmondson	38	Miner	Aldingham, Lancashire
William	Alexander	30	Miner	Overkellet, Lancashire
Joseph	Stables	32	Miner	Dalton, Lancashire
George	High	28	Miner	Ulverston, Lancashire
James	Bateman	39		Isle of man
Myles	Postlethwaite	34	Miner	Colton, Lancashire
Edward	Truscott	45	Miner	Cornwall
Richard	Faulkner	42	Miner	Liverpool, Lancashire
Thomas	Birkett	28	Miner	Isle of man
Thomas	Lace	30	Miner	Coniston, Lancashire
Thomas	Tyson	28	Miner	Kirkby, Lancashire
Frederick	Bent	31	Fireman at	
Ann	Canell	33	Servant	Isle of man
John	Rigg	30	Labourer	Lancashire
Edward	Wilson	26	Miner	Ulpha, Cumberland
Samual	Birkett	43	Miner	Ulverston, Lancashire
Micheal	Cavanaugh	30	Miner	Ireland
Mathew	Welch	57	Miner	Ulverston, Lancashire
John	Livesey	36	Miner	Blackburn, Lancashire
William	Miller	45	Miner	Keighley, Yorkshire
Joseph	Jackson	36	Agricultural labourer	Dalton, Lancashire
Robert	Barrow	38	Miner	Milnthorpe, Westmorland
William	Welsh	32	Miner	Cornwall
Robert	Ham	23	Miner	Scotland
Thomas	Chester	50	Platelayer	

Sarah	Chaplain	8	Charwoman	
Thomas	Christopherson	51	Miner	Colton, Lancashire
Robert	Dyson	34	Miner	Dalton, Lancashire
William	Wilcock	40	Miner	Lancashire
James	Miller	44	Labourer	Yorkshire
Elizabeth	Foster	36	Labourer	Durham
William	Higgin	38	Miner	Lancashire
William	Mason	55	Miner	Westmorland
Thomas	Park	27	Miner	Millom, Cumberland
Christopher	Myers	28	Miner	Dalton, Lancashire
George	Kitchen	38	Miner	Millom, Cumberland
John	Smith	28	Miner	Ulverston, Lancashire
William	Cox	36	Miner	Suffolk
Ellen	Kerwin	44	Charwoman	Isle of man
William	Marshall	30	Miner	Ulverston, Lancashire
Ann	Walker	38		Lancashire
John	Bell	46	Miner	Staffordshire
Mary	Donnally	60	Horse keeper	Ireland
James	Martin	30	Miner	Kirkby, Lancashire
Thomas	Johnson	31	Blacksmith	Kirkby, Lancashire
John	Johnson	28	Blacksmith	Kirkby, Lancashire
William	Pattinson	55	Miner	Lancashire
Ann	Sharpe	12	Servant	Egremont, Cumberland
Thomas	Birkett	33	Miner	Hawkshead, Lancashire
James	Woodend	32	Miner	Lancashire
Thomas	Raven	24	Miner	Ulverston, Lancashire
John	Procter	49	Blacksmith	Lancashire
John	Parkinson	41	Miner	Cartmel, Lancashire
Thomas	Walmsley	48	Miner	Millom, Cumberland
William	Williamson	35	Miner	Lancashire
James	Fallows	38	Miner	Millom, Cumberland
William	Nicholson	57	Miner	Ulverston, Lancashire
Mathew	Thirkell	16	Labourer	Ireland
James	Chaplain	37	Miner	Broughton, Lancashire
William	Woodcock	41	Furnaceman	
Joseph	Ellison	45	Labourer	Shrewsbury, Shropshire
William	Tyman	20	Yardsman at ironworks	Cumberland
John	Leyborne	37	Engine driver	Cumberland
Joseph	Hodgeson	38	Miner	Cumberland
James	Mathews	60	Miner	Westmorland
Thomas	Forsythe	28	Miner	Lancashire
William	Fleming	18	Miner	Lancashire
William	Coward	24	Miner	Lancashire
Mathew	Harrison	34	Labourer	Blackburn, Lancashire
John	Robinson	28	Labourer	
William	Kellet	41	Labourer	Dalton, Lancashire

Brian	Newby	33	Labourer		Broughton, Lancashire
Henry	Batty	16	Boiler smith		Middlesbrough
Thomas	Walker	16	Miner		Coniston, Lancashire
William	Cree	20	Miner		Kirkby, Lancashire
Ann	Hornby	44	Servant		Kirkby, Lancashire
Peter	Ward	32	Furnaceman		Ireland
John	Vickers	38	Miner		Ulverston, Lancashire
Ann	Strickland	31	Dress maker		Dalton, Lancashire
Thomas	Wearing	49	Miner		Ulverston, Lancashire
Patrick	Currain	48	Miner		Ireland
John	Murphy	26	Miner		Ireland
Christopher	Slater	40	Miner		Broughton, Lancashire
James	Rowley	26	Boiler maker		Staffordshire
James	Jones	25	Boiler maker		
James	Yates	27	Iron miner		Ireland
James	Miller	36	Miner		Ireland
Mary	Gregan	67	Horse keeper		Ireland
Micheal	Gregan	30	Miner		Ireland
Henry	Miles	58	Labourer		Cumberland
Charles	Spry	43	Miner		Cornwall
William	Dixon	55	Miner		Coniston, Lancashire
John	Walker	3	Scholar		Lancashire
William	Sharpe	54	Miner		Dalton, Lancashire
Hugh	Cross	29	Miner		Leyland, Lancashire
Mark	Nicholson	31	Labourer		Cartmel, Lancashire
Thomas	Pratt	43	Joiner		Ambleside, Westmorland
William	Crewdson	21	Joiner		Coniston, Lancashire
James	Crawley	27	Miner		Scotland
Thomas	Davis	41	Furnaceman		
Robert	Pitt	49	Furnaceman		Staffordshire
William	Pitt	71	Labourer		Staffordshire
John	Williams	32	Miner		Cornwall
Richard	Metcalfe	43	Miner		Yorkshire
John	Wilson	36	Miner		Kendal, Westmorland
Robert	Nelson	24	Miner		Coniston, Lancashire
John	Thompson	4			Dalton, Lancashire
Issac	Clarke	38	Furnaceman		Workington, Cumberland
John	Scoth	33	Bricklayer		Manchester
William	Muncaster	26	Miner		Lancashire
John	Bowker	35	Miner		Lancashire
Thomas	Fryson	47	Labourer		Kirkham, Lancashire
Micheal	Donal	30	Miner		Ireland
Arthur	Miller	33	Miner		Ireland
Peter	O'Neil	26	Miner		Ireland
William	Ward	23	Miner		Lancashire
Daniel	Lewis	36	Miner		Westmorland

William	Burkett	37	Miner	Cumberland
David	Farrer	39	Miner	Cumberland
Charles	Lackley	32	Miner	Stafford
Richard	Woolcock	21	Miner	Coniston, Lancashire
John	Johnson	49	Miner	Dalton, Lancashire
Joseph	Ride	26	Tailor	Salford, Lancashire
James	Chapman	60	Miner	
Henry	Edmondson	25	Miner	Dalton, Lancashire
John	Marr	22	Miner	Carnforth, Lancashire
Thomas	Strickland	29	Miner	Isle of man
Robert	Park	46	Miner	Lancaster
Robert	Park	39	Fitter	Ulverston, Lancashire
John	Carson	33	Furnaceman	Scotland
Richard	Hornby	34	Iron miner	Broughton, Lancashire
William	Berry	49		Dalton, Lancashire
John	Slater	3	Scholar	Millom, Cumberland
Robert	Milburn	32	Furnaceman	Lancashire
Robert	Gilchrist	26	Miner	Scotland
Elizabeth	Procter	4		Dalton, Lancashire
Thomas	Gilmour	33	Engine driver	Cumberland
Daniel	Mullan	38	Labourer	Cumberland
William	McLain	45	Labourer	Ireland
William	Kendall	41		Dalton, Lancashire
Robert	Derby	35	Miner	Cornwall
John	Dixon	49	Miner	Norfolk
Ann	Reid	57	Housekeeper	Ireland
Andrew	Neil	29	Miner	Ireland
William	Wilkinson	13	Labourer	Kellet, Lancashire
Henry	Lund	29	Labourer	Westmorland
Henry	Spry	45	Miner	Cornwall
William	Birch	23	Miner	Ireland
Richard	Parnell	36	Painter	Wales
Thomas	Richardson	22	Miner	Wales
Richard	Kendall	32	Miner	Dalton, Lancashire
Richard	Line	32	Grocer	Cornwall
William	Thompson	47	Furnaceman	Staffordshire
John	Wilson	45		Broughton, Lancashire
Thomas	Storey	23	Labourer	Scotland
Micheal	Satterthwaite	36	Miner	
George	Reid	36	Labourer	Ireland
Edward	Smith	24	Labourer	Ireland
William	Reid	23	Labourer	Ireland
Patrick	Hennesy	22	Labourer	Ireland
Thomas	Rayner	25	Labourer	Ireland
Peter	Lindal	42	Labourer	Coniston, Lancashire
Ann	Burns	41	Dress maker	Lancaster

Sarah	Ormandy	86		Broughton, Lancashire
Richard	Chapman	84		Cartmel, Lancashire
Henry	Chandler	36	Furnaceman	Staffordshire
Robert	Jackson	40	Engine driver	Dalton, Lancashire
John	Pearson	60	Miner	Westmorland
Adam	Jones	44	Grocer	Yorkshire
Robert	Dawes	31	Miner	Wales
Henry	Kidd	26	Miner	Westmorland
Joseph	Dogarty	22	Miner	Ireland
George	Clarke	20	Miner	Ireland
Martin	Williams	26	Labourer	Cornwall
John	Richardson	25	Miner	Ambleside, Westmorland
Edward	Barron	34	Miner	Coniston, Lancashire
William	Fullard	28	Furnaceman	Staffordshire
George	Kidd	37	Platelayer	Milnthorpe, Westmorland
William	Sargeant	34	Miner	Kendal, Westmorland
James	Pope	39	Miner	Cornwall
Mary	Lowther	36	Charwoman	Kirkby, Lancashire
Joseph	Winder	23	Miner	Lancaster
Thomas	Tomlinson	31	Labourer	Dalton, Lancashire
Issac	Roberts	30	Inn keeper	Wales
Jane	Edmondson	14	Domestic servant	Dalton, Lancashire
Thomas	Watson	33	Furnaceman	Staffordshire
Martin	Finnagan	24	Furnaceman	Ireland
George	Clarke	23	Furnaceman	
Willam	Crossley	32	Manager of ironworks	Halifax, Yorkshire
Margaret	Bell	26	Governess	Durham
Sarah	Atkinson	21	Cook & Domestic servant	Colton, Lancashire

THE LOTS/ASKAM

NAME	SURNAME	AGE	OCCUPATION	PLACE OF BIRTH
Thomas	Wright	33	Miner	Chester
James	Whitehead	32		Manchester
John	Rogers	51	Brick maker	Worcester
Robert	Griffiths	34	Miner	Flintshire, Wales
Edward	Walker	26	Painter	Dalton, Lancashire
William	Mackereth	18	Engine driver	Kirkby, Lancashire
Samual	Rogers	18	Brick maker	West Bromwich, Staffordshire
John	Rogers	15	Brick maker	West Bromwich, Staffordshire
Charles	Richards	14	Scholar	Dalton, Lancashire
Edward	Walker	4	Scholar	Dalton, Lancashire
James	Culburt	30	Rigger	Belfast, Ireland
George	Rawlinson	32		Worcestershire
Mary	Cole	40		Alderley, Cheshire
Joseph	Bowness			Thwaites, Cumberland

Daniel	McThie	35	Blacksmith	Scotland
William	Crossbeck	25	Builder	Robin hood bay
James	Wilson	21	Miner	Dalton, Lancashire
Noah	Roberts	37	Miner	Wales
Edwin	Roberts	20	Miner	Denbighshire, Wales
Peter	Hewitt	35	Boot maker	Gosford, Yorkshire
Hannah	Rodwell	37	Sales woman	Bradford, Yorkshire
Alfred	Ramsden	23	Brick maker	Lancashire
John	Parsons	27	Shoe maker	Cornwall
Nicholas	Mandall	28	Master plumber	Loughrigg, Westmorland
Annie	Carruthers	22	Dress maker	Egremont, Cumberland
Mary	Lindal	16	Servant	Cumberland
James	Wilson	30	Engine driver	Cumberland
John	Atkinson	28	Engineer	Durham
William	Antwhistle	25	Labourer	
David	Duncan	29	Miner	Cumberland
James	Mclean	24	Furnaceman	Ireland
Adam	Read	26	Furnaceman	Ireland
Henry	Martin	30	Miner	Ireland
Hannah	Lindsay	14	General servant	Dalton, Lancashire
John	Brown	29	Engine driver	Scotland
Joseph	Watson	24	Engine driver	Ireland
William	Mandall	30	Grocer	Loughrigg, Westmorland
Richard	Howorth	25	Engine driver	Garforth, Yorkshire
William	Jenkinson	28	Labourer	Lancashire
Patterson	Tebay	64	Labourer	Westmorland
Mary	Cain	8	Scholar	Penrith, Cumberland
Thomas	Cooper	19	Brick maker	Wolverhampton, Staffordshire
Joseph	Ireland	17	Brick layer	Folkstone, Kent
Thomas	Harrison	50	Labourer	Millom, Cumberland
William	Sharpe	38	Platelayer	Aldingham, Lancashire
Joseph	Gilbanks	19	Furnaceman	Kirkby, Lancashire
John	Duckworth	46	Brick maker	Bolton, Lancashire
James	Brown	20	Labourer	Kirkham, Lancashire
William	Newsham	30	Labourer	Glasson, Lancashire
James	Brown	46	Labourer	Kirkham, Lancashire
Abraham	Sharpe	34	Engine driver	Dalton, Lancashire
Charles	Wood	24	Labourer	Duckingfield, Cheshire
William	Cook	44	Clerk to the iron ore works	Bolton-le-sands, Lancashire
John	Gribben	39	Labourer	Isle of man
James	Foy	24	Miner	Ireland
Samual	Danson	26	Brick layer	Dorsetshire
Daniel	Shackleton	33	Brick layer	Manchester, Lancashire
John	Graham	22	Furnace keeper	Workington, Cumberland
Edward	Roberts	21	Tailor	Denbighshire, Wales
Sarah	Wright	16		Manchester, Lancashire

John	Lamb	35	Coal dealer	Cartmel, Lancashire
Henry	Hind	46	Grocer	
John	Williams	26	Labourer	Denbighshire, Wales
Elizabeth	Wright	13	Servant	Dalton, Lancashire
William	Simpson	33	Labourer	Nottinghamshire
William	Mashiter	39	Labourer	Lancaster, Lancashire
Robert	Warwick	28	Joiner	Westmorland
John	Dowbyn	40	Miner	Ireland
Mary	Dowd	26		Ireland
John	Kearhey	39	Miner	Chillwell, Lancashire
Willam	Cooper	22	Brick maker	Manchester, Lancashire
Issac	Graham	34	Labourer	Ireland
Thomas	McMillan	30	Labourer at ironworks	Ireland
Rachel	Chester	48		Ireland
Hugh	McMillan	29	Labourer	Ireland
William	Forsyth	40	Builder	Liverpool, Lancashire
James	McMally	25	Furnaceman	Ireland
Issac	Weeks	26	Joiner	Cumberland
John	Hamilton	35	Labourer	Ireland
John	Emms	61	Labourer	Worcestershire
Robert	Fairclough	53	Engine man	Heaton, Lancashire
Thomas	Richardson	29	Labourer	Westmorland
John	Barr	20	Labourer	Roanhead, Lancashire
John	Kirkby	23	Labourer	Westmorland
Charles	Parry	34	Gardener	Derbyshire
John	Black	38	Furnace labourer	Hawkshead, Lancashire
Richard	Atkinson	52	Labourer	Barton, Westmorland
Wilson	Thompson	26	Tailor	Patterdale, Westmorland
Robert	Parry	29	Joiner	Denbighshire, Wales
James	Curry	49	Labourer	Workington, Cumberland
Thomas	Powell	23	Painter	Wolverhampton, Staffordshire
Henry	Rogers	53	Blacksmith	Lancashire
John	Holdins	57	Engineer	Bolton, Lancashire
William	Thompson	34	Labourer	Cheshire
William	Brewer	31	Labourer	Arnside, Westmorland
Martin	Reynalds	40	Labourer	Cumberland
Thomas	Roberts	57	Miner	Lancashire
William	Hendley	26	Blast furnaceman	Shropshire
Thomas	Atkinson	23		Westmorland
Robert	Gibson	21	Furnaceman	Westmorland
Nathanial	Dawson	42	? Machine	Millom, Cumberland
George	Hay	44	Furnaceman	Westmorland
George	Gabbert	41	Furnaceman	Denbighshire, Wales
Jacob	Sayer	36	Miner	Wiltshire
William	Jackson	39	Blacksmith	Ulverston, Lancashire
Thomas	Mclamb	29	Labourer	Ireland

Thomas	Cowen	25	Engine fitter	Isle of man
Thomas	Holmes	47	Miner	Millom, Cumberland
Thomas	Calvert	32	Police constable	Yorkshire
Alexander	Lewis	28	Police constable	Derbyshire
Margaret	Wilson	50	Grocer	Lancashire
Robert	Kendall	66	Mining agent	Aldingham, Lancashire
James	Boyd	28	Miner	Ireland
Frederick	Eccles	38	Labourer	Dalton, Lancashire
John	Cameron	57	Analitical chemist	Glasgow, Scotland
John	Creary	73	Labourer	Dalton, Lancashire
Elizabeth	Shaw	65	Nurse	Dalton, Lancashire
Hugh	McDonald	64	Furnace manager	Scotland
George	Reading	35	General ? England f.co.l	Kent
Alexander	Williams	17		Beverley, Yorkshire
William	Hindle	11	Scholar	Dalton, Lancashire
William	Fletcher	24	Labourer	Bolton, Lancashire
Joseph	Picthall	34	Miner	Dalton, Lancashire
John	Sandham	21	Miner	Ulverston, Lancashire
John	Miller	46	Miner	Ireland
John	Hughes	35	Miner	Ireland
Paterick	Cunningham	27	Miner	Ireland
James	Fay	35	Miner	Ireland
John	Taylor	50		Bacup, Lancashire
William	Simmonds	28	Stoker to engine	Shropshire
Jonathan	Hodgson	21	Labourer	Dalton, Lancashire
Jonathan	Leigh	54	Labourer	Chorley, Lancashire
Henry	Cross	31	Engine driver	Lancashire
David	McEwan	28	Furnaceman	Ireland
John	Allinson	24	Labourer	Ireland
William	Lockhard	20	Labourer	Ireland
Samual	McMillan	20	Labourer	Ireland
William	Townson	23	Labourer	Dalton, Lancashire
Nicholas	Riley	26	Labourer	Ireland
Mary	Edwards	31	Housekeeper	Ramsey, Isle of man
William	Dixon	28	Miner	Kirkby, Lancashire
Mary	Tyson	13	General domestic	Broughton, Lancashire
Thomas	Close	21	Fitter	New York, America
Charles	Wilson	26	Brick layer	Leicester, Leicestershire
Francis	Townson	32	Engine driver	Coventry
John	Bradley	27	Engine fitter	Worcestershire
James	Backhouse	47	Joiner	Garforth, Yorkshire
John	Standing	16	Labourer	Galgate, Lancashire
Charles	Walker	17	Labourer	Lancaster, Lancashire
Mathew	Johnson	37	Miner	Ulverston, Lancashire
Robert	Bradley	28	Shoe maker	Cartmel, Lancashire
William	Haughton	34	Miner	Lancashire

William	Shepherd	30	Miner	Millom, Cumberland
Paterick	Sloan	25	Miner	Ireland
Daniel	Bradford	25	Labourer	Ireland
Samual	Holmes	29	Labourer	Ireland
Richard	Pilkington	44	Platelayer	
John	Creary	41		Dalton, Lancashire
Richard	Wilson	45	Labourer	Lancashire
Joseph	Dudson	51	Labourer	Bedford
William	Smith	36	Labourer	Scotland
John	Dixon	27	Blacksmith	Bolton-le-sands, Lancashire
William	Lamb	68	Retired farmer	Broughton, Lancashire
Joseph	Stables	43	Miner	Coniston, Lancashire
George	Postlethwaite	23	Miner	Sparkbridge, Lancashire
Thomas	Barnstable	56	Labourer	
John	Lysons	24	Labourer	Shropshire
Joseph	Brockbank	41	Inn keeper Askam hotel	Greenodd, Lancashire
Harriet	Ashburner	16	General servant	Woolwich
Jane	Jones	17	General servant	Wales
James	Brockbank	51	Grocer	Egton-cum-Newland, Lancs
George	Unsworth	45	Agent for iron & steel works	St Austell, Cornwall
Mary	Miller	40	Formerly housekeeper	Isle of st Lawrence
Thomas	Allinson	29	Miner	Preston, Lancashire
Nathan	Greenhalsh	21	Labourer	Bolton, Lancashire
Charles	Davis	37	Joiner	Carmarthen, Wales
William	Hutchinson	44	Labourer at ironworks	Westmorland
Jane	Crumb	56		Manchester
Thomas	Keith	34	Engine driver	Carlisle, Cumberland
James	Jenkinson	33	Labourer	Lancashire
Henry	Kendal	52	Brick setter	Chester, Cheshire

This was the first census since Askam's birth in 1865, and I'll admit it's not a fully comprehensive list as some of the original writing was illegible to me. So, I apologise if I have missed anyone's relatives. I have also only included the head of the household or anyone else living in the same house under a different surname to the head, as the list would have gone on and on and on with everyone on it!

The overall population in 1871 was 2,690 persons in Askam and Ireleth combined, compared to an estimated 400 in 1865 by the Rev. J. S. Padley, incumbent of Ireleth, (Barrow Herald, 2 August 1873).

The 1871 census is in three parts, Ireleth Village, Ireleth Gates/Ireleth Marsh (railway station) and Ireleth Marsh/The Lots, the details here follow:

Ireleth Village; had 141 houses, 137 inhabited, 1 uninhabited and 3 being built, 398 males, 345 females so 745 persons.

Ireleth Gates/Ireleth Marsh; had 204 houses, 1 uninhabited, 645 males, 491 females so 1136 persons.

Ireleth Marsh/The Lots; had 141 houses, 2 uninhabited, 468 males, 341 females so 809 persons.

There are a few interesting things about the census, one is the amount of surnames now absent from Askam's population today. This was due mainly to them coming in on a temporary basis to help construct the settlement and then moving on to the next town and so on. Another factor is that families would come to work in the mines or ironworks and when the industry was on lean times, they would move on looking for work elsewhere and rightly so. With this I have found "Askam" families then becoming Millom or Dalton or Barrow families as they resettled. In my own family I'm related to Thompson's that firstly came to Askam from London, they settled and had children here to then move on years later to Millom to work in the ironworks there, while our ironworks was shut. That family have stayed in Millom ever since. I have no doubt that some of you reading this now can relate similarly where this has been the case in your own family too. Obviously, families moved further away from Furness also, to other parts of the UK and even across the world. The population to this day is still shifting and moving about with folk coming in and folk leaving for whatever reason.

One myth that has always been wrongly attributed to Askam and Furness in general is that the iron miners were Cornish to the point that they made up a majority of the population. Well the 1871 census above and further censuses proves otherwise, in fact the majority of the workforce in the village was made up of local Lancashire, Cumberland and Westmorland workers and yes there was a proportion that were Cornish, but the censuses show us that there are even more Irish miners than Cornish and there were many other groups from all over the UK including the Welsh, Scottish and Manx as well as others too, funny how this myth has stuck due to other historians narratives.

I've come across claims that Roose and Mouzell are of Cornish origin too, again these are false claims, both places can be proven to well predate the industrial revolution and the appearance of Cornish miners in Furness. And while I'm at it the Cornish do scones completely wrong too! – its cream and then jam! Not jam and cream, the whole of Devon would agree with me on that one. Ha ha.

ASKAM RAILWAY STATION

Askam Station. (Courtesy of Mark MacLean)

Askam Station. (Courtesy of Walter Jinks)

Furness Railway constructed its first ever line from Kirkby to Barrow going straight through Ireleth Marsh in 1846. Because of this, the Sands Road (Duddon Road) now crossed the railway line, so the company had to put in gates at the level crossing to keep people and animals off the line. With it now being gated at the crossing the area simply became known as Ireleth Gates, and for a great length of time it was just a simple stop without a station. We have had two stations, the first opening April 1st 1868 and was known as Ireleth Station. However, this station wasn't suitable for the number of passengers using it. The Furness Railway finally built the Swiss chalet styled station and other buildings in 1877 to Lancaster Architects, Paley and Austin's designs, this is the station building we know of today. While researching for this book I had found it could of looked completely different again as there were plans for a sub-way and for a bridge similar to the White bridge on Lots Road and also a metal footbridge was proposed too but obviously these never came to anything.

Barrow Herald, 14th July 1866.

TRESPASSING ON THE RAILWAY.

Michael Murphy was charged with trespassing on the Furness Railway, at Ireleth, on the 7th of July, and with assaulting a porter at the Askham Station, named Brockbank, who stated that he saw the prisoner on the line near the Askham junction. He would not come off the line till he reached Ireleth gates. He returned in about half an hour and said he would again go on the line. He kicked Brockbank and also got a piece of iron ore with which he struck him, making him very ill.

Mr. Miller stated that he saw Brockbank put out his hands to stop the prisoner going on the railway, upon which Murphy kicked the porter in the side. Witness forced Murphy to the ground. Brockbank never struck the prisoner, and was very grossly assaulted.

Fined £2 10s., and in default of payment committed to prison for two months.

The same prisoner was then charged with doing damage to the value of 10s. to the lock-up at Dalton, where he had been confined. P.S. Barlow said the prisoner was so violent that he had to tie him. Fined £2 10s., also to pay the damage 10s., or two months' further imprisonment.

Barrow Herald, 28th March 1868.

THE FURNESS RAILWAYS.

Opening of New Station at Ireleth.

THE New Station at Ireleth will be opened, for Passenger Traffic, from the 1st April, 1868. The following Trains will stop at the New Station to take up and set down passengers :—

Up Trains—Nos. 4, 7, and 8.
Down Trains—Nos. 1, 3, 5, and 6.

BY ORDER.

General Offices, Barrow-in-Furness,
26th March, 1868.

Soulby's Ulverston Advertiser, 24th August 1876.

A meeting of the Furness Railways shareholders.

The Rev. J. S. Padley, of Ireleth, did not desire to cause any discord in the meeting, but he wished to call the attention of the directors to the passenger accommodation at Askam. They had both an up and a down platform, but they were simply wooden railings with gravel banks. These were useful platforms, as they were used not only for passengers but for cattle. On one side of the line there was some slight covered accommodation, but in bad weather this was so thronged with men smoking and spitting that it was not suitable for ladies. On the other side there was no covered accommodation whatever, but the Stationmaster, like all other officers connected with the railway, was very kind to the public. By allowing them the same use of the only room he had for cooking and living in. He hoped the directors would devote some attention to the subject, and make better provision for the poor starving creatures who had to use Askam railway station.

The Chairman replied that he had never seen Askam station only when he had passed through on the train, but he thought the directors might claim credit for having made the stations on the railway much better than they had been, though they might not have actually done all they ought to have done. They had shown no indisposition to furnish the public with due accommodation, for they had laid a large sum of money out in the improvement in stations generally, during the last two or three years, but as things were they did not wish to expend more of the shareholders money than was actually required. If the station was not sufficient for the requirements of the place, he was sure the managing director would give the subject his attention, and that improvements would take place in their proper turn.

Sir James Ramsden thought he might remind Mr. Padley that the Local Board were desirous there should be a bridge over the railway at the station, and until this bridge was settled they were unable to deal with the station. He thought Mr. Padley would also be aware that one set of plans have been made for this station.

The Rev. J. S. Padley said he had never seen or heard of a plan of any kind whatever, and was not aware the matter had been before the Local Board, but he understood that the Board would object to a sub-way if one was proposed. He afterwards referred to the station at Roose, from which very few houses could be seen, and then to Askam, where there was a deal of passenger traffic, and where hundreds of houses could be seen from the railway, and said at the latter place a more convenient station was necessary.

Barrow Herald, 10th February 1877.

NEW RAILWAY STATION FOR ASKAM.

On Friday evening las a public meeting of the inhabitants of Askam was held in the National Schoolroom, for the purpose of taking into consideration the desirability of memorialising the Furness Railway Company with respect to the station and other accommodation for the rising neighbourhood, of which Askam is centre. The room was well filled by tradesmen and others of the district, W. Crossley, Esq., presiding, that gentleman being supported on the platform by Messers. Weston and Mandall.

The Chairman, who on rising was greeted with applause, said they all knew what they had met about, which was a subject of great importance to the people living at Askam and its neighbourhood. It was thought that the accommodation at Askam Station was not a sufficient one, and that the footroad for instance was a source not only of inconvenience but of danger. He said that since that meeting had been proposed he had received a letter from Sir James Ramsden, of which the following is a copy;-

Barrow-in-Furness, Lancashire,

31ST January 1877.

ASKAM STATION.

My dear Sir, - I am sorry to learn, that after all the delay that has taken place, your friends will not accept the bridge offered by the company with a 10ft. 6in. headway. I conclude from what you say that we must give up all idea of getting rid of the Level Crossing at present. The plans for the station have been ready for some time, but it was not considered desirable to commence the work until the question of the bridge was settled. Pray tell your friends that they need not incur the trouble of a public meeting, our engineer having been instructed to proceed with the building without further delay. – Yours, very truly,

James Ramsden.

W. E. Crossley Esq.

He did not know (proceeded the Chairman) that the railway company were entirely to blame in the matter, for he knew that, for a considerable time past, they had been most anxious to proceed with this railway accommodation, but under conditions which, had he been consulted, he could not recommend the people down there to accept. The proposal made by the company originally was to build a station which, he believed, would amply satisfy the requirements of the place. The scheme had been drawn up two years ago, but unfortunately the matter got out, and some building speculators stepped in, and purchased some land belonging to Mr. Sharp, or the town would have for some time possessed a station with all needful advantages. But it so happened on which it was intended to commence subway was bought at a price which the company could not give conscientiously, because it would be unfair to the shareholders, and would greatly have increased the cost of the undertaking.

The next proposal by the company, this land having been taken from them, was that a subway should be made on the south instead of the north side. To do so would not near so dangerous as at the other place, and during the whole investigation the Dalton Local Board had taken cognisance of the matter, and hesitated to sanction such a level crossing as was proposed. For, according to the present arrangements of the company, they could only give them 10ft. 6in. height, and 20ft. 6in. breadth of the bridge, with cast-iron girders over. But it was considered that such a way was not only to low, but also too narrow. It was afterwards thought that height might be accepted, but it was felt that it would not do to accept the width. He had seen Sir James Ramsden and Mr. W. Schnieder (sic Henry Schnieder) on the subject several times, and on two occasions he had got them to come down to Askam station and inspect the place, and they agreed to make the way 30 feet wide, but without a distinct drain they could not give more than

10ft. 6in. headway. Matters continued in that way until Mr. Weston called upon him and asked his opinion as to having a meeting at which the opinion of the inhabitants could be freely expressed; and when he (Mr. Crossley) was asked to attend that meeting he thought it was right to inform Sir James Ramsden definitely that it was useless for the Railway company to ask the inhabitants to accept a 10ft. 6in. headway for the subway, and in reply received the letter from Sir James which had been read.

When he received that letter he consulted Mr. Mandall and Mr. Weston, as the promoters of the meeting, and asked if they thought it desirable to proceed in the matter as the company intended at once to proceed with the station, and from his knowledge of the plans he believed there would be adequate accommodation. A matter had been mentioned to him since coming into the room, and it was whether, while they were about it, it was not desirable to make it a thoroughly efficient goods station as well as a passenger station.

At present the people were put to great inconvenience in this respect, and had not the same conveniences as at other places. At Kirkby, for instance, goods could be packed in a manner that they could not be here, as this was not a clearing station, and it was desirable they should insist on the railway company making them a goods station, the same as at Kirkby, and such as is required for a growing and thickly-populated place like this. (Hear, hear.) When the station was built it was intended for convenience of only a few people, but there were now from 2,000 to 3,000 inhabitants, and they had to accommodate a good deal of business apart from supplying grocers, drapers, and others with goods, and he believed fishermen had made it an important place during the last few years.

Certainly it was a nuisance occasionally to have to go on the platform, but if this branch of trade furnished revenue to the company, there ought to be suitable accommodation for it. The traffic at the station was now very considerable and deserved greater attention than it had received up to this moment. He did not know what would be the best course to adopt under the circumstances. He had attached the meeting in a neutral capacity, and should like to hear the views of persons present, but he did not think it necessary to give expression to strong feelings. He thought the proper course, now the company had agreed to erect a station, would be to appoint a committee to meet Sir James Ramsden, or anyone appointed by the railway company, to inspect the place and see how far they were likely to meet the requirements of the place in a proper form, and otherwise assisting the company to arrive at a proper conclusion. At the same time he hoped that anything he had said would not have the effect of stopping discussion. He wanted everyone to express his opinions freely, to get the opinions of all, and to arrive at the truth of the matter. They had not met because they were antagonistic to the company, or believed the company had been antagonistic to them, but he thought the company had been a little negligent, and that a little pressure put upon them would secure all that was necessary. (Cheers.)

Mr. Mandall then rose to propose a resolution, and said that before putting it to the meeting, he might allude to one or two things which he thought the town required. They wanted a good crane for one thing. There were plenty of stations with a five or ten ton crane, and grocers and others had frequently goods of considerable weight to load and unload. He intended to propose that a committee be appointed to see the plans proposed by the company, for the level crossing wanted seeing to more than anything else, for at nine o'clock there were two trains due, and he had seen children creeping through the wheels of stationary carriages when the other train was due and there were some narrow escapes. No doubt this committee when they saw the plans would see what they could do to get all that was required. He proposed that a committee be formed to see the plans and make all necessary arrangements.

Mr. Weston seconded the proposal, believing that a committee would see every thing necessary done both for a suitable passenger and goods station. If goods came in on such a night as that and no cover on them, what a loss was made. He had many times had goods spoiled, and there ought to be a goods station. They ought to see the plans and express their opinion on them. (Hear, hear.)

Mr. Fell thought they ought to study the interests of the sand leaders. A great deal of sand was taken from Askam, and he thought arrangements should be made by which carts might be drawn close to the wagons. He did not know that anything more could be said, but what had been expressed by the gentlemen who had preceded him was what was required.

The Chairman, in putting the resolution, said there had been some very desirable expressions of opinion.

The motion was unanimously agreed to.

The Chairman said the next matter would be the nomination of a committee, which should be carefully selected from those who had had an opportunity of knowing what were the requirements of the place. He should suggest that they select a small committee, in order that they might meet together readily, and have an opportunity of learning from others what it is desirable to do. He certainly thought that if they were going to have a level crossing for both foot passengers and vehicles the station would not be adequate for the purposes intended, and that the company ought to make either a sub-way or a bridge over the railway, for the present plan was a most dangerous and inconvenient one, and that some accident would at some time occur there was not the slightest doubt.

Mr. Bell inquired whether the matter would not come under the cognizance of the Dalton Local Board.

The Chairman, in reply, said he did not think it would, unless the highway was interfered with.

A committee, consisting of Messers. Melling, Crossley, Mandall, Bell, Stevenson and Weston was then unanimously appointed.

The Chairman said there was no other business before the meeting, but he might say that he had a plan with him which he would leave with Mr. Weston, if anyone wished to see it. It had been prepared by Mr. Fox, and included an underground subway, and a bridge over the railway. The gradients were easy, but it was rather a roundabout way for foot passengers.

It was then agreed that the committee consider all points raised, and embody them in their report to the next meeting.

A vote of thanks to the chairman was then proposed and heartily adopted, in responding to which Mr. Crossley expressed his desire at all times to do anything in his power to further the interests of Askam. The meeting then broke up.

After this it seems the Furness Railway did proceed ahead with replacing the earlier station like James Ramsden stated they would do in his letter. Whether this committee in the article actually had any influence at all seems very unlikely indeed, and so the station buildings, including the goods shed and signal box, were built in 1877. And apart from losing staff and the goods shed and its sidings and the cattle platform and siding on the down line the station has remained largely unchanged.

Furness Railway signs. (Kevin Alexander collection)

Askam station 1910. (Cumbria Archive Centre, Barrow. BDB 86/1/6852. Sankey Collection)

Furness Railway crossing sign and wagon label. (Kevin Alexander Collection)

Barrow Herald, 13th October 1883.

NARROW ESCAPE AT ASKAM STATION.—A woman named Constable, living in Marsh-street, Askam, had a very narrow escape at Askam Station, on Saturday night last. The woman had been travelling by the 7-4 down train, and on the arrival of the train at Askam she, under the erroneous impression that it had stopped, stepped out on to the platform, her back being towards the engine. She was instantly thrown down, falling between the platform and the carriage. She was caught round the body by the step of the carriage, and was rolled over three or four times before the train stopped. She was so tightly fixed that it took the stationmaster and his assistants seven minutes to extricate her, and it was only by the merest chance that she was not killed. As it was, however, she got off with severe bruises on the body. There was great excitement at the station during the time they were getting the woman on to the platform.

Soulby's Ulverston Advertiser, 22nd November 1894.

FATAL ACCIDENT ON THE FURNESS RAILWAY.

Askam people were considerably startled on Thursday evening to learn that a sad accident had befallen a young couple on the railway line, this being the first serious accident which has occurred at the Askam Station. Thomas Nicholson, farm servant, and Frances Ann Fisher, domestic servant, Marsh Grange, were returning from Ulverston alighting at Askam they left the platform with the intention of walking up the line to Dunnerholme crossing. Instead of taking the path on the left hand side of the metals it appears the young couple walked in the four-foot way. The special train, which was bound for Millom, left the station shortly afterwards, and it is surmised that the young people were so engrossed in conversation that they failed to hear the approach of the train, and were knocked down and run over. The driver pulled up instantly, and sent a message to the Askam Station.

P.C. Temple and others were soon on the spot. They found Nicholson lying on the left side of the four-foot, his right arm being almost severed from the wrist, and he had two severe scalp wounds. Fisher was found in the four-foot, the engine had two carriages having passed over her, her right foot being nearly severed across the instep. First aid was rendered by P.C. Temple, Mr. Steele, and Mr. Jennings, pending the arrival of Dr. Challinor. Stretchers were secured from the Police Station and the Ironworks, and the injured persons were removed to the North Lonsdale Hospital, Barrow, several men from the cleaning shed of the Railway Company at Barrow assisting in the removal of the injured on arrival at the old station. P. C. Temple and Mr. Jennings accompanied the injured people to Barrow.

Nicholson succumbed to his frightful injuries at 12-20 on Friday afternoon.

THE INQUEST.

The inquest touching the death of Thomas Nicholson, was held on Saturday at the Barrow Hospital before Jno. Poole, Esq., coroner, and a jury of which Mr. Crouch was the foreman. Mr. H. Cook, of the Furness Railway Company, was also present.

Wm. Nicholson said he was brother of the deceased, and lived at Roanhead. Deceased had been living at Roanhead Farm, and died at the hospital from the injuries he had received. Deceased had told him he thought he was going up the shunting line. Later on witness saw him and he said his legs were cold, and he was worse. He had been up the line several times, and had lived at Marsh Grange for 12 months.

A Juror: Has it been customary for people to use the footpath?

The Coroner: This witness does not know; we will get that later.

William Sergeant said he was an engine driver in the employ of the Furness Railway.

On Thursday evening he was running a special passenger train, and left Askam at 7-50. While at Askam Station he saw deceased with a young woman going past the engine, and he asked them if they were going along the up north line. He said, "You must look out there for we are coming up that way." Deceased never spoke.

The Coroner: Is there a footpath about there?

There is a footpath, but it is not a public road.

It is about a half mile up the line.

Is there anything like a footpath at the side of the line? -Yes, there is at one side, and it is very much used by the public. It is on the west side.

They would have to cross the line to get to Marsh Grange? - Yes

Are people allowed to go up that side? – They are not expected to go up, but they do. There is a notice saying that trespassers will be prosecuted.

There is a notice board? – Yes, there is.

But persons do walk on the line side? – Yes, regardless of the notice boards.

Of course they have no real right to go on? – Well, no.

The foreman: Are the Railway Company responsible for trespassers, or is it their duty to prosecute trespassers?

A Juror: I think if there is a notice board there is no right of way.

The Coroner: If the jury want to say anything it is for them to ask questions and put in a rider after the verdict.

Thomas Steele said he was station master at Askam, and had been there for eight months.

The Coroner: Do many persons come up the side of the line by the footpath from Marsh Grange? – A good many. There are a number of men who go up and down to and from their work at the pits. We warn them if we see them.

Are they miners? – Yes, chiefly miners.

There is plenty of space on the west side for persons to go up safely? – Yes, quite safely.

Do you know why space was left? – I do not, except it was for permanent way purposes, and then again there is the post office place. There is a road to that.

That is where you take the bags from? – Yes.

What the jury want to know is do you as a rule warn people about going there, and do you stop them? – Well, when I see anyone I warn then, but they chiefly go without my knowledge.

The Foreman: This is a private road? – It is the company's property.

They were trespassing then? -Yes.

You did not see them walk on? – No, I did not, or I would not have allowed them, especially as the train was going out, and it was very dark and there was a train coming the other road.

P. C. Temple said he was stationed at Askam. On Thursday night about 7-50 he heard of the accident and went to the place and found deceased and a young girl lying near the platform. The deceased had a scalp wound, and his right hand was only hanging by one of the leaders. He was then conscious. He asked him how he accounted for it, and he answered that he could not tell. He had been walking along the line and had mistaken the way. He said he never heard anything until he was struck by the engine. There was another train on the down line, but not just then. Dr. Challinor attended him and went with him to the hospital.

The Coroner: Do many persons use this road? – Yes, especially in the early morning; mostly people going to and from Kirkby.

Miss Boulton, matron at the Hospital, said that the man died at 12-20 on Friday. Deceased never said how the accident happened.

The Coroner: In summing up, gave a resume of the evidence. The engine driver had told the deceased when he passed the engine to look out as they were going up the line. No doubt the couple were completely oblivious to either trains or anything else. Deceased had told his brother and the police constable that he had mistaken the line, and he did hear the train until he was knocked down.

These were the facts, and the jury would find a verdict to the effect. There had been a question raised by one of the jury as to the road on the side of the line. About a quarter of a mile up the line there was a footpath to Marsh Grange. It seemed deceased had been a servant at Marsh Grange, and this girl was going up there. The footpath it appeared was used greatly during the night, for it cut a very great distance off, and he daresay any of the jury or himself would use it if going that way. The station master had told him that parties were warned, and that there was a notice board but up stating that trespassers would be prosecuted. So far the notice board was concerned he did not consider it was very important, because when there was a notice board which said trespassers would be prosecuted and they were not, that notice board amounted to nothing.

They knew it was a common error that there should be a notice board to prevent people trespassing. Parties knew that they had no right to go on other people's property, and it was most absurd that anybody should be asked if there was a notice board up. Deceased himself knew perfectly well that he had no right to go that way. This was one of those unfortunate accidents that happened from time to time through persons being in a state of forgetfulness. There was no one to blame. It was a very sad case indeed, but it was one for which deceased was blameable, and no one else.

The Jury returned a verdict of "Accidentally killed."

We understand that Frances Fisher is progressing very favourably.

ASKAM CO-OP

Dalton Co-operative Society's Askam Branch, 9 Duke Street. (Lord Street corner)
(Courtesy of Garry Glew)

The first meeting of the Dalton Co-operative Society was held in Dalton, at the George and Dragon public house on 11th March 1861. The society was made up of a small group of iron ore miners of the town, whom wanted to emulate the successful Rochdale Co-operative which was the first ever co-operative society being founded in 1844. No doubt the Dalton society was spurred on when Barrow had formed a society the year before in 1860.

The society expanded into Askam in 1873, where land was purchased at Sawmill field and a new store and cottages were built. The price tendered being that of £2,369 12s. 9d., the contractor being William Gradwell and the Architect was Thomas Bennett, both of Barrow-in Furness. The store was situated on Duddon Road on the corner with Walker Street and directly across from the London House. The cottages built along with the store made up what is now Walker Street, however prior to 1901 the street was known as Co-op Street, or Co-operative Street for the obvious reason. In 1876 the manager was William R. Kellet at the Duddon Road store, although by 1882 the store was now at number 9 Duke Street at the corner of Lord Street, it had its butchers on Lord Street at the side separate to the rest of the store. The Duke Street store has greatly increased over the years taking over the three shops adjoining it, numbers 3, 5 and 7. Interestingly, I found that the Co-op supplied a reading room in 1893 upstairs, with 15 daily and 37 weekly papers and 10 monthly magazines were supplied along with 2,700 books in circulation. Askam didn't get a public library until 1904 and that was placed directly to the rear of the Co-op store on Lord Street, where it still serves the public in that capacity still.

Soulby's Ulverston Advertiser, 7th January 1875.

FURNESS MINERS' SOIREE AT ASKAM.

On New Year's Day the annual soiree and ball in connection with the Furness and Cumberland Defensive Association of Miners came off in the large room at the Dalton Co-operative Society's branch store at Askam. The room was gaily trimmed for the occasion, garlands of holly hanging from the ceiling and decorating the walls. Upon the walls appeared the following among other mottoes:—"God save the Queen," "Soothe the orphan and dry the widow's tear," "Union is strength," "A happy new year."

Ulverston Mirror, 12th September 1885.

ASKAM.

BURGLARY AT THE CO-OPERATIVE STORES.— On the manager of the Dalton Co-operative Stores at Askam proceeding ro open the premises on Saturday morning last, he discovered indications of its having been broken into during the night. A square of glass in the back window was broken, and the sash fastener unloosed, the shutter bolt broken, and to all appearance the depredator had obtained access to the entire range of the establishment. Nothing of any importance was missed, the money all being locked up in the safe, which did not appear to have been tampered with.

Barrow Herald, 22nd July 1911.

ASKAM.

Askam "Co-op." also celebrated the Jubilee on Saturday, and the affair was crowned with success. Upwards of 600 children took part in the procession. The girls, who looked extremely pretty in their white dresses and various-coloured sashes, were under the superintendence of Mrs. Hayes, assisted by other ladies, and the boys by Mr. Quine and members of the committee. At the appointed hour the procession started, preceded by Mr. Cowley, one of the oldest Co-operators, and Mr. Mason, the manager, headed by the Askam Brass Band, and paraded the streets of Askam, the Lots, and the village of Ireleth, returning to the Co-operative Stores to receive their Jubilee mugs. These were presented by Messrs. Sam Lewis, Sam Riley, Sam Hayes, and Jos. Quine. The children afterwards proceeded to the field, placed at their disposal by Mr. J. E. Greenop. They subsequently sat down to tea, each child receiving milk and a bag of cakes. There were many interesting events. The tussle of "Are you there?" was responsible for many aching sides. The other events were equally amusing. Results:—

60 Yards Flat Race (boys 5 and 6).—E. Fallows, M. Sewell, Jos. Johnson, Wm. Askew, W. Glenden, W. Wilson, Norman Johnson, E. Leece, W. Jardine, E. Chaplin, J. Pentherer, John Wilson, N. Wharton, John Johnson, John Kirkby, Norman Seward, R. Constable, —. Blackburn, W. Dixon, T. Wilson, and R. Riley.

Ditto (girls 5 and 6).—Connie Carter, Eva Wood, Alice Gill, Amy Park, Agnes Morris, Dora Turford, E. Welch, V. Kneen, E. Kitchen, R. Waterhouse, C. Shuttleworth, H. Newton, B. Leece, A. Kewley, E. Park, —. Denny, J. Rigg, F. Graves, S. Duncan, A. Tyson, E. Milligan, N. Douglas, L. Basterfield, M. Ormandy, W. Dent, A. Fallowes, Smith, E. Black, E. Kitchen, J. Turford.

80 Yards Flat Race (boys 7 and 8 years of age).—A. Blackburn, M. Langhorn, J. Noble, J. Dockeray, J. Riley, T. Dixon, T. Webster, T. Crawley, J. Blackburn, J. Kirkby, J. Newton, J. Kneen, F. Webster, F. Marshall, F. Kidd, F. Newby, Cloudsdale, J. Mossop, Robinson, Edmondson, M. Coulson, W. Wilson.

Girls' 80 Yards Flat Race (7 and 8 years old).—M. Newby, M. Robinson, M. Wilson, E. Cattier, M. Benson, L. Satterthwaite, A. Robinson, L. Myers, E. Fallows, Milligan, Buxton, and Duncan.

Boys' 100 Yards (9 and 10).—Berry, Blackburn, Kirkby, Kidd, Tyson, Robinson, Dockeray, R. Walker, J. Walker, H.

Blackburn. J. Coulson, H. Woodrow, J. Kewley, Walker, Coulson, Dixon, Blackburn, Fallows, Langhorn, W. Fox.

Girls' 100 Yards Race (9 and 10).—Alice Butcher, D. Bath, M. Tyson, A. Stonehouse, L. Duke, A. Lloyd, A. Foster, W. Wharton, V. Steele, R. Rigg, M. Bashfield, M. Park, E. Black, M. Nutter, B. Foster, O. Duncan, F. Marshall, E. Atkinson, E. Boothman, C. Barr, L. Mason, J. Gillbanks, M. Robinson, W. Graham, L. Lewis, G. Huddleston, Park, Seward, J. Eccleston, A. Kewley, M. Fox, M. Sharp, Nellie Brown, C. Townson, H. Park, M. J. Mawson, A. Edmondson, N. Barker, M. Graves, B. Stables, J. Myers.

Boys' Marathon Race.—H. Woodrow, H. Blackburn, H. Langhorn.

"Are You There?"—J. Coulson, J. Dixon, J. Wilson, S. Brown, J. Dickinson and J. Greenop.

Tug-of-War.—W. Tyson's team beat H. Holmes's team.

Ditto (ladies).—Mrs. Pope's team beat Mrs Jardine's team.

There were also one or two bouts of wrestling.

Women's Race.—1, Mrs. Fallows; 2, Mrs. Blackburn; 3, Mrs. King.

At the conclusion of the sports Mrs. W. Mason and Mr. J. W. Lewis presented the prizes. During the afternoon and evening the Askam Brass Band played selections on the field, and also played for dancing in the evening, thus ending a pleasant afternoon's enjoyment.

THE WATER FOUNTAIN

(Miles Lewis Collection)

(Courtesy of Mark MacLean)

Askam's canopied drinking fountain is an unusual landmark in the village, it is one of three that were purchased by Dalton Local Board in 1875 at £30 each (£2,925, at 2024 prices). Dalton's was placed by the Castle, and is still in situ today, the other was on Abbey Road, Barrow, which has long since gone, it was placed in Barrow as at the time of being ordered Barrow was still part of Dalton, apparently this fountain was later moved to Paxton Terrace across from Barrow's Town Hall.

The fountain is design number 8, from the Walter Macfarlane & Co.'s catalogue and was manufactured at the Saracen Foundry, Possilpark, Glasgow. The structure stands at 9 foot and 6 inches high and is cast iron and sits on a stone plinth, it consists of four fluted columns with griffin terminals at the capital, holding up an ornate pierced umbrella canopy topped with a crown finial, however once over a large gas lamp sat on top extending the height of the structure by several feet more. The columns hold four ornate arches, set above these arches are plaques or cartouches, two depict herons and one is a portrait of Queen Victoria, whilst the last one has the inscription;

"ERECTED IN MEMORY OF HER MAJESTYS DIAMOND JUBILEE 1897." Above two of these plaques is the inscription "KEEP THE PAVEMENT DRY."

The fountain font itself sits in the centre of the stone plinth beneath the columned canopy, on a clustered column with a large scalloped edged broad bowl for the water, the central urn once had a large crane bird sat on top of it with drinking cups attached to chains, these are now missing.

The fountain holds two secrets, interestingly one is that when it was first placed in Askam it wasn't situated where it now stands. It's also a lot older than the dated inscription suggests. It was originally placed on Duke Street on the pavement by the Furness Tavern across from the Steel Street junction in 1875. This was where in the 1850's map a spring was located and no doubt this was at the time the source for the drinking water, it wasn't until Queen Victoria's Jubilee that the Dalton Local Board decided to move it where it is now and then dedicate it to the 1897 jubilee.

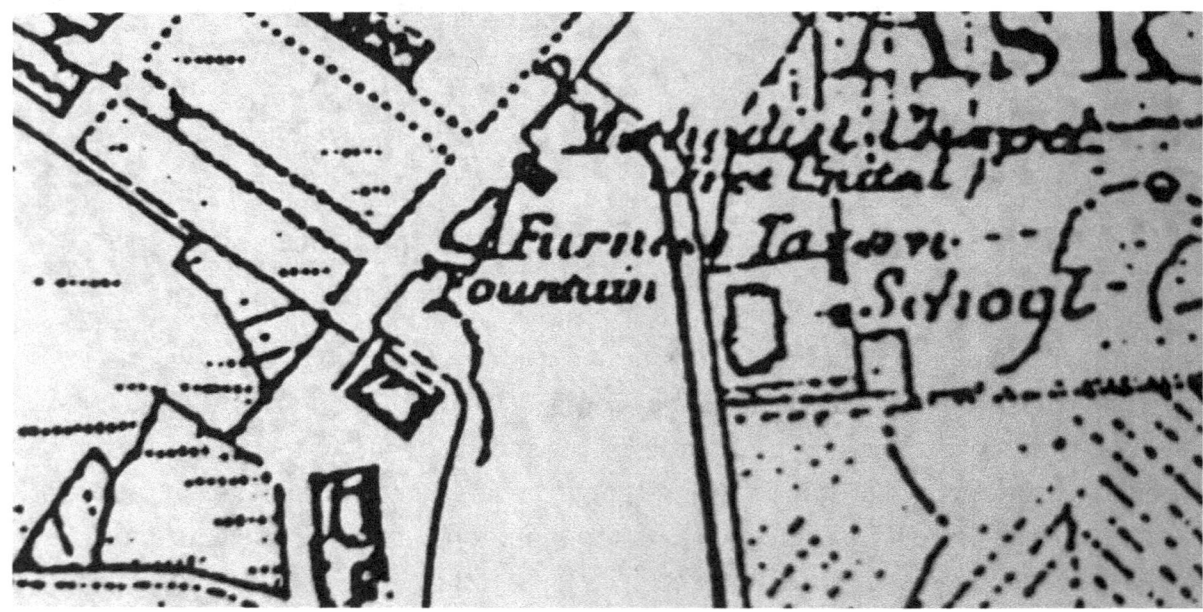

The fountain's original location on Duke Street, and opposite Steel Street. From the 1890s Ordnance Survey map. (Courtesy of Janice Cumming, Askam History Club)

Barrow Herald, 7th August 1875.

DALTON LOCAL BOARD.

The ordinary monthly meeting of the Dalton Local Board was held in the Burial Board-room, Cemetery, Dalton, last Monday afternoon, when there were present—Dr. Hall, presiding, Messrs. Wilson, Hosking, Fargher, Turner, Sharpe, Mandall, Mason, Ashburner, Askew, Robinson, Ashworth, Fisher, and Postlethwaite.

WATER FOUNTAINS.

A report was read from a committee appointed to consider the desirability of erecting water fountains in various parts of the Local Board district. The places suggested were—Tudor Square, the junction of the roads at the Railway Arms, and in the market place at Dalton; Sandy Lane at the junction of Steel Street, and a second at the junction of the Dalton and Ireleth roads were named as the most desirable places for the erection of fountains in Askam.

Soulby's Ulverston Advertiser, 9th September 1875.

THE REPORT OF THE DRINKING FOUNTAIN COMMITTEE

Stated that they had selected a design for three canopied drinking fountains, two to be put up at Dalton and one at Askam, the estimated expenditure to be £30 per fountain, exclusive of erection. They also recommended one fountain at Dalton and one at Askam, to be built into the wall similar to the one put down by the Barrow Corporation at the junction of Brestmere Beck Road and the road to Dalton, the estimated expenditure being £12 each, exclusive of erection.

Mr. Robinson, in moving the adoption of the report, said the Committee could have obtained fountains at less cost, but they were of opinion they ought to have something decent, and that was why they had made the selection they did.

Mr. Wilson seconded the report, which was adopted.

Soulby's Ulverston Advertiser, 3rd June 1897.

DALTON LOCAL BOARD JUBILEE COMMITTEE MEETING.

That the water fountain at present near the Askam Iron Works entrance, be removed to a more suitable site, and placed in effective condition.

Soulby's Ulverston Advertiser, 30th September 1897.

DALTON LOCAL BOARD JUBILEE COMMITTEE MEETING.

Askam Fountain: The surveyor reported having secured an arrangement with the Furness Railway Co. for the provision of a site for this fountain, near to the Railway Crossing on the east side of Duke-street, on terms of payment, by the Council, of the sum of 10s. per annum, the tenancy being determinable by six months' notice by either party.

All four sides. (Kevin Alexander Collection)

BRICK MAKING

Mention bricks and naturally you would think of the brickyard of Furness Brick on Dalton Road by Greenscoe. However, the story of brickmaking in Askam did not start there Instead it started on the site of the ironworks in 1865, when the Furness Iron Company put out adverts in newspapers locally and afar asking for "BRICKMAKERS, BUILDERS, & OTHERS" to supply "THREE MILLIONS MORE BRICKS," this was for the building of Askam itself. Underneath Ireleth Marsh you see was a layer of Boulder Clay left behind by the glaciers of the ice age, an ideal cheap and readily available building material, and the extraction of this clay on the ironworks site was also beneficial to the company by creating reservoirs needed for the iron making process.

Barrow Herald, 3rd June 1865.

TO BRICKMAKERS, BUILDERS, & OTHERS.

THE FURNESS IRON COMPANY, situated on the Duddon, near Ireleth, Lancashire, are desirous of having THREE MILLIONS MORE BRICKS made upon their Ground this Season than are already made, for the Erection of Cottages, and will be glad to have TENDERS for the same Counted out of the Kiln when Burnt, or the Labour to be paid for by the 1000, and the Company providing materials.

Apply personally or by letter to C. J. CLARKE, C. E., Furness Abbey, Hotel, Lancashire.

Brick making in the early 19th Century was still a basic process not much different than that of the first makers of bricks in Britain, the Romans. The bricks were literally made by hand in a field, where the raw clay was thrown into wooden moulds and then the bricks left to dry in stacks under primitive shelters for a few weeks before being fired in temporary small kilns of various designs. The most popular by far at that time was the clamp kiln, where the dried "green bricks" were stacked in a rectangular pile with semi-fired bricks surrounding them, the outer bricks are then covered with a layer of clay called "Daub" to help hold in the heat when fired. At the bottom of the clamp several "Burn holes" were left so that the kiln burner could feed the kiln continuously for about a week, stoking the fire 24 hours a day. Once the selected period for the burn was over, the kiln was left to cool slowly for a further week or two. After this around 30,000 bricks were then ready to be used in building.

We know that Benjamin Carruthers won the contract to build the ironworks, and he would have been the main manufacturer of bricks in Askam at that time. The majority of the builders mentioned in the "Building Askam" chapter no doubt made their own bricks too, however I have not been able to source the definitive evidence, like the Duke of Buccleuch's royalty reports for brickmaking from the 1860s so I can only assume that most of the builders did manufacture their own. Although bricks were also brought in from Barrow too, as my next-door neighbour's house from 1867 had a rare stamped Rawcliffe brick amongst its walls, and I have come across Caird, Ormsgill and Gradwell Bricks amongst the ironworks rubble.

Barrow Herald and Furness Advertiser, 1st December 1866.

ALLEGED THEFT OF A WHEELBARROW.

Wm. Hewitson, Newby, was charged with stealing two wheelbarrows, the property of H. Forshaw, builder, of this town.

John Clarkson said: I am a brickmaker, at Ireleth Marsh; I had some wheelbarrows there; they belonged to Mr. Forshaw, and were in my care, I took a contract from him to make bricks, and he supplied materials to work with; I missed one wheelbarrow about two months ago, worth about 10s,; I missed the other last Thursday, it is of the same value; I tracked the wheelbarrow on Friday morning to some new houses belonging to Mr. Madeley, Ireleth Marsh, where I found both of them in the front place. I afterwards went again to the house, and found the prisoner bringing one of the wheelbarrows away, it was the last one stolen; he was taking it back to where he got it from, I asked who told him to get them; he said no one, and that he would take a barrow if he wanted one. I asked him what he had done with the other which he took two months ago; he said that he had not taken it. I told him I had searched all through Ireleth, and could not find it; it must have been hid. He said he had found it, but made three different statements as to where. I then gave him to custody.

By Mr. Postlethwaite: Did not know that prisoner had been working for Mr. Forshaw for two years; had never seen the man before he found him with the barrow; he did not say that after he had taken the first barrow, he had lost it, and then found it at another place; the barrows had Mr. Forshaw's name on them; he took them at dinner-time, when we were all out of the field. I did not report to Mr. Forshaw that I had lost them; I told him on Saturday, when he said that the prisoner had done a few odd jobs for him.

The case was here adjourned till next Thursday, for the production of Mr. Forshaw, bail being extended.

Barrow Herald, 8th December 1866.

ALLEGED LARCENY.

Wm. Hewitson Newby, of Ireleth, was brought up on remand from last week, on a charge of stealing two wheelbarrows. A portion of the evidence we gave last Saturday. The case was remanded for the appearance of Mr. Forshaw, the owner of the wheelbarrows.—Mr. T. Postlethwaite appeared for the defence.

Mr. Forshaw said Clarkson, the prosecutor, was in his employ as a brickmaker; I had all materials to find him; I should not take any article from him without first telling him; when parties in the same employ are working near each other they often borrow each other's barrows; defendant is a paviour, and has been occasionally in my employ; he was not working for me when the barrows were taken; the defendant always bore a good character.

The Chairman said he hoped defendant would be careful in future; he had a very narrow escape. They dismissed the case, believing there had been no fraudulent intention.

Ulverston Mirror, 16th May 1874.

ASKAM BRICK COMPANY.

This Company is prepared to execute orders for their superior BRICKS, and deliver the same at any Station on the Furness Line, or at the Works.—Apply at the Works, or to Mr. R, PEARSON, Gill, Ulverston.

Interestingly the above company manufactured its bricks in the most surprising of locations and most people don't realise it had even existed. As per the advertisement they could deliver to any station, this was because they were sited on the corner of Dalton Road and Ireleth Road, right across from the railway station, a separate platform on the down line would have served them as well as being used later for cattle, it can be seen in the photographs in the Railway Station Chapter and can be seen from the crossing today.

I have not been able to ascertain when this company was started exactly, only that it belonged to Robert Pearson of Ireleth. He originally was a stonemason before becoming the owner and inn keeper of the Bay Horse, Ireleth, until in 1866 when he lost his licence to serve beer due to "keeping a house of ill repute." He then rented out the Bay Horse and I imagine it was at this point with all the building going on in Askam he started making bricks.

Unfortunately, Robert died in 1874 aged 76 and his estate came up for sale soon after marking an end to the company.

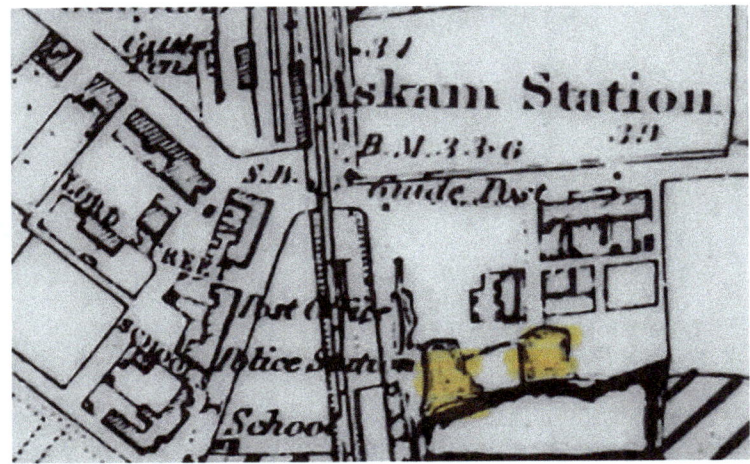

Above in yellow are the flooded clay pits of the Askam Brick Company from the 1890s Ordnance Survey map. (Courtesy of Askam History Club)

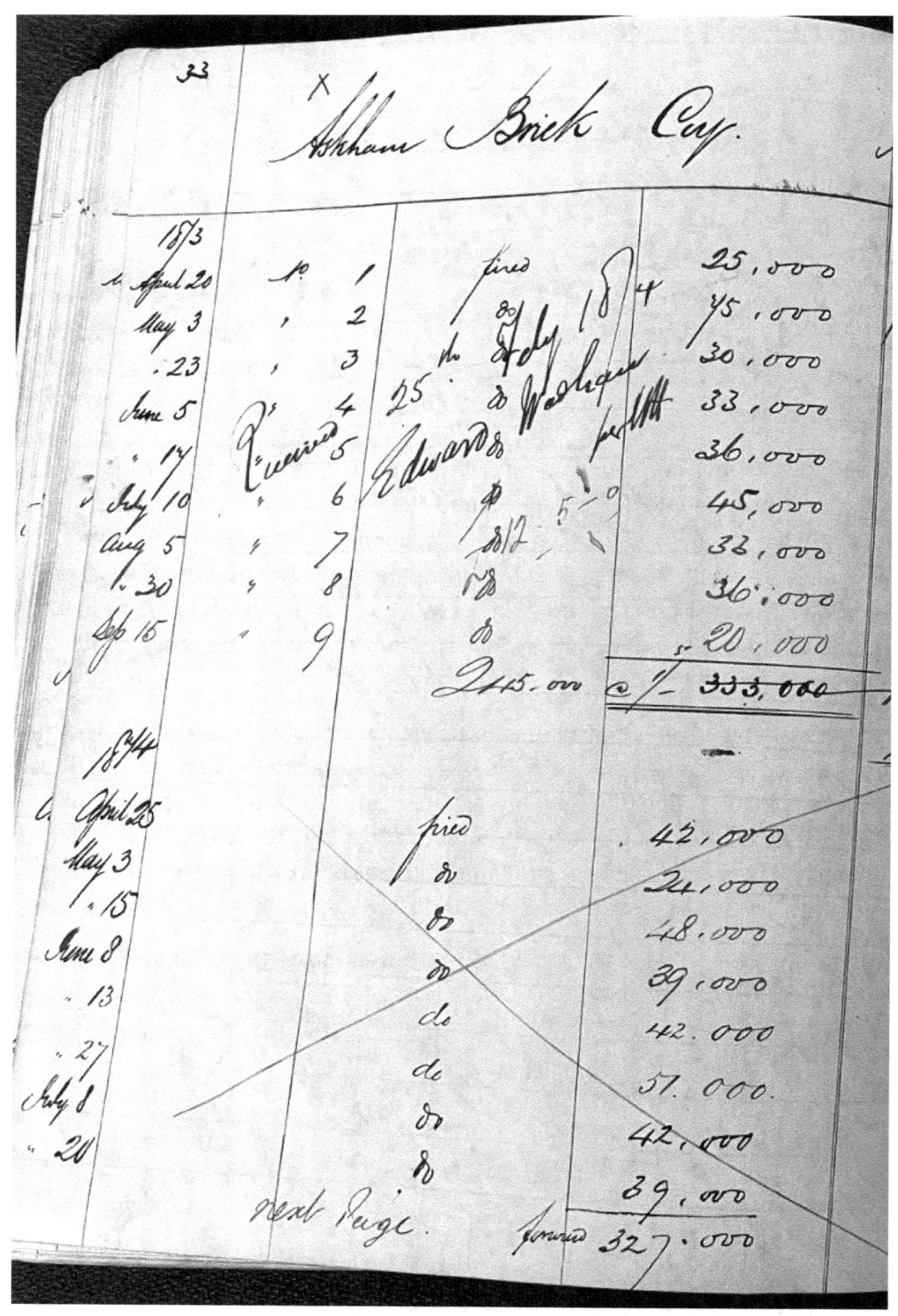

Above is the "Askham Brick Co, Ireleth," entry in the Duke of Buccleuch's Royalty Book for brickmaking, showing the number of bricks made, 333,060 bricks in 1873 and 327.000 bricks in 1874. (Courtesy of James Collinge, Furness Brick)

Ulverston Mirror, 31st October 1874.

Inn, Dwelling-houses, and Building Lots at Ireleth and Askam for Sale.

TO BE SOLD BY AUCTION,
By Mr. ROGER DODGSON,

At the house of Robert Turner, known by the sign of the "Bay Horse," at Ireleth in Furness, in the County of Lancaster, on Wednesday, the 25th day of November, 1874, at Six o'clock in the evening, in the following or such other lot or lots, and subject to such conditions and plans as may be produced at the time of Sale :—

Lot 1. All that well-accustomed INN, with the Stable and Premises belonging thereto, called the "Bay Horse," situate at Ireleth, aforesaid, and now in the occupation of the said Robert Turner, as tenant thereof.

Lot 2. Also all those TWO COTTAGES and GARDEN adjoining Lot 1.

Lot 3. Also all that detached COTTAGE and Premises near to Lot 1.

Lot 4. Also all that Dale or Parcel of LAND situate in Town Meadow, in Ireleth aforesaid, now in the occupation of Robert Turner.

Lot 5. Also all that Close or Inclosure of LAND as laid out in Building Lots, and adjoining the main road leading from Askam to Dalton, a portion of which is at present used as a Brick Yard, belonging to the Askam Brickmaking Company, and contains about 3 Acres.

All further particulars as to Lots 1 to 4 may be known on application at the offices of Mr. PARK, Solicitor, Ulverston and Barrow; and Plans may be seen and all particulars known as to the remainder of the property at the office of Mr. SETTLE, Surveyor, Ulverston.

October 30th, 1874.

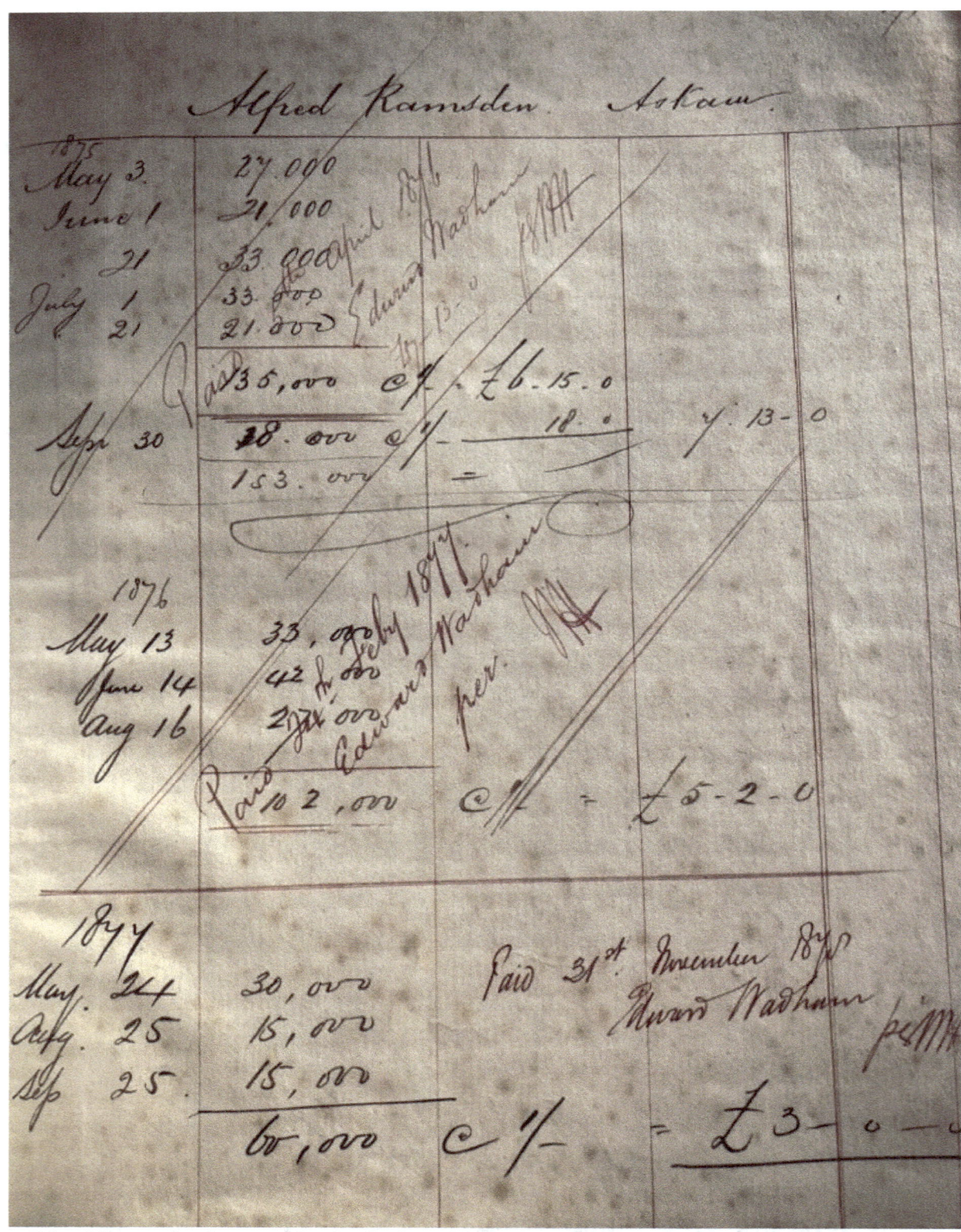

Alfred Ramsden's entry in the Duke of Buccleuch's Royalty Book for brickmaking, showing the numbers made and the royalties paid.

(Courtesy of James Collinge, Furness Brick)

Another small brickmaker in Askam was Alfred Ramsden, who married his wife at Ireleth in 1866, so I can only presume he came to Askam in the boom to make bricks, he was listed as a brickmaker in the 1871 census aged 23. I imagine he initially made them on the ironworks site and as time went on, he would have made them where he was building at the time, it looks like he was responsible for a lot of the shops on Duke Street, although by 1876 he was getting a reputation of being a dodgy builder as it would be worded now. He apparently would mortgage against a property then would run off with the money, he left Askam for Australia in 1879 where he made bricks and was a builder, buying more property with more mortgages and then moved on to New Zealand in 1882 where he did exactly the same again, he moved back to Australia in 1884 where he stayed and became a hotel owner but he soon became bankrupt in 1886 when his mortgages caught him up. Later he moved across Australia doing the same as before and in 1891 had £97,000 of debts! He carried on being in and out of jail for his debts and false cheques, indecency charges and being drunk, he abandoned his family too and was committed to an insane asylum where he escaped and went on the run! He went on to be a general nuisance, right until he died in 1923.

Company motif of the second Askam Brick Company formed in 1899, at the current Furness brick site, Dalton Road. (Courtesy of James Collinge, Furness Brick)

An Askam Brick Company Brick found during kiln repairs, Furness Brick.
(Kevin Alexander Collection)

Soulby's Ulverston Advertiser, 31st August 1899.

DALTON URBAN DISTRICT COUNCIL.

The usual monthly meeting of this Council was held at the Council Offices on Monday evening. There were present Councillors C. Kirkbride, J.P. (chairman), Donald, Robinson, Cowan, Polkinghorn, Lewney, Myers, Hamer, Backhouse, Kay, Ashburner, Wardley, and Lawn.

HIGHWAYS AND LIGHTING COMMITTEE.

Tramway Cross, Park-road : Resolved that the application by Mr. Mellon for the construction of a level crossing by tramway over the Park-road public footpath at a point near to and north of Park Farm House—such tramway being for the purpose of conveying materials from Park Farm Quarry to the proposed new brick works abutting on the railway near Greenscoe—be acceded to in accordance with the plan submitted.

The reports were accepted on the motion of Councillors Kay and Wardley.

The Askam Brick Company became a registered company on the 9th December 1899, and held their first official Directors meeting on the 29th December 1899, at the "Offices" of the proposed site. Present at the meeting were; R. F. Matthews, G. S. Heath, John Field and Henry Mellon. Construction of the works started on the 29th January 1900, and was undertaken by builder, Thomas Brown for an initial sum of £171-11-9. (£18,569.08 at 2024 prices) to build the two chimneys.

Here's some information taken from the company's minute book held by Cumbria Archive Centre, Barrow. (Reference; BDB 15/5/1).

People and companies involved during the construction period;

W. Gradwell - Timber.

H. Burt - Carter.

Furness Brick & Tile – supply of bricks and two brick machines (machines; £712 the pair. £73,955.28 at 2024 prices).

R. Balfour – Coal supplier.

R. B. D. Bradshaw – Solicitor.

Thomas Mitchell & Sons – Machine supplies.

Rimmington Bros – Oil.

A. J. Crawford – Leather belting.

D. Cairds Foundry – Supply of ironwork.

C. Whittaker & Co – Brick machinery.

R. F. Case – Alcoholic beverages.

Furness Railway Company – Transportation of goods, and connection of the line.

George Butterworth – Boiler and fittings.

H. Mellon – Civil & mining engineer.

W. R. Pickup – Plumbing.

J. Winder.

John Mills.

J. Dixon.

Joshua Birkett.

A. Cottam.

W. Bell.

W. Barratt.

W. Winder.

J. Tyson.

(Kevin Alexander Collection)

H. Gaythorpe – Engraver.

W. Dawson.

Askam Porphyry co.

Kennedy Bros.

J. Thornton.

Messer's. Ashburner.

John Fisher & son.

The company's first bricks began to roll out of the machines on the 1st December 1900, and on the 28th the company agreed to order coal for the kilns and for the boilers to further power the machines. On the 31st January 1901 an order to seal up the forth kiln without further delay was made, showing that production was truly up and running. However, a special meeting of the Directors was held on the 22nd November 1901, declaring that the company had debts totalling £4179-13-9. (£434,071.77. at 2024 prices).

"It was agreed that the leasehold, buildings, machinery, stock in trade, book dept, cash in land, and bank, chattels and effects of the company be disposed of to the Furness Brick and Tile Company for the above mentioned sum of £14179-13-9 in cash and for 3138 ordinary shares in the Furness Brick and Tile Company, to be issued out if a contemplated issue of 4000 additional ordinary shares of the Furness Brick and Tile Company. And resolved that an extraordinary meeting of the shareholders be called for the purpose of carrying the above resolution."

The meeting was held at 2pm on the 28th February 1902, passing Director R. F. Matthews as the liquidator of the Askam Brick Company for the purpose of voluntary winding up the business and that Furness Brick and Tile company take over the business. R. F. Matthews I must point out that he was also the managing director of the Furness Brick Company.

A final winding up meeting on the 4th April 1902, marked the end of the Askam Company and the beginning of Furness Brick at Askam.

(Courtesy of James Collinge, Furness Brick)

Furness Brick's Askam site in the 1930s. (Kevin Alexander Collection)

Furness Brick and Tile Company Limited began in 1898, being incorporated on 20th September of that year, however, the company's origins date further back to 1845.

Richard Frederick Matthews firstly started out with a brickyard on Thwaite Street, Barrow, he went on to acquire the brickmaking firms of Richard Platt on Walney Road, Barrow, and the Ormsgill Brick Company, Ormsgill, and sold his original site in 1897. He then sold the other sites to the Furness Brick and Tile Company for £17,500. (£19,221,876.83 in 2024 prices). A company whom he was the managing director and the main shareholder too.

(Courtesy of James Collinge, Furness Brick)

(Courtesy of James Collinge, Furness Brick)

(Kevin Alexander collection)

As already mentioned with the Askam Brick Company, Furness Brick took over the site and company on the 4th April 1902, with R. F. Matthews as the managing director. An interesting note is that the Askam site is completely different and unique to all the other brick yards in the Furness area, as instead of using boulder clay, the material used for the bricks here was shale, a rock basically halfway in-between being a slate and a clay which lays underneath Greenscoe and Greenhaume in abundance. This material is far superior to the boulder clays and with that you get a more superior brick of better quality in strength and appearance and because of this, all the facing bricks stamped "Furness brick - Barrow" were made here in Askam, while at the Barrow sites the cheaper common bricks were made.

Also, the kilns and accompanying buildings are substantially larger and more permanent than what had been used before in Askam, the site had the most modern and efficient Staffordshire transverse arch type kiln built, originally it had 12 chambers with a slate roof on timber frames, and the main chimney measured 220 feet tall (now 200ft). During the early years they fired intermittently due to supplying only the high-quality bricks and because of this the site fell into a state of disrepair with some arches having to be propped up to stop collapse. During the 1930's it was decided to make a modern rustic brick through the extrusion process, these extruded wire-cuts became quite popular to the point where a large housing estate in London was built along with many housing estates in the local area.

After the second world war in 1945 the kilns were completely rebuilt from the ground up and they decided to have 18 chambers instead of 12, this was to cope for the increase in production after the war. The roof of the kiln was rebuilt at that time too, using a steel frame and corrugated asbestos roofing sheets, as was common on post war buildings (this being completely replaced a few years ago). The company has continued to adapt to the market and carry on improvements right up to the present date where many other brick companies have not been able to carry on. This company can now offer many different types of bricks, from any shape or size, smooth or textured and in many colours too, this success has been largely due to the Collinge family and their involvement in Furness Brick over four generations! From W. G. Collinge starting out as the company secretary in the 1890s and then his son Bill amassing a majority share, Bill's sons Roger, John and Richard then ran the company, and now Richard's sons James, Nick and Mark are now at the mantle.

Soulby's Ulverston Advertiser, 31st August 1912.

SLEEPING OUT AT ASKAM.—A tramp named John Harris was charged with sleeping out without any visible means of subsistence at Askam the previous night.—P.C. Shaw spoke to finding prisoner asleep in the brick kiln at Askam Brickworks at 12-45 that morning. He had no visible means of subsistence.—Prisoner, who pleaded guilty, was committed to Lancaster Castle for seven days.

Barrow News, 23rd July 1938.

RUNAWAY LORRY CRASH

driver of this lorry crawled from his cab unhurt when the vehicle crashed into a bank at the side of the after running away on Greenscoe Hill, Askam, yesterday. The lorry ran backwards for about 300 yards, was turned into the roadside by the driver, overturned and caught fire.

It looks as though it was carrying a cargo of bricks up the hill towards Dalton on the old Dalton road.

"Donkey" train or narrow-gauge train at the brickyard quarry at Park. This was the last working train at the works, it was a 20hp diesel built in 1946 by Motor Rail Ltd. (Courtesy of Peter Holmes)

The same train with empty wagons heading to the quarry. (Courtesy of Peter Holmes)

A first world war 'Simplex' train at the quarry. (Courtesy of Peter Holmes)

The loco was built by the Motor Rail & Tramcar Co Ltd of Bedford under their trade name 'Simplex' in 1917, WD number 2182. It was of the Simplex 'Armoured' design and looked like a little tank, it would have seen service bringing supplies and ammunition to the trenches. Furness Brick bought it in May 1921 from the War Department Disposals and Liquidation Commission at Richborough, Kent. This replaced an earlier unreliable "Donkey" train, possibly the first the company had from 1899, however it is unknown whether this was a steam engine or an early petrol engine however I believe it to be the latter. Amazingly both trains pictured are still in existence and have both been restored since leaving Furness Brick in 1970/1.

HOW BLACKS POND GOT ITS NAME

Blacks Pond, formed because of subsidence of the Woodhead mine.
(Kevin Alexander Collection)

Soulby's Ulverston Advertiser, 8th April 1909.

PATHETIC CASE OF SUICIDE AT ROANHEAD.

"I SHALL DO SOMETHING TO MYSELF."

SAD OCCURRENCE.

A painful sensation was created in Askam and district about noon on Saturday, when it became known that Mrs Jane Black, wife of Richard Black. Had committed suicide in one of the water lodges near to Woodhead Pit. Deceased was well known in the district and much respected. It was a great shock to her many friends when they heard of her sad untimely end.

THE INQUEST.

An inquiry took place at the deceased's home, Big Field, Roanhead, on Saturday evening, before Mr. Poole (Coroner) and a jury, of which Coun. Alfred Jackson was foreman.

Mary Ann Black was the first witness, and said she resided at the Ship Inn, Kirkby. The deceased, Jane Black, was her sister-in-law, and was 47 years of age. Her husband's name was Richard Black. He was a miner. She (witness) only came to Roanhead the previous day, and had intended to go back the same night, but her sister-in-law asked her to stay all night. The deceased had not been well for a long time. She could not say how long. She had been attended by Dr Cook for depression. She had to be well looked after. They had breakfast together about eight o'clock, and after that they sat on the bedside. The deceased went out about 10.10 the same morning, which was as near as witness could tell, to fetch some eggs. She left the bedroom, and she (witness) and the family thought deceased had gone into the kitchen. Rose, one of her daughters said "Where is mother!" They found she had gone, and went to look for her. Witness said she examined the bedrooms and other rooms in the house. The window of the room in which witness and deceased were sitting was shut, but the one next to that room was open at the bottom. When she did not find her in the bedroom witness, went out to look across the shore to see if she could see anything of the deceased. She sent to Mr Hunter's, and also to Mr Burn's. She did not seem to be any more depressed that morning than usual.

The Coroner: Had she ever threatened to do anything to herself on any previous occasion.

The witness, who had been giving her evidence with much difficulty, completely broke down when she said that the deceased had told her that if they took her to Ambleside "I shall do something to myself."

WHAT THE ENGINE DRIVER SAW.

John Molyneux said he resided at Sandscale Cottage. He was an engine driver. He was coming over to this end of Roanhead to get through his usual routine of work. He saw Mrs Black's two daughters hurrying across the field towards Mrs Burn's. He thought something must be wrong, and very soon he saw Mrs Bath, and he asked her what was to do. She said that Mrs Black had got out of the house and they were looking for her. In a short time he saw Mrs Bath standing on a stone heap near to Woodhead Pit, waving a white handkerchief. He went towards Mrs Bath, as she said she had seen some of Mrs Black's clothing on the edge of the water at Woodhead Pit. She was frightened to go *down, so she asked witness. He described the wearing apparel which the deceased had apparently kicked off, as the clothing was scattered about. He looked into the water and saw the body quite distantly. This would be about 11 o'clock, or soon after, as the morning shift men were leaving their work. The body was lying about 10ft from the side, and in about 5ft or 6ft of water, but added witness, it would be hard to tell, as it was broken ground. They commenced to use some grappling irons, but as soon as they started dragging for her the water went muddy. He asked some workmen to get a hook. Some men who were coming to work also helped. Witness held a man called Nicholas Atkinson, who managed to reach the body with a hook until it floated to the edge of the water. She appeared to be quite dead. He assisted in placing the body on a stretcher, but he did not assist in taking it home.*

The Coroner then briefly summed up, the jury returned a verdict that "The deceased drowned herself whilst temporarily insane."

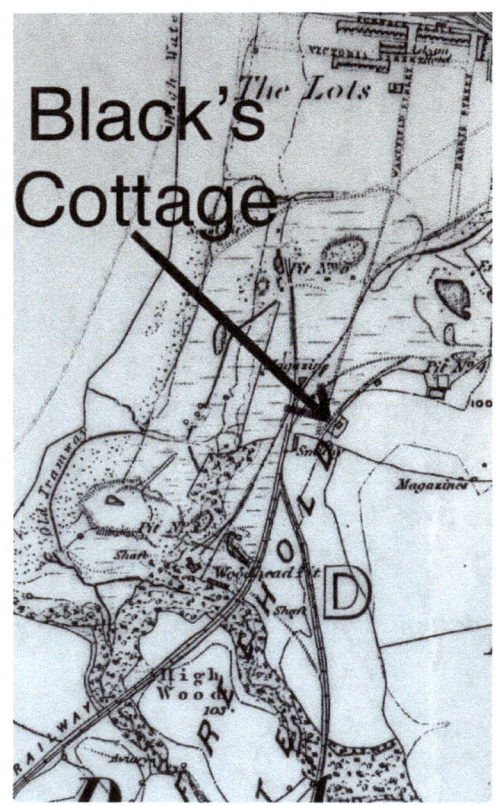

(Courtesy of Janice Cumming)

(Kevin Alexander Collection)

THE RUGBY

Askam 'Football' Club as it was originally known by was officially formed in September 1879, and they held their first ever game a month later against Barrow on 25th October where Askam unfortunately lost. I have found that they were playing games from 1877 amongst themselves. Members of the founding Askam club were also playing cricket for both Ireleth and Askam and Askam Good Templars Cricket teams, and similarly to what occurred at Ulverston went on, where the cricket lads at the end of the season decided to carry on meeting up and played 'football' instead.

Of course, you may have noticed the 'football' mentioned instead of rugby and you will see this further on! You see, all were football teams in the beginning, the difference only being what rules the club decided to play by. Some even played both rules - association rules (soccer) or rugby rules. I've not found Askam to have ever played under association rules until a separate association club did in 1904. However, as time went on, clubs became more definitive to what they played. Association football simply became known as football with hardly anyone referring to it as soccer anymore. By 1895 there was a split between the rugby playing clubs and a separate rugby organisation was set up called the Northern Union (later known as Rugby League in 1922), and those who didn't break away stayed in the Rugby Union, Askam only joined the Northern Union on 20th August 1897, after all the other local clubs had already done so!

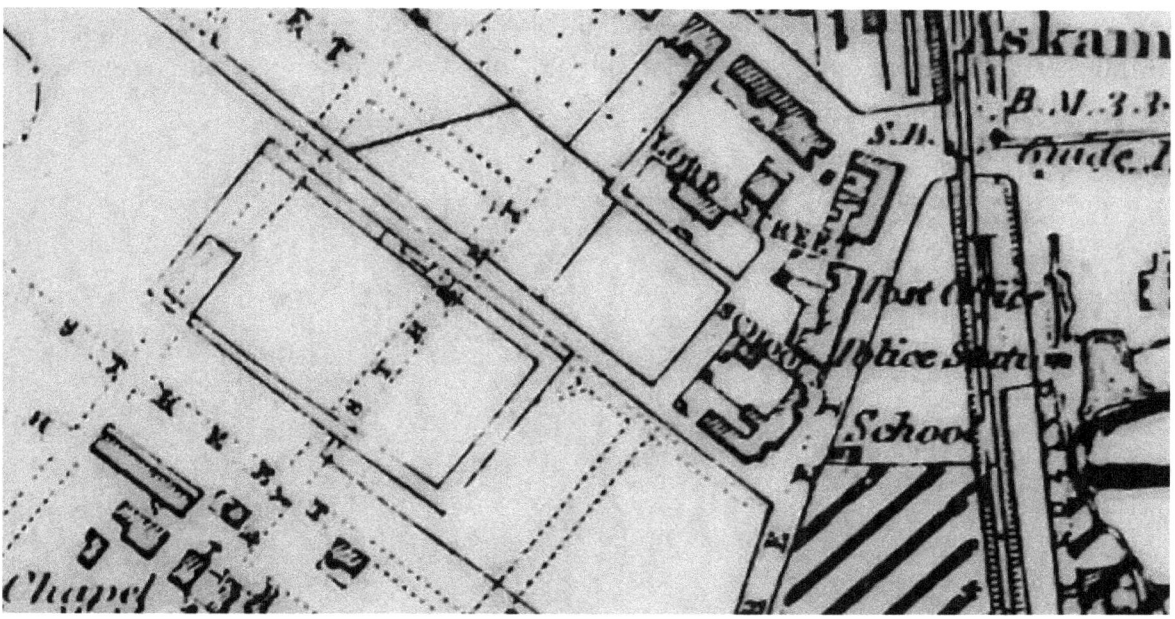

Askam's rugby pitch marked out on the 1890s Ordnance Survey map with the planned streets crossing it. (Courtesy of Janice Cumming, Askam History Club)

From 1879, Askam played their matches in a field off Sandy Lane (Duke Street) known only as an enclosure or Marsh field, the current name of Fallowfield Park was not adopted until a much later date. With only renting the field it seems the club were at risk of being kicked off, and in 1895 this became the case when Mr Anthony Clark gave notice to T. H. Relph, the Secretary of Askam Football Club, to quit Marsh Field. However, I believe a deal must have been made as I have found the club to have continued using the ground up until 1906 where an article states that the Club became "defunct," this was short lived for I have them playing again in 1907. Possibly instead of being defunct it could just be that they ended up being evicted and then without a pitch until one was found on Duddon Road in 1907, whether this new home was the ground of the present-day Askam United Football Club or the grounds of the Duddon Sports and Social Club I am not sure. The Rugby ended up purchasing their original ground in 1924 where they have remained ever since.

I cannot for sure declare what the club's original colours were from the earliest of days, as its simply not mentioned unfortunately. Although the club has in its possession a really old photograph, taken I believe at the club's formation in 1879, and after careful studying I believe it is the oldest known one of the club. It appears to be taken outside of the Ironworks offices in Askam - this makes sense with the President of the club in 1879 was William Crossley, who was also the Manager of the Ironworks. I'd like to imagine the colours were green and gold (yellow) with white shorts, but we will never know for sure. What we do know is the club adopted to wear a white shirt in 1882 with white "drawers" these later changed to blue, the socks remaining brown. The white shirt was kept right up until the late 1930s and early 40s when the club changed to the green kit, they are well known for wearing now.

(Both photographs courtesy of Janice Cumming, Askam History Club)

Earliest known photograph of Askam Rugby Club circa 1879. (Courtesy of Askam Rugby. Picture originally donated to the club by Bridget Benson)

Known players are, Dick Williams, Stephen Trenwith, Jack Dixon, Roger Sharp, Stephen Troughton (holding the ball), Jack Myers, Jim Sharpe, J. Kidd and Jos Anderson.

Soulby's Ulverston Advertiser, 25th September 1879.

ASKAM.—FOOTBALL CLUB.—A largely attended meeting has been held in the National Schools for the purpose of forming a football club. The following officers were elected for the ensuing season:—President, Mr. Wm. Crossley; vice-president, Mr. H. Mellor; captain, Mr. Stephen Troughton; committee, Messrs. Jno. Trenwith, J. Stockwell, R. Woodburn, J. Fleet, R. Bell, Jas. Guthrie, G. Postlethwaite, and R. Galloway; hon. sec. and treasurer, P. Postlethwaite. Mr. J. Lamb has kindly allowed the club to occupy a field for practice. The club now numbers some forty members, and promises to be a very flourishing one. It has been decided to arrange matches for the ensuing season with clubs in the surrounding district.

Barrow Herald, 1st November 1879. (Askam's first ever game)

ASKAM FOOTBALL CLUB.—MR. G. ASHBURNER'S TEAM (BARROW) v. ASKAM.—This the opening match of the season (and the first match of the Askam club since its formation) was played on Saturday, at Askam, in the presence of a large number of spectators. The weather was fine, and the ground in splendid condition, despite the recent heavy rain. Ashburner kicked off for his side at three o'clock. The ball was well returned, and a series of scrimmages were contested in the Barrow half of the ground, in which it was seen that Ashburner's team had the advantage in weight. The game was very even up till about three minutes before the call of half time, the visitors having scored one touchdown. However, just before half time the Barrow forwards took the ball, by some good passing up to the Askam goal, where a fierce scrimmage was fought out of which Lindow, getting the ball, scored the first try for the team. The try was taken by Atkinson, who kicked a neat goal; afterwards half time was called. On the ball again being started, the Askam forwards played up with great vigour, and, aided by some good runs by their backs, succeeded in causing the visitors to touchdown in self-defence. The game continued to be very even, neither side gaining any advantage for some time. The superior condition of the Barrow forwards began to assert itself, and they worked the ball down to the Askam goal line, and T. Carlton getting the ball out of a scrimmage, ran in and obtained the second try for his side. The try was again converted into a goal by Atkinson. Askam again played up vigorously, under this second reverse, and succeeded in keeping their opponents at bay till call of time, the score being then—Ashburner's team two goals and two touchdowns; Askam, one touchdown. For Ashburner's team, Smythe, Carlton, and Gradwell (forwards), and Atkinson and Jones behind played a good game, and Cook, W. Guthrie and Spencer (forwards), and Johnson, Troughton, and Trenwith behind, showed good form for Askam. It was discovered at the close of the game that the visitors had been playing 16 men to Askam 15, which makes the *debut* of the Askam club a very creditable one. The next match in connection with the A.F.C. will be played on November 15th, at Askam, against the Victoria Club, Newbarns. The following are the names of the players:—Ashburner's team: Backs, Atkinson and Kendall; three-quarter backs, E. Jones and T. Bell; half backs, T. Carlton and A. N. Other; forwards, Lindow, J. Carlton, Smythe, Gradwell, Brown, Rogers, Presow, Ashburner (captain), and Mawson. Askam: Back, F. Johnson; three-quarter backs, S. Troughton (captain), and W. Dodgson; half backs, F. Gibbs, and J. Trenwith; forwards, J. Stockwell, R. Spencer, Cook, Hewitson, W. Guthrie, junr., J. Guthrie, G. Gott, A. Macdonald and S. Kendall.

Barrow Herald, 12th February 1881.

ASKAM RANGERS v. DALTON SECOND FIFTEEN.—A match was played between these two teams on Saturday, Feb. 5th, on the ground of the former. Lindsay won the toss, and chose to play with the wind. McDonald kicked off for Askam. The ball was not returned and several scrimmages were formed in Dalton 25. The Dalton team, however, prevented Askam from scoring anything. By the good kicking of Milligan, and running of Rowley, Hill, and Nicholas, the ball began to approach Askam goal line. After some loose play in Askam ground, Hill, Chamber, and Jones broke away with the ball, and driving it across Askam goal line, Jones fell upon it and secured what seemed to be a fair try. McDonald said that he had his hand on the ball at the time when Jones touched down, and a maul followed in which he got the ball and touched down. The ball was again put in motion. Four touch downs followed rapidly in favour of Dalton through the good play of Harper, Todd, and Askew, and kicking of Jackson and Milligan. Just before half time was called, Rowley got the ball, and by a good run passed Askam forwards, but was brought to the ground by Lewis. On the game being resumed, Lewis got past the Dalton forwards several times, but he always found either Milligan or Backhouse in the way. Askam now played in good style, and compelled Dalton to touch down twice. Some long kicks by McDonald were loudly cheered by the spectators. One of these sent the ball into Lindsay's hand, and although in Dalton 25 he passed Askam forwards, went up the field, followed by McDonald, and secured the first try that was got during the game. Milligan brought out the ball and Linsay kicked, but just as the ball rose the wind caught it, and the result was a poster, and Askam touched down. After kick out, Askam gradually began to draw near Dalton goal line. Farran kicked the ball into touch, and McDonald threw it out into Lewis' hands, but as it was said not to have been thrown out straight Dalton did not attempt to stop him; the result was that he secured a try (which Dalton disputed), and, although disputed, McDonald would kick, and converted into a goal. This terminated the game, Dalton claiming the victory, and having to their credit one poster and six touch downs to Askam's one disputed try and two touch downs. Teams:—Askam: Back, T. McDonald (capt.); three-quarter backs, J. Guthrie, Hugh Saunders; half backs, J. Lewis, R. Lewis; forwards, M. Backhouse, L. Backhouse, G. Griffiths, J. Wilson, R. G. Graham, Wm. Quail, J. Pope, R. Hodgson, T. Cross, T. Trembles. Dalton: Back, S. Milligan; three-quarter backs, W. Backhouse, T. Jackson; half backs, J. Lindsay, W. H. Rowley; forwards, J. Hill, J. Todd, W. Harper, T. Chambers, J. Thompson, J. Jones, W. Backhouse, C. Nicholas, J. Askews, W. Hill.

Barrow Herald, 15th February 1881.

FOOTBALL AT ASKAM.

Sir,—Would you kindly allow me space in your valuable paper to make a few remarks on the match played at Askam, on Saturday last. It is usually the case that when one team visits another for the purpose of playing a match, they generally look to be treated with kindness and respect; but I think from what I saw and heard at Askam on Saturday, I may come to the conclusion that the people of Askam do not practice that respect which they expect from others. First, I would mention the language used by some of the Askam team, which I may say was disgusting. I have witnessed many matches, but never did I hear such language used by any team as that used by the Askam team on Saturday. Next I would say that of the many matches I have seen played I never yet saw so much unfair play, the visitors having repeatedly to submit to anything that was said by the Askam captain. Lastly I would mention the conduct of the spectators, which was anything but creditable to themselves, and which made it most uncomfortable for the visitors. I may say I have heard it reported that Askam was a rough place to play a match at; and I am sorry to say, from what I saw on Saturday that the said report was not without foundation. I hope that when the next match is played at Askam, the team as well as spectators, will conduct themselves in a more respectful manner than they did on Saturday. Hoping I have not too far intruded on your valuable space, I remain yours, &c,

A PLAYER.

Barrow Herald, 26th August 1882.

ASKAM FOOTBALL CLUB.—The annual general meeting of the above club was held in the National Schools, on Wednesday. Mr. Massicks occupied the chair. The finances of the club show a balance in hand of £4 12s. Mr. Massicks was elected president, Mr. Mellon vice-president, Mr. S. Troughton captain, Mr. J. Trenwith vice-captain, Mr. H. T Hosking hon. sec. and treasurer, with a committee of twenty. The chief business of the meeting was the changing of the colours of the club. It was decided to have white jerseys with a red rose on the left breast, white drawers, and dark brown stockings. It was also decided that the club should travel north this season and meet the Whitehaven, Cockermouth, Maryport, and Workington teams. Several new members have joined, and altogether a successful season is anticipated.

Askam colours. (Kevin Alexander Collection)

Barrow Herald, 18th November 1882.

DEATH ON THE FOOTBALL FIELD.

THE INQUEST.

On Monday afternoon the Coroner of the District, Mr. J. Poole, held an enquiry at the Vulcan Hotel, Askam, as to the cause of the death of Robert Askew, of Dalton. The following composed the jury:— Messrs. Matthew Wilson (foreman), Joseph Thompson, Henry Waiting, William Atkinson, Robert Parker, William S. Jervis, John Dixon, George Trenwith, Daniel Holmes, James Hodgson, Jonathan Dixon, and William Fell.

It appears that about three o'clock in the afternoon of Saturday last a football match came off between a fifteen of the Dalton White Star football club and a fifteen of the Askam club, on the ground of the latter. The game had not been in progress more than a few minutes, when the deceased was observed to make a grasp at a member of the Askam club who had possession of the ball, but missing his grasp he fell forward and did not rise again. The cry of "a man down" was raised, and Dr. McMillan Challoner, of Askam, who happened to be on the field watching the game, ran towards the deceased and found him unconscious, breathing very slowly, "not more than five times a minute" as the Dr. said, but his heart beating terrifically. In five minutes he was quite dead. Various rumours have been current, such as that he fell upon the ball and injured himself internally; that he had been tripped up, and had received concussion of the brain, &c., &c.; but the medical man's evidence sets at rest all such rumours, for he says that there was not a sign of a rupture or a bruise upon him. It is somewhat remarkable that the only witness called to give evidence concerning the actual fall of the deceased was the young man who was playing on the part of the club which was opposed to that in which deceased was playing. There might at least have been some one or more of his fellow members produced at the inquest to state whether the deceased had shown any symptoms of weakness before, or had ever made any complaint of weakness in their hearing. The father of the deceased emphatically says he never did any such thing, but was always strong and hearty. The sad event has created a strong public sympathy with the family of the deceased, and also promoted a feeling against the game played according to the "Rugby Rules."

The first witness called was a member of the Askam Football Club named John Woodburn, who, being sworn, said: I and others were playing football on Saturday, deceased was amongst us. We had been playing about three minutes. I saw him stretching out his hand to catch hold of one of the Askam men, and I turned round to watch the ball, when I heard the cry, "A man down," and I went up to the deceased, who was already surrounded by the doctor and others. He had been running. He did not catch hold of the man, he was trying to. I do not know whether he had ever played before or not. We play under the Rugby rules. His mates had said that in the dressing room he did not feel in very good trim for playing. He was removed to the Vulcan Hotel, but he was dead before he left the field. He had been joining in the game for a few minutes previous to his death. The ball was near the deceased when he fell, but there was no one near him. We had no scrimmage or rough work.

The first witness called was Samuel M'Millan Challoner, surgeon, of Askam, who deposed: I have this day made a *post mortem* examination of the body of the deceased, and have found all the organs healthy with the exception of the heart and the brain. The wall of the right side of the heart was thin; one portion seemed to be giving way, as of some of the muscular fibres. It was not a complete rupture. The brain was very much congested, and showed hemorrhages externally the cause of death was congestion of the brain with these small hemorrhages, due to a weak heart, coupled with excitement brought on by the exertion of running. There was no fracture or rupture of the bladder or of any organ whatever. I was present on the field when the playing was going on and the first thing I noticed of him was him lying on the ground with some men rubbing him. I went up to him and found him almost stopped breathing. He was not breathing more than five a minute. His heart was beating vigorously, as I could feel by the pulse. I tried artificial respiration, but he died with five minutes after I saw him. I ought to say that I asked the captain of the team if he had complained of anything and he replied that deceased had told him that he was in very good form. The cause of death was not assignable to any violence except that of the excitement of the game and the running. I could not say that he might have complained before he played. The walls of the heart were thin, which was probably due to disease.

Thomas Askew, of Dalton, miner, said: Deceased was my son and he was aged 18 last birthday. He played at football last winter and also this season so far. He never complained of having any pain at the heart, but he has always been strong and healthy. He had never been at home ill for a week.

The Coroner in reviewing the case to the jury said this being the second case which had arisen from the football field within about a month, he thought it best to hold an inquest, although he had reason to expect the evidence that had been given, as it might have been thought to have occurred from rupture of the bladder, or some other organ. Death has been caused prematurely, or to the deceased having a weak heart and that coupled with the excitement of the game, and to the running causing congestion of the brain from which the deceased died, and the jury would find a verdict in accordance with that fact. There did not seem to be any one to blame, that deceased had been thrown down nor received any injury. He might say that this game as played under the Rugby rules appeared to him to be an excessively dangerous one. It was very different to the game that used to be played when the ball was put down and kicked to the goal.

The jury immediately brought in a verdict of "died from natural causes."

Barrow Herald, 13th October 1883.

ASKAM 3RD XV. V. BARROW EXCELSIOR CLUB.—These teams met at Askam on Saturday, and the result was a win for the Askam team, by one goal, two tries, five touchdowns, to one touchdown. The Excelsiors although lighter than their opponents, played a very plucky and good game, and there was little in the choice between the two for the first twenty minutes, the ball being generally in neutral ground. Brown, of Askam, then secured the first try, which was converted into a goal by Woodburne. Two other tries were got, one by Brown, and the other by Newby, but were not improved upon. For the winners Brown, Kelly, Bettany, Woodburne, Sharpe, and Duncan played very well, whilst for the losers Hayton (captain), McColl, Clayton, and Cochran, played pluckily, trying hard to avert defeat.

The club at this point doing well with three teams!

Barrow Herald, 9th April 1889.

The return match between Askam and St. Helens was played at Askam, on Saturday, before a good attendance of spectators. The kick off did not take place until 5-15 p.m. In the first half Sharpe gained a try for Askam, the kick at goal failing. The score at half-time was:—Askam, 1 try, 4 minors; St. Helens, nil. On the change of ends Askam had the best of matters, and Kendal scored twice after good runs, but the attempts at goal failed. The Askam team played in their best form, and at the call of time were left winners of a grand game by 3 tries, and 3 minors; to St. Helens, 1 minor. Kendal, Pope, Lewis, and Vickers, were perhaps the pick of the winners, whilst Lund, Cross, Borthwick, and Foreman were most conspicuous for the losers.

Soulby's Ulverston Advertiser, 21st November 1889.

ST. HELENS v. ASKAM.

At Askam. Soon after the start Alexander scored for Askam, and very soon after again ran in. Half-time score: Askam, two tries; St. Helens, one minor. Re-starting, Dearden ran over, but the point was disallowed. Halton soon after scored a splendid try for St. Helens, from which a goal was kicked. Final score:—Askam, one goal, two tries, and two minors; St. Helens, one goal and three minors.

EDWARD ALEXANDER is 22 years of age, and is the smallest man in the team. He is only 5ft. 6in. in height and in weight is 9 stone 7lb. He came from Askham to Walkden three years ago and partnered Jones at half-back. He soon became a general favourite, and his style of play is most effective. For a short distance he has a wonderful turn of speed, and his trickiness is always a source of great amusement with the spectators. He is a coal miner.

Teddy moved to Walkden because of the ironworks strike at Askam in 1889, he played for Walkden until they folded in 1899. (Courtesy of Dave Huitson)

Soulby's Ulverston Advertiser, 24th April 1890.

ASKAM FOOTBALL CLUB.

Record of matches for the season 1889-90:—

Points for.			Played against.	Points against.		
G.	T.	M.		G.	T.	M.
0	0	4	Leigh	1	0	8
3	4	10	Whitehaven	0	0	5
4	5	4	Ulverston	0	0	2
1	1	2	Manchester Rangers	1	3	4
1	1	3	Shipley	0	0	3
1	1	4	Egremont	0	2	3
1	0	4	Millom	0	2	2
1	1	3	Kendal Hornets	0	0	3
1	2	1	St. Helens	1	0	2
3	4	3	Workington	0	0	1
1	0	2	St. Helens	0	4	4
1	0	2	Kendal	1	1	2
0	0	1	Millom	1	0	4
0	2	4	Morecambe	0	0	2
1	0	1	Lancaster	1	0	3
0	1	0	Tyldesley	3	7	0
0	1	2	Kendal	0	0	1
2	0	2	Egremont	1	2	2
0	0	2	Barrow	1	1	5
2	1	2	Morecambe	0	0	4
0	0	8	Whitehaven	1	3	4
1	1	6	Ulverston	1	0	4
1	2	4	Lancaster	1	0	5
1	0	6	Barrow	0	0	4
1	0	8	Workington	0	2	4
1	0	1	Kendal Hornets	1	2	6
0	1	4	Leigh	0	0	3
3	2	3	Manchester Rangers	1	0	0
3	4	2	Dewsbury	0	2	2
7	2	3	Shipley	0	0	2
41	36	101		16	31	94

Won, 20; Lost, 9; Drawn, 1.

Scorers. W. C. Kendall, 16 tries; J. Pope, 12; T. Vickers, 1; J. Tomkinson, 8; S. Troughton, 6; T. Mylrea, 3; J. Anderson, 3; E. Alexander, 3; J. Dixon, 2; J. Sharpe, 2; R Sharpe, 2; T. Townson, 1; J. Woodend, 1; T. Whittaker, 1; D. Thompson, 1; R. Case, 1. Pope dropped seven goals; Vickers, four; R. Lewis, two; and Kendall, one. Lewis also placed 23 goals from tries.

Barrow Herald, 12th July 1890.

ASKAM FOOTBALL CLUB.

The annual general meeting was held at the Vulcan Hotel on Wednesday week, the captain, Mr. W. C. Kendall, presiding. The yearly financial statement showed the club to be in a satisfactory and healthy condition, the balance—after meeting all disbursements—exceeding £31. The report showed that the club had enjoyed an exceedingly successful season. The balance sheet and report, which were presented by the secretary (Mr. W. Tyson), were unanimously adopted. Mr. R. Todd-Newcombe was elected president for the ensuing season; hon. treasurer, Mr. James Trenwith; hon. secretary, Mr. W. Tyson, 3, Lord-street, Askam. Mr. W. C. Kendall was unanimously re-appointed captain, it being remarked that the success of the past season was mainly due to his influence and consistency. Mr. Roger Sharp was re-elected vice-captain. For the reserves Mr. T. Huddleston was chosen captain, and Mr. R. Cole vice-captain. The following committee was appointed:—Messrs. S. Troughton, J. Anderson, J. Sharp, R. Greetham, T. McDonald, R. Sharp, J. Trenwith, J. Woodburn, J. Barnes, J. Rylands, John Tyson Townson, J. Park, and T. Relph.

Thirty-four matches have been arranged for the coming season, against 28 last season.

Champions-Lancashire Junior Challenge Cup and North-Western Junior League 1900-01. (Courtesy of John Clegg) Photo taken back of Vulcan Hotel.

A. Cottier.   W. Wadeson.   F. Lewis. (Treas.)   S. Barr.   R. Kendall.   J. Heather.   J. Dobb. (Sec.)

   W. Cottier. (Vice-capt.)   L. Barr.   E. Gill.   H. Fulton.   J. Constable.   J. Kidd.

T. Mawson.   C. Barnes.   R. Holmes.   H. Wilson. (Capt.)   J. J. Mylrea.   J. Barr.   W. Dixon.

S. Lewis.   E. Conner.   W. J. McGivern.   R. Lewis.

North-Western League Winners 1904-5. (Courtesy of John Clegg)

Soulby's Ulverston Advertiser, 12th December 1912.

THE ASKAM MASCOTS.

The above reproduction is that of Messrs. J. Lishman, Kirkby, J. Benson, H. Holmes, and Fallows, who accompanied the Askam Football Club to Wigan recently on the occasion of the club's splendid victory.

On the face of it you would think this relates to the mighty Wigan, unfortunately, no. They actually beat Wigan Athletic instead, that club is now known for playing football, they switched sports in 1932. Askam won 13-6 on the day.

North-Western League Winners 1913-14. (Courtesy of John Clegg) Photographed at the rear of Vulcan Hotel.

Soulby's Advertiser, 7th May 1914.

NORTH-WESTERN LEAGUE.
FINAL.
ASKAM v. SEATON.

ASKAM THE CHAMPIONS.

Played at Railway Meadow, Dalton, in ideal weather, before a big crowd. Askam turned out as selected, and Seaton were at full strength. Mr. Hestford, of Broughton, Manchester, was the referee. Askam faced the wind and sun in the first half, and were early penalised, Seaton finding touch well up. Barnes replied, and being thrice penalised Seaton fell back. Brown was held on the line, but Askam got off-side. A drop at goal by Lewis was low, another by Grice going wide. Askam had had the best of matters so far. Lewis, in vain, claimed a try, and then Barnes marked, Lewis landing a goal. Seaton attacked, and Askam were penalised, but the kick was charged. Barnes held Moore after fine play by Brown. Again Lewis landed a penalty goal. Spry again led the attack, and the succeeding play was splendidly contested. Half-time:—

Askam ... ... 4 Pts.
Seaton ... ... Nil.

Seaton were repeatedly in possession in the second half, a round of passing failing when Moore knocked on, while a capital tackle by Lewis kept Fletcher out. Grice lacked speed in a breakaway, and Askam had again to defend. First Brown and then Fletcher made brave bids for the line. With the Askam forwards away, Lewis missed a penalty, then another round of passing by Seaton took Moore over with a try at the corner, Pepperill missing the goal. Another attack by Seaton; a fine kick by Barnes that found touch at half-way; a gallop by Lewis, another by Spry that took him to the line, and the Cumbrians were beaten. Result:—

ASKAM ... ... 4 Pts.
SEATON ... ... 3 Pts.

Mr. Nixon, chairman of the Cumberland Commissioners, presented the cup to Charlie Spry, the Askam captain, amid scenes of great enthusiasm.

GREAT RECEPTION OF CUP WINNERS.

Not since the days of Steve Troughton and other stalwart Askamites has there been so much enthusiasm displayed as that witnessed at Askam on Saturday. During the week, the "boys" in white had been getting themselves into form, and all with one accord were agreed on one thing—that Askam would come out on top. True the score was not a big one, neither was the margin a wide one, but it was sufficient to spell "win." Of course, the weather played a great part in the game, and Askam went with the full determination to win, and the players were all bred and born in Askam, and all good, clean "sports" at that. All who could go, went to Dalton by train, cycle, shank's pony, and—car? It was a busy time for the milliners; one shop sold nearly 300 white rosettes before noon, so one can imagine the feeling that pervaded the stalwarts of Askam. People in Askam were waiting with bated breath for the result. News leaked through at half-time that Askam were leading 4pts. to nothing, and this caused quite a flutter. When the "final" news arrived that Askam had won, everyone you met wore a joyous smile. The enthusiasm was great. Between the presentation of the cup and the arrival home of the team, Askam was getting into form to give the team and cup a jolly good welcome. The route between the station and the headquarters was crowded with spectators. As the train steamed into the station, cheer after cheer was raised, hats and caps were flying in the air, and all kind of songs were sung by the youngsters, for it seemed as though the whole of Askam had turned out. The team and their supporters, headed by the Askam Town Brass Band, then marched to the headquarters, Vulcan Hotel. The cheering was deafening, and the enthusiasm was of such a nature that it took some time to cool down. Hearty good fellowship reigned supreme. At the various places where men do congregate, the health of the winning team was pledged with musical honours— and even the "cup" was not forgotten. It was a great time, and one that will not easily be forgotten by the young and rising generation in Askam for for many years to come.

(Inset) J. Boyd   R. Myers. J. Gill. J. W. Lewis,(CHAIRMAN) C. Houghton.   (Inset) E. Lewis.

R. Seward. D. Newton,(TREASURER) Evan Lewis,(SECRETARY) E. Ainsworth. S. Wallace. H. Woodend.

T. Pope,(TRAINER) J. Fullard. J. Houghton. W. Alexander. Geo. Dixon. T. Kirkby. J. Peutherer. J. Gilchrist. W. Walker,(TRAINER)

E. Bodley. W. Kirkby. T. Wharton. J.D. Wharton. W. Barnes,(CAPTAIN) T. Dixon. J. Pope. T. Walker. T. Fell.

James Wharton.   R. Coulson

North-Western League Winners 1919-20. (Courtesy of John Clegg) Photographed to the side of the Vulcan Hotel.

The Askam vs Bradford programme. (Courtesy of Askam Rugby Club)

Askam Football Club.

President: MYLES KENNEDY, Esq., J.P.

Vice-President: Capt. J. M. CHALLINOR, M.C.

Hon. Secretary:
EVAN LEWIS, 22, Stafford St., Askam-in-Furness.

Headquarters: DUDDON ROAD. Colours: WHITE

OFFICIAL PROGRAMME.

PRICE ONE PENNY.

NOTES:

It is just 20 years since Askam were last drawn at home in First Round Proper, Northern Union Cup, Widnes being the visitors on that occasion and winning by a try to nil.

To-day we entertain Bradford Northern in First Round of the Northern Rugby Football Union Challenge Cup. The West Riding Team occupy a rather low position in the League List, this evidently being one of their lean years. They are, however, dogged Cup-fighters, and we confidently look forward to a thrilling contest well and capably managed.

It might be of interest to note that Bradford has figured in two Challenge Cup Finals, with the following results:—

1898—BATLEY 2 goals, 1 try; 7 points—BRADFORD nil.

1906—BRADFORD 1 goal, 1 try; 5 points—SALFORD nil.

THEY SAY—

That a certain Askam Forward took his North Western League Medal ('19-'20) to a Barrow Jeweller to be engraved. Upon being informed that centre piece would not stand much pressure, he naively remarked to the Jeweller "If it should happen to break, shove a bit of glass in, and I'll use it as a ruddy monocle"!!!

That Fearless Forward, Fell, figures frequently for fine footwork.

That Jimmy Pentherer has lately gained some re(pent) with his goal-kicking capabilities.

That nobody is more interested in to-day's match than our old friend Jamie Woodend (Copper-Nob).

That our 'Soccer' friends are holding another of their successful Dances in the Assembly Rooms this evening. Everything from "Imagination" to a "Dream of Romance" is included in their repertoire.

That the Askam Town Band's Instrumental Contest takes place next Saturday evening. Make a note of this date.

That entries for the Dalton Rugby Club's Knock-out Competition close in March. Entry forms and terms from Jimmy Welby, Bank, Dalton.

That our friends across the water, the best of luck in their the Cumberland Cup.

Colours are White, Knickers Blue,
Bradford to-day we're on view;
you predict,
team be licked,
we shall meet in Round 2?

Askam's Cup-Winning Years:

North Western League—1900-1, 1904-05, 1906-07, 1913-14, 1919-20.

Lancashire Junior Cup—1900-1.

Lancashire Junior Cup (Runners up)—1899-1900.

Also Winners and Holders of Cup for 9-a-side teams.

Askam Players who have made their mark:

Bobby Lewis, Jont Whitehead, Jack Kidd, Jim Metcalfe, Ike Lathom, Tom Mylrea, Geo. Whitehead, Jack Dixon, Roger Sharp, Jack Beetham, Jack Wharton, Jim Vickers, Joe Pope.

(All the above, I think, secured County Honours).

OTHERS:

Steve Troughton, Bob Crawley, Jamie Woodend, Fred Lewis, Joe Anderson, Jack Woodburn, J. Trenwith, Tom Vickers, Teddy Alexander, Tom Fell, Wilse Cottier, Hughie Fulton, Tot Mawson, Jud Edmondson, Tom Constable, Billy McGivern, Pete Vickers, Billy Mason, Jim Constable, Ned Connor, Jimmy Barr, Fred Trenwith, Billy Grice, Walter Barnes, Ike Woodend, Tom Wadeson, Jimmy Wharton, Sam Lewis, Dave Lewis, Jack J. Townson, J. J. Mylrea, Bill Dixon, Jack Benjamin, Louis Barr, Jos. Cain, Arthur Sirett, Dick Townson.

(With apologies to those whose names have been omitted).

CUP TIE NOTES.

The record 'Gate' previous to last year for the Northern Union Final was at Headingly, Leeds, in 1903, between Salford and Ha— when £1,834 8s. 6d. was taken at the turnstiles. The atte— was 32,506.

The smallest 'Gate' for a Final Tie was at Salford in 19— Broughton Rangers and Wigan only drew 8,000 spectators and —

The Draw for the Second Round of the Northern — Competition, to be played on March 12th, will be made durin—

(Inset) J. Boyd.   R. Myers. J. Gill. J. W. Lewis,(CHAIRMAN) C. Houghton.   (Inset) E. Lewis.

R. Seward. D. Newton,(TREASURER) Evan Lewis,(SECRETARY) E. Ainsworth. S. Wallace. H. Woodend.

T. Pope,(TRAINER) J. Fullard. J. Houghton. W. Alexander. Geo. Dixon. T. Kirkby. J. Peutherer. J. Gilchrist. W. Walker,(TRAINER)

E. Bodley. W. Kirkby. T. Wharton. J.D. Wharton. W. Barnes,(CAPTAIN) T. Dixon. J. Pope. T. Walker. T. Fell.

James Wharton.   R. Coulson

North-Western League Winners 1919-20. (Courtesy of John Clegg) Photographed to the side of the Vulcan Hotel.

The Askam vs Bradford programme. (Courtesy of Askam Rugby Club)

Askam Football Club.

President: MYLES KENNEDY, Esq., J.P.

Vice-President: Capt. J. M. CHALLINOR, M.C.

Hon. Secretary:
EVAN LEWIS, 22, Stafford St., Askam-in-Furness.

Headquarters: DUDDON ROAD. Colours: WHITE

OFFICIAL PROGRAMME.

PRICE ONE PENNY.

NOTES:

It is just 20 years since Askam were last drawn at home in First Round Proper, Northern Union Cup, Widnes being the visitors on that occasion and winning by a try to nil.

To-day we entertain Bradford Northern in First Round of the Northern Rugby Football Union Challenge Cup. The West Riding Team occupy a rather low position in the League List, this evidently being one of their lean years. They are, however, dogged Cup-fighters, and we confidently look forward to a thrilling contest well and capably managed.

It might be of interest to note that Bradford has figured in two Challenge Cup Finals, with the following results:—

1898—BATLEY 2 goals, 1 try; 7 points—BRADFORD nil.

1906—BRADFORD 1 goal, 1 try; 5 points—SALFORD nil.

THEY SAY—

That a certain Askam Forward took his North Western League Medal ('19-'20) to a Barrow Jeweller to be engraved. Upon being informed that centre piece would not stand much pressure, he naively remarked to the Jeweller "If it should happen to break, shove a bit of glass in, and I'll use it as a ruddy monocle" ¦¦¦

That Fearless Forward, Fell, figures frequently for fine footwork.

That Jimmy Pentherer has lately gained some re(pent) with his goal-kicking capabilities.

That nobody is more interested in to-day's match than our old friend Jamie Woodend (Copper-Nob).

That our 'Soccer' friends are holding another of their successful Dances in the Assembly Rooms this evening. Everything from "Imagination" to a "Dream of Romance" is included in their repertoire.

That the Askam Town Band's Instrumental Contest takes place next Saturday evening. Make a note of this date.

That entries for the Dalton Rugby Club's Knock-out Competition close early in March. Entry forms and terms from Jimmy Welby, Bank Buildings, Dalton.

That we wish our friends across the water, the best of luck in their endeavour to lift the Cumberland Cup.

THAT—
Our Colours are White, Knickers Blue,
'Gainst Bradford to-day we're on view;
Now can you predict,
Should this team be licked,
Who the deuce we shall meet in Round 2?

Askam's Cup-Winning Years:

North Western League—1900-1, 1904-05, 1906-07, 1913-14, 1919-20.

Lancashire Junior Cup—1900-1.

Lancashire Junior Cup (Runners up)—1899-1900.

Also Winners and Holders of Cup for 9-a-side teams.

Askam Players who have made their mark:

Bobby Lewis, Jont Whitehead, Jack Kidd, Jim Metcalfe, Ike Lathom, Tom Mylrea, Geo. Whitehead, Jack Dixon, Roger Sharp, Jack Beetham, Jack Wharton, Jim Vickers, Joe Pope.

(All the above, I think, secured County Honours).

OTHERS:

Steve Troughton, Bob Crawley, Jamie Woodend, Fred Lewis, Joe Anderson, Jack Woodburn, J. Trenwith, Tom Vickers, Teddy Alexander, Tom Fell, Wilse Cottier, Hughie Fulton, Tot Mawson, Jud Edmondson, Tom Constable, Billy McGivern, Pete Vickers, Billy Mason, Jim Constable, Ned Connor, Jimmy Barr, Fred Trenwith, Billy Grice, Walter Barnes, Ike Woodend, Tom Wadeson, Jimmy Wharton, Sam Lewis, Dave Lewis, Jack J. Townson, J. J. Mylrea, Bill Dixon, Jack Benjamin, Louis Barr, Jos. Cain, Arthur Sirett, Dick Townson.

(With apologies to those whose names have been omitted).

CUP TIE NOTES.

The record 'Gate' previous to last year for the Northern Union Cup Final was at Headingly, Leeds, in 1903, between Salford and Halifax, when £1,834 8s. 6d. was taken at the turnstiles. The attendance was 32,506.

The smallest 'Gate' for a Final Tie was at Salford in 1911, when Broughton Rangers and Wigan only drew 8,000 spectators and £376.

The Draw for the Second Round of the Northern Union Cup Competition, to be played on March 12th, will be made during next week.

Programme for To-day—26-2-21.

BRADFORD NORTHERN v. ASKAM

AT DUDDON ROAD.

Kick-off 3 p.m.   40 minutes each way.

TEAMS: **ASKAM.**

1
W. BARNES.

5　　　　4　　　　3　　　　2
T. BURROW.　W. KIRKBY.　T. DIXON.　J. POPE.

7　　　　　　　6
R. COULSON.　　　T. WHARTON.

8　　　　　　9　　　　　　10
J. PEUTHERER.　J. BOYD.　T. KIRKBY.

11　　　　　12　　　　　13
J. NANSON.　W. ALEXANDER.　T. FELL.

Referee: Mr. F. FAIRHURST, of Wigan.

13　　　　　12　　　　　11
MANN.　　DOBSON.　　HALFORD.

10　　　　　9　　　　　8
MYERS.　　HOLMES.　　DOLAN.

7　　　　　6
MORTIMER.　MELLING.

2　　　　3　　　　4　　　　5
SMITH.　LAUGHLIN.　SURMAN.　TREHARNE.

1
OLIVER.

BRADFORD NORTHERN.

TOUCH JUDGES:

Messrs. W. M. Gabbatt (Barrow) & Jas. Atkinson (Dalton)

The Askam Town Prize Band

Will play Selections on the Field from 2 to 3 p.m.

The Game that the programme was from, ASKAM vs BRADFORD NORTHERN:

Barrow News, 5th March 1921.

THE CUP NOT FOR ASKAM.

(BY "Line-out.")

Without a doubt, the spoils went to the better side at Askam. Ardent supporters within hearing of the press table - a very "comfy" little arrangement, for which many thanks – freely admitted it. Truth to tell, the Villagers never looked like winning. It may be that they played just as well as the opposition allowed them, or it may be that they were over-impressed by the importance of the occasion; but certain it is that Askam did not give of their best. Even the seasoned Barnes made mistakes; nothing serious, or that in any way let his side down, but still he wasn't the Walter we know.

Throughout, Bradford held the whip-hand. The dividing line between a First Division team, however lowly, and a junior team was well marked. To a man, Askam worked like Trojans; all solid hard graft, but not always to the best effect. Over-eagerness cost them the Bradford try. The halves and centres did not link up successfully. Coulson performed cleverly; doubling round the scrum on one occasion, he all but got through. But some of his passes lacked direction, and were altogether too lightening-like for Wharton, Dixon, and Kirkby. All praise to the defence of Burrow and pope; scoring chances, practically nil. The forwards were all heroes alike; little wonder that the energy expended during the first half left them lacking towards the finish.

The Yorkshiremen, too worked hard. They were desperately intent on winning; so much so, in fact, that towards the finish one lost his head to the point of being sent off. They had a decided pull in the weights, and were the better tacticians. Their first goal, from outside half-way, was a beauty. Their second was the result of over-zeal by an opponent, and their try was somewhat of the "gift" order. With the last kick of the match, Askam scored a goal; they went close for one in the first half, and had luck when, now and again, chances offered.

So that, after all is said and done, the Askam lads deserve congratulation on having coming through with a good deal of credit.

Barrow News, 15th March 1924.

FOOTBALL FIELD PURCHASE.—The Askam Northern Union Football Club are to be heartily congratulated upon purchasing, with the assistance of the Northern Union, their original football ground. Negotiations have been in progress some time, but the transaction was completed this week, the vendor being Mrs. Barr. The ground, which is situated off Duke-street, is about three acres in area, and will permit of a full-sized playing pitch being laid with plenty of room for the spectators. It is proposed to fence it off and to bank up one side. Certain parts of the field will require to be levelled, but it is expected that it will be put into first-class trim for next season. A certain amount of the money required to complete the purchase has been advanced by the Northern Union on generous terms, and the club has opened a 500 shillings subscription list to defray part of the expenditure. The purchase will mean a big saving in rent to the club, and it is hoped to make it one of the best football grounds in the district. It was on this ground that the Askam Rugby team played soon after it started in 1875, and it was the football ground up to 1906, when the club became defunct. In the days of Barlow-Massicks and Stephen Troughton the sods were raised, and it was relaid as level as a billiard table, and it has the reputation of being the dryest football field in the district. After the Askam club was re-formed, they played on the Duddon-road field, but even greater things are expected when a return is made to the old venue.

Barrow News, 10th May 1924.

HELP FROM ABROAD.—On reading that Askam Rugby Club had acquired a playing field Mr. George Dixon gathered dollar subscriptions from a number of Askamites now in America, and with the result that the club's exchequer has benefited to the extent of about £4. The subscribers included Mr. George Dixon, Mrs. Dixon, Mr. Geo. Fisher (of Millom), Mr. James Brown, Mr. Harry Brown, Mr. Wm. Brown, Mr. W. Cullen, Mr. W. Edmondson, Mr. W. Kelly, Mr. Harry Jackson, Mr. David Twiname, Mr. Tom Twiname, Mr. F. Quirk, Mr. John Dickinson, Mr. Joseph Dickinson, Mr. James Dickinson, and Mr. Joseph Dixon.

Askam's original badge. (Courtesy of Ray and Jane Alexander)

Lancashire Junior Cup Winners 1930-31. (Courtesy of Jeanette Shepherd)

D. Kellet. J. Sanderson. _Procter _Colthurst. W. Chester. Tom Martin. G. Coulson.

T. Lawley. C. Raven. R. McGivern. W. Kewley. J. Procter. D. Thoroughgood. S. Stevenson. A. Stevenson.

G. Neild. C. Kellet. W. Thoroughgood.

H. Johnson.   H. Rawlinson.   N. Kitchen.

ASKAM WINNERS OF LANCASHIRE JUNIOR CUP, 1930-31

(Courtesy of David Robinson)

Barrow News, 15 January 1938.

NORTH-WESTERN RUGBY LEAGUE CUP

ASKAM PRESENTATION

The North-Western R.L. Cup was presented to Askam (the winners) at a social gathering at the Railway Hotel, Askam, on Tuesday, by Mr. W. Gabbatt, a member of the Rugby League Council and the Barrow R.F.C. Committee.

Mr. J. Bourne received the cup on behalf of the club, and suitably acknowledged Mr. Gabbatt's congratulations. A hot-pot, at which the club entertained members, was first served, followed by a smoking concert.

Thanks were expressed to Colonel R. Thompson, Mr. Gabbatt, Mr. W. Kellett, Mesdames Blezard, Benson, Stables, Bradley and Irving and Mr. F. Benson for his entertaining.

Barrow News, 29th January 1938.

ASKAM 17pts., MARSH HORNETS nil

The game commenced at a fast pace, with Askam continually hammering Hornets' defence. The pace was kept up and after a half-hour's play Newton converted a free-kick for the home side. This score was shortly followed by a smart try by McGivern, who puzzled the Hornets' defence and crossed the line, the goal kick failing. Shortly before half-time Gee, of Askam, made a strong dribble from half-way and touched down at the corner for a very hard-earned try. The goal kick failed.

The Hornets commenced the second half without the services of F. Pratt, injured. The game proceeded on similar lines to the first half, with Askam holding the upper-hand. F. Newton obtained a try and kicked two goals, and a fine drop-goal, from half-way, came from McGivern.

Dyson, Bourne, Newton, Newsham, McGivern, and N. Starkie were prominent for the home side with Stevenson and Gee whole-hearted workers. For the visitors, Wharton, a real bundle of tricks, Johnson, and Scott were outstanding, and Pratt was fine up to his injury.

Barrow News, 22nd January 1938.

THE NEWS SATURDAY, 22 JANUARY, 1938.

ASKAM R.F.C., who won the North-West Lancashire area final of the Rugby League Challenge Cup, but lost to Maryport, the pick of the Cumbrian section, in the play-off for progress to the first round proper.

NEARLY THERE.—Scene in the Askam v. Maryport Rugby League Challenge Cup area final qualifying round at Askam, which Maryport won 6pts. to nil. In a Maryport raid on the Askam line, the referee has awarded Askam a free-kick for obstruction.

THE IRONWORKS

(Furness Year Book 1905)

The Furness Iron and Steel Company was formed in 1864, when Edward Thomas Wakefield and John Shapter, both London barristers of Middlesex and civil engineer John Harris of Durham all decided they wanted to start a company for the purpose of manufacturing iron and steel in the Furness district at Ireleth Marsh. A 32-acre site was selected on Chapman's lot because of its proximity to the large ore fields and limestone quarries, E. T. Wakefield had also bought 28 acres of Chapman's lot separately to the company for his 'town' project and to acquire a portion of the ore field. The construction of the works was begun by April 1865 however there was one problem! The site was near but not directly connected to the Furness Railway mainline. The company needed access to the land of their neighbour William Alexander MacKinnon, a Scottish clan leader and recently retired Middlesex politician who owned 500 acres of the Greenscoe and Greenhaume Estates to be able to transport materials in and out of the works.

The company must have made quite the impression on their neighbour during negotiations for the use of his land as for March 1866, a new company was incorporated; The Furness Iron and Steel Company Limited, which took over the assets of the previous company. The new company had an authorised capital in shares of £70,000 (£7,069,282.51 in 2024 prices.) in shares of £1000 (£100,989.75), 65 shares were taken up, 35 shares were distributed between the original company partners and the rest by the new partners W. A. MacKinnon (senior), W.A. MacKinnon (junior), Lauchlan Bellingham MacKinnon, Daniel Henry MacKinnon, the father Willam Alexander MacKinnon (senior) became the Chairman of this new company.

Barrow Herald, 1st April 1865.

IRELETH.—The blast furnaces, so long a matter of gossip in this neighbovrhood, are soon to become a reality. During the past week upwards of 40 men have been employed upon the site. It is said that the first proceeding will be to build about one hundred cottages for the workmen, and no doubt Ireleth will soon become a flourishing place.—*Cor.*

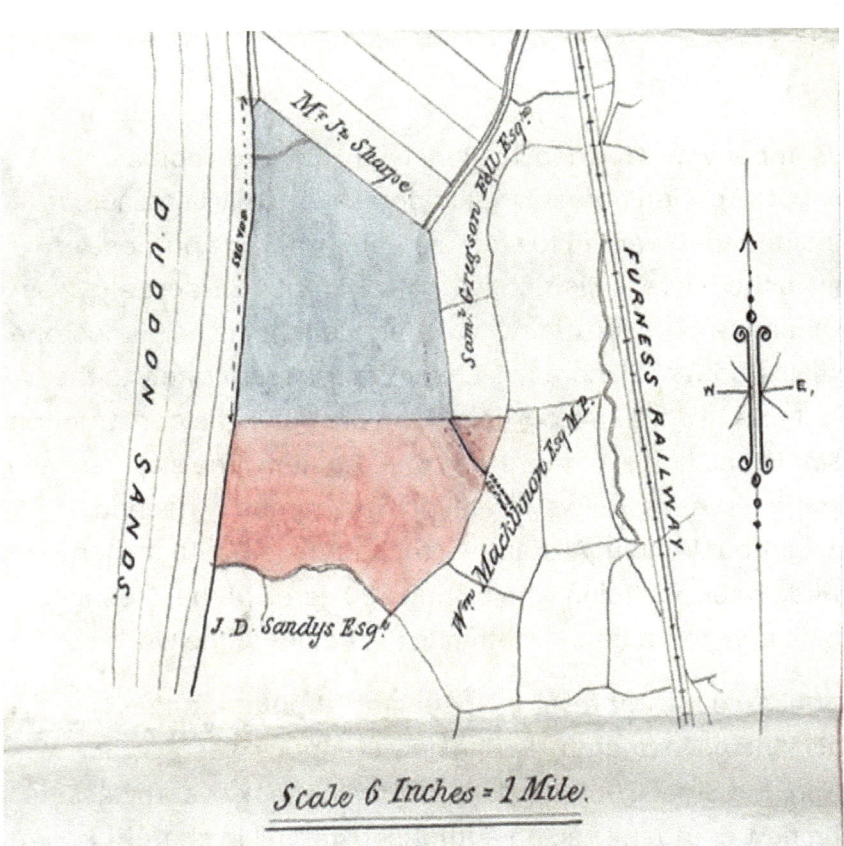

The original size of the ironworks site marked in blue, prior to the MacKinnon's joining and the buying of Mr Fells land. (Kevin Alexander Collection)

Barrow Herald, 12th August 1865.

IRELETH IRON AND STEEL WORKS.—On Tuesday last the foundation stone of the chimney of the Furness New Iron and Steel Works at Kirkby Ireleth, was laid by Mrs. Wakefield, wife of one of the firm. The men, numbering about 200, all suspended work for the time, and Mrs. Wakefield, attended by Mr. Wakefield, Mr. Clarke, of Furness Abbey, Mr. Peascod and Mr. Carruthers proceeded to lay the stone in its place, which she did in a very graceful and skilful manner. After the laying of the stone, Mrs. Wakefield said :—I express a wish and hope for the success and prosperity of the Furness New Steel and Iron Company. I thank you for coming to assist me in laying the first stone of these buildings, and for the labour you have bestowed on the work. I pray that the undertaking may contribute to your welfare, and I will conclude with the German proverb —" What is well begun is half done."—Three hearty cheers were then given for Mrs. Wakefield and heir, one for Mr. Wakefield, and one, for the firm. At the close of the interesting proceedings the whole of the workmen were supplied with refreshments.

Barrow Herald, 14th July 1866.

FURNESS IRON AND STEEL COMPANY
(Limited.)

Anyone who knew Ireleth twelve months ago, and paying a visit to it now would feel a strange sensation of utter bewilderment. Then it was a small but beautiful village lying on the side of a vast and barren valley on the shore of the sea, and even now it is marked upon the ordnance maps as a large rabbit warren. Now it is the scene of busy and extensive works. The change is as sudden as it is surpassingly complete. Through the enterprise and capital of Messrs. Wakefield, Mackinnon, and Company, what was once a barren waste has become a beehive of industry. Where furse luxuriated only six months ago, beautiful houses and streets now stand; where the seamew laid her eggs, and rabbits ran wild, shops and stores now stand. *Then* there were

   * * * laughing bowers,
Where by twining elms, a pleasant shade
At summer noon is made;

But *now* there is

   * * * the incessant din
Of iron hands, and roars of brazen throats,
Joining their unmingled notes,
While the long summer day is pouring in,
Till day is gone and darkness does begin.

We paid a visit to the new works of the above company on Tuesday last, and were quite struck with the vast changes that had taken place in this quiet out-of-the-way spot. The first object that strikes the eye as we approach this really wonderful place is the tall chimney which rises to an altitude of 109 yards. It was built, from the design of Mr. Clark, the manager of the iron department, by Mr. J. Carruthers of this town, and is one of the neatest and most substantial we have ever seen. We believe there is only one larger in Great Britain—that at Glasgow. At the base is inserted a tablet, bearing the following inscription:—

     Hic Lapis a
A. Florence W. Wakefield, D.
    die 8 mo. Augusti,
   Conjugo Carvet dilectissimo
18   et unico filio   65.
     astantibus

Through the kindness of the officials we were enabled to ascend to the top of the tall column, the view from which is truly grand, and we see the village of Ireleth (the old village) constitutes but a few houses, compared with those which have arisen within the past few months, and taking a bird's-eye view of the whole we can see that the ground is laid out for a large town, which, with the wealth of the district and the well-known enterprise of the proprietors, will ere long be completed. Just outside the buildings, and within two or or three hundred yards of the steel works, ore is being brought up from the bowels of the earth in large quantities, and as far as we could judge it appears to be of the purest and best kind. The ore after being dug up is carried to the slips or stores, within a few feet of the furnaces, two of which are already erected, and foundations laid for two more. Two exceedingly powerful engines are fitted up in a chastely-built engine-house, in which is room for two more to be fitted up shortly. Further on are the walls of the steel works, which, when completed will be very extensive, and fitted up 12 blowers, rollers, sheers, hammers, &c., &c. The steel department is under the management of Mr. H. Haywood, the furnaces under that of Mr. C. J. Clark, and the whole under the general management Mr. Allan Meredith. Mr. James Carruthers, of this town is the contractor for all the buildings. There seems to be everything in the immediate neighbourhood for carrying on these extensive works but coal. They have on the ground plenty of clay, limestone, water, ore, and wood, and we learn that it is expected that the manufacture of iron and steel will commence in earnest about October next. From what we saw on Tuesday last we have no doubt the works will be highly prosperous, and that Ireleth will at no distant date be a populous and thriving town, and that Messrs. Wakefield and Co., will have the pleasure of seeing the bleak and barren desert converted into an important and prosperous hive of industry and a place of wealth.

Ulverston Mirror, 8th September 1866.

The Furness Iron and Steel Company, Limited,

ASKHAM, DALTON-IN-FURNESS, LANCASHIRE.

DIRECTORS:

CHAIRMAN: W. A. MACKINNON, ESQ., London;

VICE-CHAIRMAN: JOHN HARRIS, ESQ., Woodside, Darlington;

W. A. MACKINNON, JUN., ESQ., M.P.;

CAPT. MACKINNON, R.N., M.P.;

E. T. WAKEFIELD, ESQ.;

JOHN SHAPTER, ESQ., Q.C.;

SECRETARY: L. A. E. MACKINNON, ESQ.;

SOLICITORS: YARKER & SALMON, Ulverston;

BANKERS: WAKEFIELD, CREWDSON, & Co., Ulverston, Barrow, and Kendal.

The works opened in August 1867, and foundations were laid for the building of the Bessemer steel plant, but work was halted as there was a national economic crisis, not the best time to commence a business I imagine and so they halted production until the economy improved. It wasn't until 1871 until the first two furnaces were put in blast. A third furnace was added in 1873 and a fourth in 1874, but the Bessemer plant was never completed and the idea of making steel at Askam was dropped completely for the company to just concentrate on making hematite pig iron.

Barrow Herald & Furness Advertiser, 1st November 1873.

On Sunday evening a valuable horse, the property of the Askam Iron and Steel Company, was severely burnt by the bursting of a slag-ball which was being taken from the furnaces.

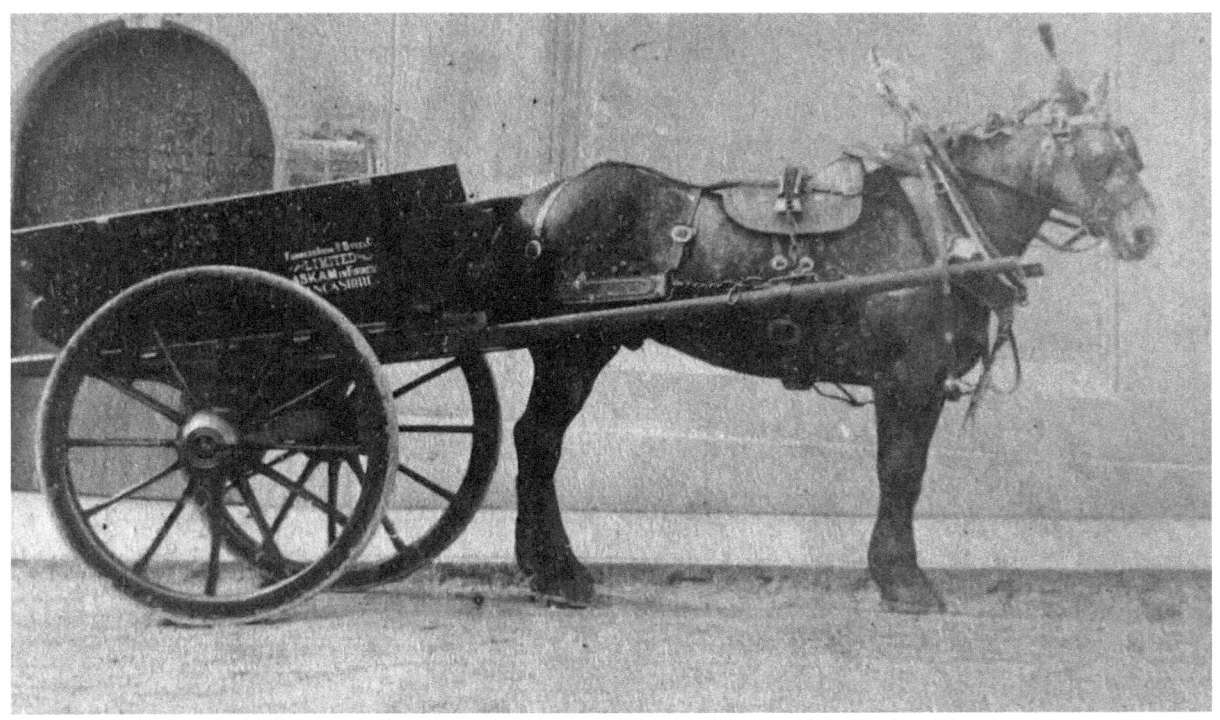

A Furness Iron and Steel Company horse. (Kevin Alexander Collection)

In modern times it seems hard to believe that horses were once used to move the slag about, but it was the case, in fact it would have been a common sight as the first roads of Askam were made up with the ironworks slag moved by the horses in large wooden carts lined with iron and brick. The slags consistency being somewhat semi molten by the time it found its way to where it was meant to go, so workers would tip it out and then rake it creating a rough road surface, sometimes the slag would cool too soon, and the now solid block would have to be broken up on the road with sledgehammers.

Broken up slag can still be seen on the unmade roads still, although only one exists in Askam today where you can still see the poured slag, and that's the shore end of Steel Street by the pavement, also poured slag was used on the sea wall of the Woodhead mine (Blacks Pond) which can still be seen today.

Furness; Past and Present. J. Richardson 1880.

A well put together write up on the Ironworks, however a big chunk comes from Mr. Crossley's own account that he wrote in the July edition of the 'Engineer' in 1871. I also point out the date of the Furness Iron Company forming is incorrect, as it was in-fact 1864. Also, Richardson purposely withholds naming E. T. Wakefield at any point, this was I suspect because the book is dedicated to the Duke of Buccleuch, and the Duke and Wakefield were rivals in a lengthy legal battle over the Askam mine on Chapmans lot.

FURNESS: PAST AND PRESENT.

The Works of the Furness Iron and Steel Company, Limited, though very considerably smaller than the famous works at Barrow, are of much importance; and, seeing that they have been directly instrumental in founding Askam, deserve some attention. It was in August, 1867, that a number of gentleman formed the company for making iron and steel from the hæmatite discovered to abound in the locality, particularly in the neighbourhood of Park and Roanhead, in which district they acquired possession of the mines discovered and worked by Mr. Kennedy. Their intention was then, as it is now, to convert the Hæmatite iron issuing from their furnaces into Bessemer steel, though this process has not been developed yet; their manufacture stopping with the convertion of the ore they raise, into hæmatite pigs suitable for forge and for Bessemer purposes. Commencing operations in unfortunate times, when the money panic of 1866 had reduced the demand for iron of all kinds very much, the company conducted their business under the greatest possible difficulty until 1869, when the prospect in the iron trade somewhat improved and when a change in the management of the works was made. Mr. C. E. Clarke who had previously been in the employ of Messrs. Gilkes, Wilson, Pease, & Co., of Middlesbro', had been the chief engineer for the construction of the Askam works, and the erection of the first two furnaces. He was followed in the management by John Whitwell, Esq., now M.P. for Kendal; and subsequently by Mr. Talbot, of Grange; this gentleman being succeeded by Mr. W. Crossley, the present managing director, who joined the company in 1869. Mr. Crossley had previously been manager for Messrs. Cochrane & Co., of Middlesbrough.

Since Mr. Crossley's connection with the Askam works they have been much extended and have greatly enlarged their operations; and have been so successful that from the time of the establishment of the works there has never been a cessation of operations not even during the great depression which characterised the autumn of 1875. The two original furnaces with which the Company started were followed by a third constructed on a larger scale, being 75 feet in height, 23 feet in width in the 'bosh;' this being then, and yet remaining the largest furnace erected for the manufacture of Bessemer iron in the Hæmatite district. It was 10 feet higher and 5 feet wider than the two previously constructed by Mr. Clarke. The new furnace worked so successfully, that the company added another of the same size to their plant. Both these larger furnaces were put up by Mr. Crossley as the result of theoretical considerations, in spite of the fact that at other works in the district every attempt at increasing the size of the furnaces had resulted in failure, and in the face of the adverse predictions of people well acquainted with the manufacture of hæmatite iron. In these four furnaces the company can make about 7,500 tons of iron per month, and in the manufacture, 8,000 tons of coke, 13,000 tons of iron ore, and 4,000 tons of lime-stone are used. The consumption of coal is very small, as the gases emitted from the consuming mass in the furnaces are utilised for heating the blast used in blowing the furnaces and raising steam to work the engines. In consequence of this profitable utilisation, the district surrounding the works is not so prejudicially affected by the gas escaping as is the case with the old form of furnace.

Within the last few years the numerous and valuable mines previously worked by Mr. Joseph Rawlinson, of Dalton, have been acquired by this company, who are thus large vendors as well as consumers of iron-ore. At their different furnaces and mines, they employ about 1,000 men, and pay in wages per week, about £1,500. The following is a more detailed description of the works.

The unusual height of the great chimney will not fail to arrest the spectators attention at once. The stack is no less than 326 feet high, and is a very conspicuous land-mark which can be seen from nearly all the high ground in the Furness peninsula, and a great distance out at sea. At the front of the furnaces are the depôts for the storage of the iron ore, coke, and lime-stone. The construction of these, render them capable of stocking the following large quantity of material:—iron-ore 30,000 tons; coke, 10,000 tons; lime-stone, 4,000 to 5,000 tons. The material used is raised by a steam-hoist, with a steam cylinder, 40 feet in length, working without gear of any kind beyond the requisite valves to shut the steam off and on. The trucks thus conveyed up to the top run along the depôts on two distinct lines of railway, and after the material they contain has been emptied, they pass on to the opposite end and are lowered by a pneumatic hoist of novel construction. The furnaces consist of the two large ones already mentioned as 75 feet high, 23 feet wide in the 'bosh,' and with a diameter of 8 feet in the hearth. The two smaller ones are 65 feet high, 18 feet wide in the 'bosh,' and 7 feet diameter in the hearth. The material is filled at the depôts into large iron barrows, which are then drawn to the top of the furnaces on inclines by two winding engines, there being a separate incline for the two different sizes of furnaces. The winding engines for the smaller furnaces were constructed by Messrs. Coupe, of Wigan, and those for the larger furnaces by Messrs. Westray, Copeland, & Co., of Barrow-in-Furness. The inclines are set at an angle of $25\frac{1}{2}$ degrees, and have a double line of railway with steps in the centre, which latter enable the men to walk to the top of the furnaces without the risk of ascending with the barrows. When the material has reached the top of the furnaces, it is charged into them by what is commonly called the cup and cone, or bell and hopper arrangement. The bell and hopper is specially contrived to close the mouth of the furnace, thus securing the collection of the whole of the gases, which are utilised as before stated in raising the temperature of the blast or to generate steam in the engines. This is a decided improvement upon the hæmatite furnaces which allow the gases to escape. This is also undoubtedly the largest bell arrangement yet adopted at any furnace in the hæmatite districts of Cumberland and Furness. The bells are lowered into the furnaces for the admission of material by an ingenious hydraulic contrivance, invented by Mr. Wrightson, of the firm of Messrs. Head, Wrightson, & Co., of Stockton. The 'tuyeres' offer a blast area of about 66 square inches to each furnace.

The blast of the furnaces is supplied from five large blowing engines of 1,300 horse power, with one spare engine which is only started in case of accident to any of the others. Three of the engines are of the most approved construction, and two of them are so arranged that the waste steam from the others (which are high pressure) are worked by means of a vacuum produced by condensation. One of these condensing engines was from the works of Messrs. Cochrane, Groves, & Co., of Middlesborough, and the other from Messrs. Westray, Copeland, & Co., of Barrow-in-Furness, both respectively reflecting the greatest possible credit upon the constructors. The engines are driven by steam raised from 16 boilers, six of which are remarkable for their great length being no less than 82 feet from end to end. The others are only single flued boilers. There are six stoves apportioned to each furnace, five of which are in constant operation, allowing one off for the purpose of cleaning and repairs. The stoves are of such construction as to be capable of raising the temperature to 75,375 cubic feet of atmospheric air per hour per furnace. The ore used is principally from the Company's mines near Askam and the Askam mines belonging to Mr. Kennedy, which are situate near to the Company's own mines. Both are connected by private lines of rail with the furnaces, there being no necessity to take the ore over the Furness Railway line. The size of the largest furnaces may be appreciated when it is mentioned that the capacity of each is 23,019 cubic feet, and that of the smaller ones 13,186 cubic feet each.

The following analyses show the component parts of the material used and of the iron produced at these works:—

ASKAM ORE.

Peroxide of Iron	83
Silica	15
Carbonate of Lime, a trace, say—	.50
Moisture	1.50
	100.
Metallic Iron	58.10

IRISH ORE.

Black Pisolotitic, from County Antrim, used as flux on account of the Alumina it contains—

Silica	6.0
Magnesia and Lime	trace
Alumina	20.37
Titanic Acid	.75
Per oxide of Iron	71.63
Protoxide of Iron	.68
Water of Combination	1.15
	100.58
Metallic Iron	50.14

LIME-STONE.

This is the local stone obtained at the Company's quarries at Goldmire, about two miles from the Askam works. The analysis determines the contents as appended:—

Carbonate of Lime	96.24
Silica	2.25
Carbonate of Magnesia	.30
Oxide of Iron	} 1.34
Alumina	
	100.13

COKE.

The very best coke obtainable from the Durham district only is used, and it contains on an average the following:—

Sulphur	.70
Ash	5.00
Moisture	.92
Carbon	93.38
	100.

PIG IRON.

The Askam hæmatite pig-iron produced from the above material has been recently analysed by Mr. Edward Riley, F.C.S., of Finsbury Square, London, and still more recently by Mr. Pattinson, F.C.S, of Newcastle-on-Tyne, who gives a much lower per centage of Phosphorus. We have been favoured with the following copies of their reports:—

"Newcastle-on-Tyne, March 14th, 1876.

"I hereby certify that I have analysed the undermentioned samples of Pig Iron and that I find the following results:—

Sample marked	No. 1
Phosphorus	0.017
Sample marked	No. 3
Phosphorus	0.016

(Signed) JOHN PATTINSON."

"Laboratory and Assay Offices,
"14a, Finsbury Square, City Road, London,
"June 7th, 1875.

"Messrs. The Furness Iron and Steel Company, Limited,

"Gentlemen,—

"Herewith I beg to forward you the results of my analyses of the two samples of Pig Iron received from you. The samples contain—

No. 1 Bessemer:—

Carbon as Graphite	3.720	} Total Carbon.
Combined Carbon	.370	} 4.090
Silicum	2.574	2.566
Sulphur	.030	
Phosphorus	.065	
Iron	92.207	
Manganese	.518	
Titanium	.503	
	99.987	

No. 3 Bessemer:—

Carbon as Graphite	3.151	} Total Carbon.
Combined Carbon	.554	} 3.705
Silicum	3.228	3.252
Sulphur	.036	
Phosphorus	.071	
Iron	92.170	
Manganese	.653	
Titanium	.244	
	100.107	

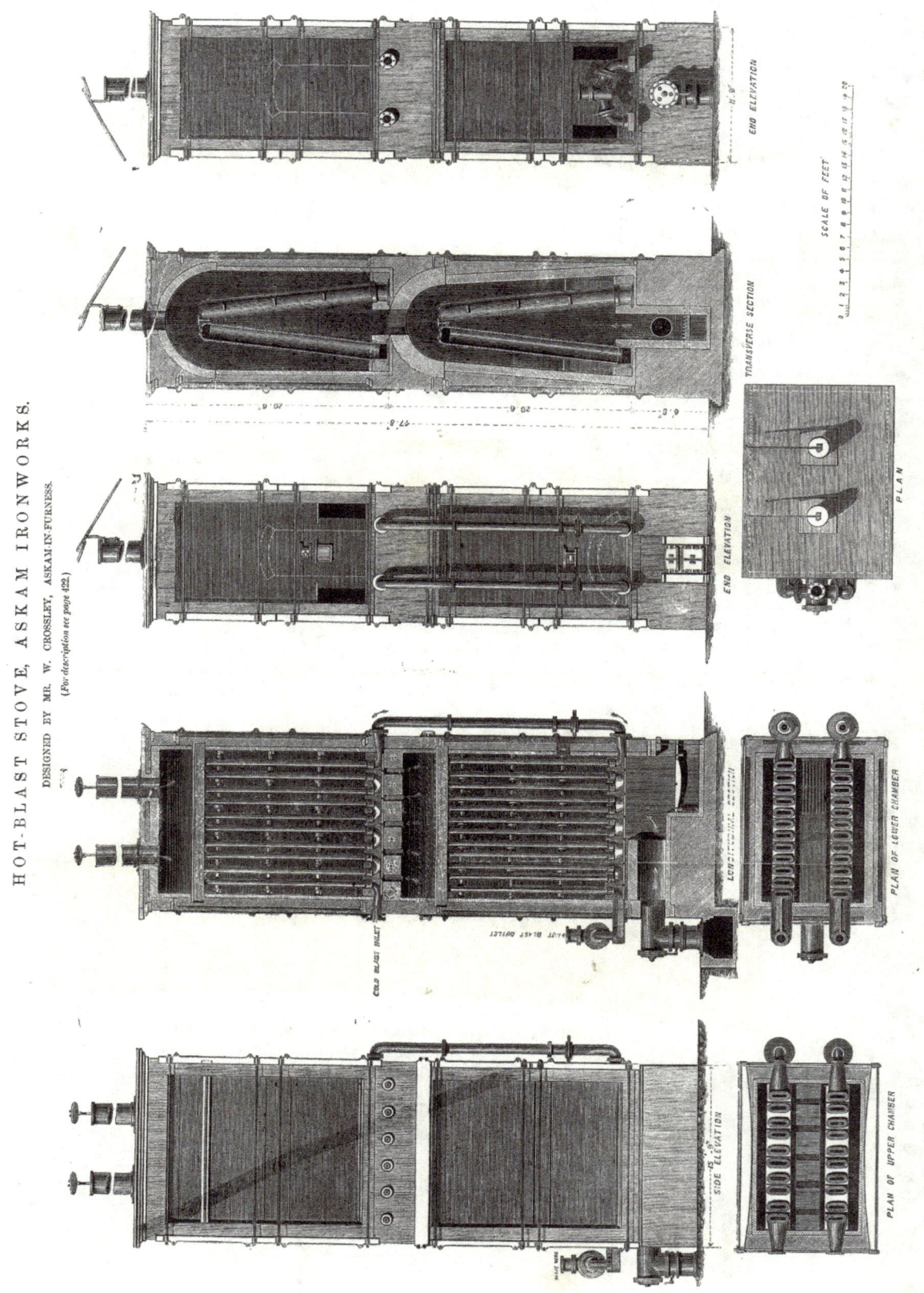

William Crossley's improved stove. (Kevin Alexander Collection)

After a relatively successful run with William Crossley as the works manager and engineer the company began to suffer financially due to a lull in the iron trade in the late 1870's and by 1879 the company ceased payments and went into voluntary liquidation, the company owing £98,335.19s.6d. (£100,989.75 in 2024 prices). The liquidators ran the firm successfully for two years until a new firm, The Askam and Mouzell Iron Company Limited took over, that company being incorporated on 11th February 1881.

Barrow Times, 26th February 1881.

THE ASKAM AND MOUZELL IRON COMPANY, LIMITED.—This new company was registered on the 11th inst., as we announced in the *Barrow Daily Times* of Monday. Its capital amounts to £100,000, in 1,000 £100 shares. The subscribers are G H Horsfall, Larkfield, Toxteth-park, 100 shares; Col. Sir Jas. Bourne, Bart., Heathfield, Liverpool, 100; G E Holt, New Brighton, Cheshire, 100; Hodgson Horsfall, 17, James-street, Liverpool, merchant, 100; Thomas Massicks, Millom, Cumberland, ironmaster, 100; John Clegg, Ulverston, Lancaster, 400; James Ashworth, Dalton-in-Furness, mining captain, 100. The company is to purchase the land, furnaces, and machinery belonging to the Furness Iron and Steel Company (Limited), in liquidation, and to manufacture iron and steel, and to carry on the business of miners, smelters colliery proprietors, fire-brick manufactures, &c. The The new firm are also owners of the valuable and extensive Mouzell Iron Ore Mines, which were purchased prior to the acquisition of the Askam Works, and held in the same proportions as given above. The capital invested in the new company may therefore be taken as upwards of £200,000.

The following is a modern article compared to the majority in this book, but it describes the Ironworks expansion under the new company brilliantly, in connecting the mines at Dalton, Lindal and Marton.

Barrow News, 6th August 1982.

THE LITTLE LINE FROM ASKAM TO DALTON. BY PETER HOLMES.

ANYONE with an eye for railway relics will know about that mysterious branch which ran between Askam and Dalton, climbing from Askam ironworks to serve the iron mines at Crossgates and Mouzell. It is more than 60 years since the last train ran, but the older people of Dalton and Askam must remember the line operating, in the days when it seemed as if it would last forever.

The Mouzell branch was an attempt to break the Furness Railway Company's monopoly on ore carriage. When the Askam and Mouzell Iron Company was formed in 1881 ("The Mouzell Company") they assumed control of Askam ironworks, and the Mouzell mines, but were entirely at the mercy of the Furness Railway for the carriage of the iron ore between the two places.

At this time all the ore raised at Mouzell, Martin and Crossgates was taken down to the main line at Dalton by a narrow-gauge railway dating from 1849. The ore was tipped into standard gauge wagons at Crooklands sidings.

Obviously any ore consigned to Askam was travelling by a roundabout route, and the new direct railway branch was designed to cut the corner. It would be worked by the Company's locomotives, and would be carried on completely independent of the Furness Railway Co.

Borrowed

The branch was built during 1882, and opened in August of that year. There was a special train on the opening day, consisting of the Mouzell's Company engine and a comfortable inspection saloon borrowed from the Furness Railway Co., so relations between the two firms cannot have been too strained at the time.

The line began in the yard at Askam ironworks, close to Lots Bridge. Crossing the main line and the road close to the brickworks, it ran steeply uphill past Greenscoe House and the granite quarry of the same name.

Crossing the road again, it ran behind Greenhaume Cottages where there was a weighing machine for the wagons. There was another bridge over the road here, and its foundations can still be seen on the east side.

Once over the road, the railway entered the mine area and branched out to reach the various pits. There was a workshop and loco shed on the hilltop, close to the large house which at the time was Mouzell mine office.

Round hill

The route wandered round past Mouzell farm and descended to Crossgates, where it met the old narrow gauge line coming down from Martin. There was an extensive network of track here, connecting a large number of pits spread around the countryside in a way which is now hard to imagine.

Some of the track had three rails, to carry both standard and narrow gauge traffic. The photograph which accompanies this article turned up just in time to commemorate a hundred years of the Mouzell Railway. The original print was recently donated to the Cumbria Record Office in Barrow, and the picture is produced by their permission, for which I am extremely grateful'

It shows Greenscoe, one of the Mouzell Company's engines, which worked the trains on the branch. She came new to the firm from the Hunslet Engine Co. of Leeds in 1876, and was probably photographed standing on the end of the branch near Lots Bridge, ready to take a string of empty wagons up the hill. She worked bunker-first to Mouzell and could manage 24 wagons up the steep bank, with steam to spare.

Greenscoe had 15 in. cylinders and was the most powerful engine owned by the Mouzell Co. In between working the trains to Mouzell, she shunted the traffic coming off the mainline at Ironworks Junction, and the wagons of pig iron waiting to go out.

She was a well-known engine locally, and was manned by an equally well-known crew. The Twiname brothers, Bill and Jack, have been mentioned in these pages before. Bill was the elder, a locoman of long time standing and minus a hand, which led to his nickname "Wingy."

HE IS REMEMBERED FOR HIS HABIT OF THROWING COAL AT ANY CHILDREN WHO HAPPENED TO WANDER WITHIN RANGE AS THE TRAIN WENT PAST.

When times were particularly hard, he would roll a large lump off the engine as it passed behind the houses at Greenhaume, and this would keep the people there in coal for quite a while.

Wingy Twiname kept a pub in Askam, and again this was referred to in the News afew years back. Brother Jack was a teetotaller – he was happy to sit in the bar of an evening but would never touch a drop.

Can anyone say whether the two men in the picture are the Twinames? Their name is so firmly associated with the engine and the works that it would be nice to find out. (It was confirmed to be the Twiname brothers).

Take a lift

During the school holidays children from Askam would take a lift on the train to go walking or blackberrying "up at Mouzell." Ernie Tyson, of Askam rode on Greenscoe *occasionally when he worked at the Ironworks, and he recalled how, in wet weather, the rain would drip off the edge of that short cab roof, straight into your eye. It was certainly "an outdoor job," and no doubt Jack Twiname was glad when he got the job of driving a new engine which had a proper enclosed cab. This was in 1895; the new engine came from Peckett's of Bristol and lived in a small shed near Mouzell offices.*

Jack Liddell, who lived at Crossgates House, remembered the little Peckett when it was sparkling new that summer, as pretty as a picture, it was Jack Twiname's absolute pride and joy.

This engine shunted the lines around the mines, while Bill and Greenscoe continued to work the trains down the hill to Askam. Some of the sections of track around Mouzell were extremely steep and sharply curved, and often it required the combined efforts of both engines to shift the wagons. The worst bit was from the valley bottom at Crossgates, near the Colorado pits, up to the level crossing at Mouzell Farm.

Jack Liddell often saw both engines struggling to lift two full wagons up this bank – they must have fairly raised the echoes from the surrounding countryside.

Mines closed

All the mines at Crossgates closed in the early years of the 20th century, and Askam ironworks closed temporarily from about 1912 to 1916. The Mouzell railway continued in use for traffic brought down from Elliscales quarry, and the engine also shunted "the North line2 which ran across The Lots to Kennedy's mines at Roanhead.

When Kennedy brothers were sending ore to Millom ironworks, it went via this line and Askam Ironworks Junction rather than via Park sidings, which were closer to Thwaite Flat. This was because the Furness Railway's rate from Park to Millom was 11d per ton, whereas from Askam Ironworks to Millom was only 9 1/2d per ton.

This difference made it worthwhile for the Mouzell Co. to keep at least one engine working even while Askam works was out of use. The Twinames and Greenscoe did this job regularly.

Track lifted

In 1915 all the track at Mouzell was lifted, and the rails were brought down to Askam for scrap. The branch itself was left as far as Elliscales quarry, but when Askam ironworks closed for good at easter, 1919 there was no hope of limestone traffic reviving, and the track was lifted as far back as Greenscoe quarry. Granite traffic from here continued until about 1936, worked by the railway company with a loco of their own.

When Askam ironworks finished, Greenscoe and her Askam sisters were sent to Millom ironworks, where they continued to work. The Twinames' old engine lasted until 1937, when it was scrapped at Millom after a useful life of more than 60 years.

After the track was pulled up the Mouzell railway began to revert back to nature, and in places it has disappeared entirely. The road bridges were removed in the 1930s as they had become a danger to the increasing volume of road traffic and today only a few of the cuttings and embankments remain to show where the railway ran.

HOWEVER ANYONE WITH A LITTLE IMAGINATION CAN STAND BY THE CUTTING AT MOUZELL FARM AND PICTURE GREENSCOE AND THE PECKETT BATTLING UPHILL ALL THOSE YEARS AGO.

Ironworks train 'Greenscoe' with the Twiname brothers Bill and Jack. (Cumbria Archive Centre, Barrow. BDP 16)

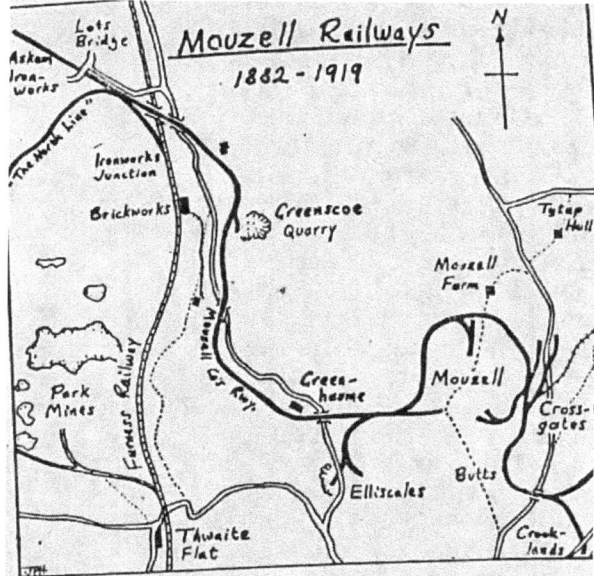

Peter Holmes map. (Barrow News, 6th August 1982)

Barrow Herald, 19th December 1882.

THE FATAL EXPLOSION AT ASKAM.

ADJOURNED INQUEST.

On Monday morning the Coroner for the district (Mr. J. Poole) held the adjourned inquiry into the deaths of the two men, Price and Edwards, who were killed by the explosion at the Askam and Mouzell Iron Works, on Friday, the 8th December. It will be remembered that on that day six men were engaged breaking up the refuse iron and slag from the bottom of two of the furnaces belonging to the said company, when suddenly an explosion was heard, and two of the men were literally blown to pieces, and the other four severely injured. The four men were conveyed to the North Lonsdale Hospital, at Barrow, and the two men who were killed were carried to their homes. On the following Monday the Coroner had a jury summoned, composed of the following residents at Askam:—John Dixon (foreman), John Seward, Henry Edmondson, Thos. Birkett, John Rylands, Oliver Lewis, Watson Milligan, Hy. Waiting, John Leyburn, Isaac Ireland, G. Stephens, J. Butcher, and Wm. Alexander. The inquiry was opened at the Vulcan Hotel, Askam, but the only evidence taken was that of George Postlethwaite, of Steel-street, Askam, who identified the bodies as being those of Price and Edwards. The Coroner issued his certificate of burial for the two men, and then adjourned the inquiry until ten o'clock on Monday (December 18th.)

Accordingly the same jury assembled at the Vulcan Hotel on the day named, and there were present:—The Coroner (Mr. J. Poole), Captain Cundill, Government Inspector of Mines, who watched the case, and will specially report upon it to the Government; Mr. H. Jackson, solicitor, of Ulverston, who attended on behalf of the Askam and Mouzell Iron Company; Mr. Massicks, senr., manager to the Company; and Mr. H. Massicks.

The Coroner having first proved the attendance of jurymen proposed that they should pay a visit to the scene of the accident previous to taking any evidence. This was done, and after an absence of about half-an-hour the jury returned, and the Coroner commenced to examine the witnesses. The first witness called was

Frederick Vale, who said: I am a contractor, and live at Barrow. I took a contract seven weeks ago for the breaking up of iron taken out of the furnaces of the Askam and Mouzell Iron Company. There is generally slag and fire clay as well as metal. I commenced work seven weeks ago to-morrow. I commenced work by boring holes and using blasting gelatine. I did not use powder or dynamite. I bored the holes with ratchet and brace. I saw all the holes exploded in every case. I was there on the morning when the accident happened, and had four men working—Bennett, Edwards, George Price, and George Corkhill. I left the works about eleven o'clock, and heard of the accident on my return home. When I left my men I instructed them to bore a hole in each of the two pieces of iron rejected by the Company.

By Mr. Jackson: The piece which exploded was not one of the pieces they had been told to bore. They had only got one of the two pieces in the position. The piece which exploded was there when I left in the morning, and had not then been operated on by me at all. It has been said that the piece which had exploded had been sent to the furnace returned. Mr. Ward told me this, but I have no other knowledge of it. I got the gelatine I used from an agent of Kitchen's, of Whitehaven, at Dalton. I buy my own. The Company does not provide it for me. I fetch it from the agent as I require it. I was not blasting on the morning of the explosion. I last got a charge from the agent on the Wednesday before the explosion. I never left any explosives with my men. I saw every hole exploded which I charged. I cannot say whether the piece which exploded was old or new.

By Captain Cundill: I have not had gelatine which ran out. I would not have bored into a piece like that which exploded. I saw the place on the evening of the explosion about 6 o'clock. Mr. Massicks went there with me. The holes had not been bored which I ordered. The piece which exploded had very little metal about it, it was mostly slag and brick, and no hole bore could have been put into it. There was no crack which I noticed before I went away. So far as I know I did not use any explosive which could have made that crack. I could not say whether any previous contractor had dealt with it. I found that Price and Edwards had been killed and the other two of my men injured by the explosion which had occurred. I did not notice any sign of drill-hole in the piece, only a crack near one end. I had had two years' experience of using explosives of this kind. Nitro-glycerine has been known to run from the cartridges and not run into the crack while it was in the furnace. My men had no explosives which they could use in my absence.

George Tomlinson said: I live at Victoria-street, Askam, and am a labourer. I was going to turn the points close to the place where the accident happened on that Friday afternoon. I was going towards the men when the accident happened. There were four men—William Edwards, George Price, John Corkhill, and Joseph Bennett. Two were striking. I saw the piece struck and the explosion occur. It was not a loud explosion. There was pretty much smoke. My brother was also injured and I took him away. I saw George Price afterwards. I did not know how he was injured. I do not know who removed the men. They were striking at the piece I pointed out to the jury this morning. I saw them strike two blows, and it was the second blow when the explosion occurred. Witness, in answer to the jury, said when he was damping he sometimes used water and sometimes damp clay. When it cracked the substance he examined for dynamite before putting in any powder.

William Townson, Staines-street, Askam, labourer, said: I was close to George Price, Edwards, Bennett, and Corkhill, I was scotching wagons and they were at the other side of the wagons. Just before the accident Price was striking with the double handed hammer,

Bennett was striking with the shafts, and the other two were lifting it when the explosion made a noise like a frap like some of the other explosions. There was no smell of gunpowder. I did not see any smoke.

John Ward, Alexandra Place, furnace manager to the Askam and Mouzell Company, being sworn said: I have been there since the Company took possession of their works. I heard the explosion and I turned to look towards the place of the report and saw the men fall. I was a hundred yards or more away. I noticed nothing different in the sound of the report to an ordinary report. I could not say whether it was an explosion from gunpowder or not, it was a very loud report, but not so loud as I have heard. I went straightaway and found Tomkinson standing with his face all bleeding; Edwards had his leg blown to his back; Price was lying with his face between two lumps of iron. Price was dead. Edwards was saying "Lord help me," when I got to him and "take me out of this." Corkhill had run away home and so had the other. I collected some men and had the injured men put on the stretcher, taken to the depot, and sent for the doctor straightaway. I stayed with Edwards until he died, about half-past four. After I had seen the iron taken out of No. 3 and 4 furnaces, since I came to the works, the charging and firing was done by the witness Davidson, under my superintendence, and I supplied him with dynamite as he required it, and I had the key of the store. The quantity varied sometimes three or four up to eight or nine cartridges; he also got the powder from me. I left the firing entirely to him, as he was an experienced man. After the iron was blown into pieces it was taken out and on to the slag bank, and mixed with what had been previously taken out, thrown at the most convenient place along the railway. I have seen the piece that was carried out since, and I cannot say whether it was a piece that was taken out by the old company or by the present company. I could not identify. We have had no contractor before Mr. Vale to break up this. I do not know that the old company had either. I do not know who took it out of the old furnaces for the old company. The clothes of Edwards seemed blown off very much, but I did not notice any sign of burning about them, nor burns upon the men, nor did I smell burning. The cartridges were all given back to me that were not used. I saw the charges fired in each case, and I myself took back the surplus dynamite and locked it up. I never saw any cartridges lying about loose. If I had seen any I should have reprimanded the men, but in all cases he gave me them back. I knew how many cartridges there were in each hole in all cases and therefore I should have known if I had not got back the remainder. I have never had any deficiency. Davison always measured the hole and asked for the number wanted. I saw him put them in. I do not know if it was all Dobell's dynamite, it was all supplied by the Mines' Company. The fragments were not broken up until Mr. Vale came.

This was the last witness examined and the Coroner summed up the case for the jury. He said it might have been satisfactory to have had a previous contractor before them in order to learn what kind of explosive he used, but as one could not be found they must take the case as presented to them. The present company took out the iron and slag from No. 3 and 4 furnaces after they had taken possession of the works. Ward had charge of it and proper precautions seemed to have been taken to see that no dynamite was left in them and that the cartridges delivered to Ward were exploded. Therefore no hole had been left nor any unexploded cartridges, and no dynamite had been left lying about the works. Previous to this, however, the liquidators of the old Iron and Steel Company had taken out the bottoms of their furnaces and had placed them in pretty much the same way and place as this was. It would have been better if it could have been shown which particular furnace this iron which was exploded came from. Mr. Vale was perfectly positive that no hole had been left in the iron slag since he came on the works, therefore they were driven to the conclusion that the particular charge must have been left at the bottom iron when it came out. There was a crack in it, but no hole when the men commenced to work, and this led them to break it up with a hammer. They struck it once, and no explosion took place, but when the iron went down a second time the explosion took place, which resulted in the death of these two men and injury to four others. Captain Cundill had said that a number of accidents had happened through glycerine getting into cracks, which might explode in four or five years after it had been left there. He (the Coroner) was afraid that through no fault at all of the parties that some of this explosive had got into the crack and this accident had occurred. The duty of the jury would therefore be to find that these men were killed by an explosion, and it did not appear to him that any blame was attached to any one.

The Coroner then ordered the room to be cleared of all except the jury, who remained considering their verdict some twenty minutes, at the end of which time the public were again admitted, and the Coroner read out the verdict which the jury had agreed upon, which was to the effect: that the deceased were killed on the 8th December by an explosion, but whether this explosion had been an unexploded cartridge left in the iron, or was part of an explosive which had found its way into the crack, had not been proved. The jury wished to say that they consider that the remaining iron should not be broken up with a hammer, but that a ratchet bit only should be used in borings.

This verdict was signed by the jury, and the enquiry then terminated.

Ulverston Mirror, 2nd February 1884.

A FEROCIOUS RUFFIAN.—On Saturday afternoon a man named James Ward went to the ironworks, and demanded money from Mr. Wilson, who had formerly employed him as pig worker. Mr. Wilson refused, and the prisoner commenced a savage assault upon him, knocking him down and kicking him in a very brutal manner. The assistance of the police was obtained, and P.C. Hind took James Ward into custody, charging him with assaulting Wilson. James Ward then attacked the constable, kicking him in a very savage manner. Hind, however, succeeded, after an half hour's struggling, in overpowering the prisoner, and getting the handcuffs on him. The sequel appears in our police court report.

SEQUEL; James Ward was fined 20s for attacking Mr Wilson and 40s for attacking P.C. Hinds.

Soulby's Ulverston Advertiser, 10th March 1887.

ACCIDENT.—On Saturday a boy named Joseph Whittle, residing at 112, Steel-street, Askam, was admitted to the North Lonsdale Hospital suffering from very severe burns to one of his legs. It appears that he had been about the slag bank near the Askam Ironworks, and had come in contact with some hot slag that had been newly tipped.

One of the biggest events to hit the ironworks and Askam was the 1889 strike, lasting over 5 months and completely changing Askam. Workers of both the Ironworks and the mines were out of work. It was at this point where Askam men began to seek employment elsewhere, particularly abroad in South Africa and America. Large numbers however moved to Walkden near Manchester, to mine the coal there. When the strike finished many came back to Askam, particularly the Walkden lads and some from abroad did too, but many stayed where they were, forming themselves new lives away.

Barrow Herald, 23rd February 1889.

THE STRIKE AT ASKAM.

THE FURNACES CLOSED.

According to their notice the workmen at the Askam Ironworks left their work on Sunday morning, and the furnaces were "damped down." About 40 men are on the works performing necessary duties, all being "union" men, but the question has not been definitely settled, although on Monday evening there was a rumour that the non-unionist had left the works, but this is incorrect. The men seem to be extremely annoyed by the action of the non-unionist, as he is said to have been the first to clamour for the formation of the union, and then when formed would not join it. He is only a recent comer to Askam, and his family have not yet joined him.

Our Dalton correspondent says:—The attitude of the men at Askam is, if anything, firmer than ever. Meetings of the members of the Branch Union have been held every day, and a mass meeting is to be held on Saturday, when Mr. Wills, who is on a lecturing tour in Cumberland, is to be with them, and speak. The non-unionist workman is still employed on the works, his duties being those of night watchman. He is little seen, except to come and go between his work and his lodgings. The persons with whom he is lodging were apprehensive that some danger might befall them if they kept him, and gave him notice to leave. The Company, however, sent information that they would stand the consequence of any damage, if there might be any committed, by the unionists. There seems, however, to be no grounds for any fears on this score. The strikers are strongly supported by the men at Barrow, Millom, and other places in Cumberland; and from various sources are guaranteed such assistance as will enable them to stand out for twelve months. Our correspondent says he is informed that the men at Barrow and Millom have given notice to their employers that any attempt to put in furnaces for the purpose of supporting the market, in place of those stopped at Askam, will be met by their notice to go on strike.

THE MILLOM AND ASKAM IRONWORKS DISPUTES.

On Tuesday evening last, a meeting of the ironworkers was held at the Devonshire Hotel, Millom, called at the instance of Mr. Walls, general assistant secretary. Nearly all the men off work attended. There were also present two delegates from Askam, who spoke of the determination of the men there to stick together and remain out for six or twelve months if necessary. The Chairman referring to the Askam difficulty said, they were all aware that their fellow-workmen at Askam had, owing to some of their mates refusing to join the union, given a fortnight's notice, and would discontinue work when it expired. They in Millom had a few members who returned their cards and by the advice of the secretary they met together to consider what steps should be taken,—whether these men should be asked to join the society, or if not, would they do the same as Askam,—give in their notices. The two places were now united and they would have to fight the one battle. He understood that some of the men who had handed in their cards, desired to rejoin the union, and it would be for the meeting to say if they would be allowed to rejoin.—A workman suggested that if all the men did not join the union they ought to leave the job.—This opinion was endorsed by several others.—The Chairman thought the men ought to have a chance to join the union.—This was the course advised to be adopted by the union. It was proposed that the men connected with the Millom blast furnaces who are at present not members of the union receive two days notice, and if they do not express their willingness to join inside of that time, another meeting would be held to decide what further action should be taken.—The delegates from Askam pointed out that according to rule 8, union men were not allowed to work with non-union men. After some further discussion, a resolution was adopted pledging those present to give every support in their power to the Askam men.—From the above it appears therefore likely, that the strike at Askam will be repeated at Millom. The Askam furnaces are all damped down, but from 50 to 60 non-union men are still at work and will, we understand, be retained by the directors who state that they feel bound to resist what they consider the uncalled for coercion of men who do not wish to join the union. Amongst the Millom men on the other hand there is a feeling that unless the non-union men join them at once the notice should be given to the employers on Saturday. The men on strike are receiving pay from the Blast Furnacemen's Association, the usual amount allowed being 1s. 6d. for each child. It is understood however, that this does not represent the amount the Askam men are getting from the Association.

Writing on Friday, our Millom correspondent says:—It appears that the company are determined to resent the alleged unionist dictation. Owing to the action of union agents in giving notice to those men who have not joined the union, the company have ordered the posting of the following notice, "Millom Ironworks, 21st February, 1889. Notice. The Blast Furnacemen's Association having served notice dated 19th inst, upon several of the workmen in our employment that unless they join the Association within two days, they will work a notice against them. The Company hereby intimate that they will continue to employ all their workmen who are not members of the Association, and also the men who *cease to belong to the Association before noon* on Saturday, the 23rd February, 1889. Workmen unwilling to continue in their employment on the terms of the Company, will receive the usual notice of 14 days from the 23rd February to the 9th March, terminating their employment, and in future *No member of the Blast Furnacemen's Association will be employed* by us at either our Millom or Askam works. For the Cumberland Iron Mining and Smelting Company Limited,

(Signed,)
Thomas Barlow Massicks,
Managing Director."

A meeting of the men was to have been held last (Friday) night at the Devonshire Hotel, when an address was to be given by Mr. Walls, general assistant secretary to the association.

Barrow Herald, 9th March 1889.

THE MILLOM AND ASKAM IRONWORKS DISPUTES.

MEETING OF MASTERS AND MEN AT MILLOM.

DETERMINED SPEECH BY MR. BARLOW-MASSICKS.

A THREATENING OUTLOOK.

On Tuesday last a meeting of the workmen engaged by the Cumberland Iron Mining and Smelting Company at the Millom Ironworks, was held in a large room adjoining the works. Mr. T. Barlow-Massicks, J.P., managing director of the Company; Mr. H. Cook, one of the directors; Mr. Horace Barlow-Massicks, manager of the works; Mr. H. I. Nicholson, and others, were present.—Mr. T. Barlow-Massicks said he was sorry that Mr. Horsfall, the chairman of the Company, was unable, through illness, to be with them that day. Mr. Cook, however, who was one of the directors of the Company, had come over that day, and he (Mr. Massicks) was there himself as the direct representative of the Company to speak to the men on the question which was before their minds at this particular time. Referring to the commencement of the Company, it began, he might say, judging from many of the faces in the room, before many of them were born—nearly 25 years ago. At that time, at the works in Cumberland, the twelve hours' system was adopted, and, of course, there was nothing else to adopt at Millom. Their manager came from Cleator Moor, and they began to work on the same lines as at Cleator Moor. Wages were 6s. per day, and times were bad then, although pig iron was £1 per ton more than it was to-day. They went on with the twelve hours' system until about 1871 or 1872, when many of the workmen complained of the long hours they had to work, especially when they had to put in "double turns," to change the shifts from night to day, as is usual, and one man, named Parke, complained at that time that he was unable to go to church. The Company then adopted the eight hours' system at Millom, being the first firm on the West Coast of England to do so, and they adopted it to a greater extent than others, because it embraced the furnace keepers, assistant keepers, slaggers, chargers, and fillers. This was not done by any other works in the country. They kept on working in eight hours' shifts until bad times came, when they had to appeal to the workmen to go back to the twelve hours' shifts, but instead of this the men agreed to accept reduced wages. In the end, however, the Company had to adopt the twelve hours' system. Neither he nor the workmen liked it. It lasted but for a short time, and the workmen went back to the eight hours' system, and from that time to this, their works had been the only ironworks in the county of Cumberland conducted on the three shift principle; indeed, this was the only Company working on this system on the West Coast, with the exception of those at Barrow, Ulverston, and Carnforth, and they followed their example at Millom. They worked twelve hours' shifts on the East Coast of England, in Scotland, and in the Workington, Whitehaven, and Maryport district. The Company at Millom had, however, worked very well all along. The Union, which had just been established in this district, was a new thing. The home of the Union was in Middlesborough, and doubtless it had worked satisfactorily there, where the works were gathered together in one common centre; but of all the parts of the country which had done most harm to the trade of this district, in which both those present and himself were so deeply interested, Middlesborough was the one, because it had done much to run one particular class of iron out of the market. This had nearly ruined the steel trade of the West Coast, and it had closed up iron ore mines which were not very flourishing ones, and, by the use of a very inferior class of pig iron in the production of basic steel, it had taken part of the market which was previously and exclusively confined to hematite iron. There were no Union men at Askam, and on Saturday next it would not exist at Millom. There would be no Union at Millom after that time. At Middlesborough it existed because there were on the directorate there two gentlemen whom he knew well, and of whom he must speak in the highest terms—Sir Lowthian Bell and Mr. David Dale, the latter gentleman having frequently acted as arbitrator in labour disputes. The company at Middlesbrough were induced by those directors to establish a union because, in their opinion, it would not be found to be a bad thing. He should not like to take advice from an enemy on any occasion, and he should not like to take advice from the East Coast of England. One side of the country was in direct antagonism with the other. Those present had heard what Mr. Snow and Mr. Walls had said about the unions in Cleveland and at Barrow, but it remained to be seen how long those advantages they claimed would be experienced. Continuing his address, Mr. Massicks said: We now come to the case of John Dutton, at the Askam works. The union at Askam, through its secretary (a man of the name of Rear), gave notice that John Dutton would be forced to join the union or be dismissed; otherwise the union would be "worked" against him. This was a tyranny to my mind which, as managing director, I could not submit to. I would not coerce any free-born Englishman, Irishman, or Scotchman, unless he liked to take a certain course of his own free will. John Dutton's case is only a test case—one out of 40 or 50 at Askam. The moment John Dutton was dismissed, we should have to dismiss all the non-union men at Askam, and all the non-union men at Millom. We will not submit to dictation of that kind. We have shut up the works at Askam, and the same will be the case at Millom if the union continues its demand. After making a suggestion as to the course to be adopted in order to avoid contact with the union, Mr. Massicks said: I am not going to get into a bad temper about this thing; you will be absolutely free, as so shall we. If you don't like the conditions which exist at these works, where so many of you have been employed for so long a time in the service of a company, so respectable, so strong, with a reputation second to none in the country —why, you are free men, to go where you like. But there has been an attempt to prevent freedom in this way. Posters have been put up at Askam and elsewhere, saying that everybody is to keep away; and there is another poster headed "Strike at Millom Ironworks" (which has not yet begun), and men are requested to keep away from Millom. Why? We always pay our wages, and good wages too. We have as short hours of labour as any iron company in the world. The difficulty at Askam will affect something like 7,000 persons, and will bring about intense misery and want. We are not quarrelling about wages or hours of labour, but with this infamous union, which wants to force everybody into it. Is there to be no freedom in the country? There is no advantage at all to you in joining the union, nor will there ever be. Be that as it may, we shall not move. I want you to carry away this conviction—that this week, next week, next month, next year, we shall not change. We will stop our works, and make the place desolate first.—Mr. B. Massicks stated at the finish that he could not agree to Mr. Snow or anybody else coming between him and his men, and that he would not see anyone connected with the union again on this matter.—Mr. Cook, Mr. Cunningham, and Mr. Jones having spoken, the meeting terminated.

A half section of an early Askam pig bar (top) and a tail off piece (below) a 50p is shown for size. (Kevin Alexander Collection)

Barrow Herald, 9th March 1889.

At no time, probably, since the laying of the foundation stone of the great chimney—the marvellous structure, with its towering height of 330 feet—in 1865, by Miss Wakefield, has the enthusiasm and excitement of the Askam people been raised to such a pitch as it now is on the great strike question. The great majority of the Askam people are connected with the Iron Works. On Wednesday, the Blastfurnacemen expected Mr. Snow, the secretary of the association. Long before the time of Mr. Snow's arrival the men had mustered in their full strength at the Vulcan Hotel, and it was arranged that they should make a tour of the town and district. Headed by the Askam Brass Band, therefore, they formed in procession, and to the inspiriting strains of lively airs, marched along the principal thoroughfares of Askam, and then proceeded along the "New-road" to Dalton. Here the sensation they caused was great. With great caution, the police had arranged to accompany them; and as the "noble three hundred" marched along they had an escort of police on each side. But whatever expectations the police may have had, there was no sign of disorderly conduct; on the contrary, everything was done in the most admirable way. After passing through the town, they returned to Askam by way of Broughton-road, coming down the village of Ireleth, and terminating their walk at the Vulcan Hotel. The next item of the day's work was the meeting of Mr. Snow, who arrived by the 2-53 train from Middlesborough. The band struck up as the train steamed into the station, and the local secretary and officers were on the platform. As Mr. Snow was seen coming off the platform, the most enthusiastic cheering commenced, and was continued as, escorted by the procession, that gentleman walked to the Vulcan Hotel. The large room there was filled. Mr. Snow's speech was mainly an exhortation to the men to be firm in the line of conduct they had taken. He strongly urged upon the men to be careful in their public conduct—not to give way to drinking, and not to to commit any offence against the law, so that no chance should be given to the masters to point to them as men undeserving of public support. (Hear, hear.) There were many, he said, who were of opinion that their line of conduct was wrong; but he believed this opinion would change when the public became more and more aware of the true nature of the dispute. There had also, he heard, been comments made that the money for supporting the men on strike would not be forthcoming; but as it was always said " the proof of the pudding was in the eating," so it was in this case; for the money was now on the table, and would very soon be in the hands of the men themselves. (Loud cheers.) He would like to reser to Mr. Massicks' speech at Millom. (Hear, hear.) Mr. Massicks had said that he would not speak to him (the speaker), nor have anything to do with him. Well, Mr. Massicks could, of course, please himself, but he, in return, would say this, that if any settlement of the disputes was to be arrived at, he (the speaker) would be the one with whom Mr. Massicks would have to settle. (Hear, hear, and applause.) So long as the men remained firm and true to the union, he (Mr. Snow) would stand by them. (Cheers.) And if Mr. Massicks wanted to have his places idle for twelve months for the purpose of crushing the union, he would find him (Mr. Snow) at his post, prepared to support the men for that time, or longer. (Renewed cheering.) The union was as firm in its resolve to stand by the men of Millom and Askam as Mr. Massicks was in his resolve not to employ union men—and perhaps firmer. (Hear, hear, and cheers.)—The distribution of pay was next proceeded with, and the members afterwards formed in procession again to escort Mr. Snow to the railway station, where he was to take the train to Middlesborough. The route was lined with spectators, and the men themselves were in the highest state of enthusiasm.

A meeting in connection with the Blastfurnacemen's Association was held on Thursday evening, at the Devonshire Hotel, Millom. There was a large attendance of the men. An address was given by Mr. Vickers, of Barrow, who advised them to "stand to their guns," and come out for their own interests. Considerable discussion took place upon the speech made by Mr. Massicks to the men on Tuesday, a good deal of which was considered as "blarney." The men firmly decided to stand by the union, and strike. The company commenced on Thursday to damp down two of the furnaces; one of the furnaces is going on still. All the unionists will, in all probability, be out by Sunday morning.

Barrow Herald, 29th June 1889.

ASKAM & MILLOM DISPUTES.

GREAT EXCITEMENT AT ASKAM.

INCREASE OF POLICE.

Our correspondent, writing on Thursday night, says:—The excitement at Askam during the week has been intense. As we stated last week, a furnace has been put in blast, and, as more hands have been turning in nearly every day since, it is believed that another furnace will be lighted before long. It is said that men of reliable ability have come from Barrow, Ulverston, and other places, but a very large number of the others are really very third-rate men, who have not the requisite skill for furnace work. Among those who have started work is a man named Kidd, who has been a very prominent man during the strike. He was, in fact, chairman at one of the meetings when Mr. Snow first attended Askam. At that and other meetings he was always an advocate of the "cling together and stand up for your rights" principle which the union men are engaged in. He was not actually a blast-furnaceman, but belonged, we believe, to the Miners' Union. However, he is now a blastfurnaceman. His commencing at the works was the signal for a hostile display of feeling. On Tuesday evening, about 8 o'clock, a procession was formed, with an effigy of Kidd in its midst. The effigy was subjected to every conceivable abuse, and was "drowned." This was not considered sufficient punishment, and after being dragged about in a rough fashion it was "rescued" by the police, who had, of course, turned out in full force to quell the disturbance. So great was the fear, that windows were barricaded and doors fastened. At the furnaces it was deemed advisable to look out for possible danger. Reinforcements of police were sent for, and later on a considerable number turned in from Dalton and other surrounding places. It is believed the Ironworks people really feared an attack on the works, for the blast was turned off for a considerable time, and it is said that several of the officials did not leave the place until it was thought safe to do so. No interference with the works was, however made, but the house where Kidd resides has constantly been the scene of uproarious proceedings, and windows have been broken. A very large section of the Union men are strongly opposed to this sort of thing, but the minority are disposed to show hostility in a determined fashion. A number of the men who have come to the furnace at Askam are those who were taken from Askam to work at the Millom furnaces. As we have previously stated, all information as to the real state of things is only to be had by dint of much sifting and side-questioning. Everyone connected with the furnaces seems to have a notion that the Company are to such an extent masters of the situation that there is no information necessary except the "Oh, tut! the strike is over!" Police supervision is now kept up with increased vigilance, and especially at nights.

Barrow Herald, 13th July 1889.

THE SITUATION AT ASKAM.

VISIT OF MESSRS. SNOW AND WALLS.

Last Monday several men applied for work at Askam, including, it is said, some of the unionists, who were prepared to surrender their membership. The strike is now virtually over, and the extra force of police will be removed.

In replying to a deputation at Askam last week, Mr. Barlow-Massicks said that he would not discharge or remove any man now in the employ of the company to make way for the men who had for so long done their best to injure and ruin the company, but that Mr. Sparrow, the manager, would start as many men as there was room for, and so soon as furnaces could be got ready, but each man must make individual application for employment. There were very many of the company's late workmen who would not again be employed. Mr. Barlow-Massicks further said that he extremely regretted that the men should have left their employment under such circumstances, and added that he would not have interfered with the Union if those who controlled its action had done so in a reasonable way.

The secretary and assistant secretary (Messrs. Snow and Walls) visited Askam again on Saturday. The events of the week had been such that their coming was looked forward to with special interest. In his address Mr. Walls alluded to the fact that Mr. Massicks had now obtained what he was determined to have at any price—non-union men working his furnaces. (Hooting.) But even with that he could not yet crush out the union—(cheers)—which still remained intact, and would remain intact probably longer even than the Askam furnaces. (Loud cheers.) Mr. Massicks had not even crushed out the Askam branch, let alone the United Kingdom. (Cheers.) They were quite willing to let him have his own way, and they could have theirs. For the most part he had taken on men at whom he would have laughed the laugh of derision if such men had applied six months ago. If these men had told him then, that they had never done any pig-lifting, nor filling, nor puddling—except sweeping "puddle" in the streets—(loud laughter)—would he have taken them on and talked about them being stalwart and able-bodied men? ("No.") And all this was because he was determined to crush out the union. (Cries of "Never," and cheers.) He (Mr. Walls) believed that Mr. Massicks would yet see a deal more fighting against the union, but for the present he was having his own way. He would urge the men to keep to their convictions, and if they believed they would in the end gain by the union, then stand firm to it. (Loud cheers.)—Mr. Snow said that anyone looking round that room would be bound to acknowledge that Mr. Massicks had a deal to do yet before he crushed the union. At their first meetings, in fact, they had very few more than were now in that room. He felt sorry that some of the "noble 200" should have been led away, but they could hardly expect but that they would have a few weak ones among them. They had endured a trial and temptation such as few bodies of men ever met with, and they had gone through that ordeal better than those in a great majority of such cases. (Cheers.) If all had stood firmly together, Mr. Massicks would not even now have had a furnace blowing at Askam, and the long holiday for the blast engines would have been longer. (Laughter.) Another interview with Mr. Massicks showed that it was fruitless to expect any reasonable treatment from him, and he would now advise them to seek work elsewhere. Let them return Mr. Massicks the compliment of saying they did'nt want him. (Laughter.) There was plenty of work in Workington and Cleveland, and they could go and be welcome, and keep to their union. (Cheers.) The union would still pay their allowance until all had got work, and then they would make a grant for the expense of removing their families. In conclusion, he urged the men to keep to their convictions, and, as Mr. Massicks would not have the union, turn round and say the union would not have Mr. Massicks. (Loud cheers.) —The usual allowance to the men was then paid, about 160 of the names being answered. Messrs. Snow and Walls were accorded a hearty reception for their attendance and speeches.

This was the end of the strike with nobody winning.

By 1890 there was a change again in ownership when the Askam and Mouzell Company was amalgamated with the Cumberland Iron Mining and Smelting Company (Millom Ironworks), creating the Millom and Askam Hematite Iron Company Limited. Unfortunately, while under this company the ironworks was quite frequently having disputes with its workers on an account of a poor trade in iron. So, the furnaces ran intermittently right up until the first world war, however during the works biggest strike lasting 11-months between 1900/1901 the company did invest £65,000. (£6,778,388. In 2024 prices) in the building of a large 90ft "American furnace" at Askam. The new manager of both Askam and Millom ironworks was a Swedish fella called Axel Sahlin, who had spent many years working in America at larger more modern ironworks and it seems he was brought in to modernise the sites and he started at Askam.

However, even after the furnace was completed the works continued to run intermittently due to repairs and a poor iron market, the site closed for 9 years in 1908 only opening again under government control in 1917 to help with the war effort, the works closed for good in April 1919.

The extent of the ironworks land in 1890. (Courtesy of Janice Cumming, Askam History Club)

Soulby's Ulverston Advertiser, 2nd October 1890.

MILLOM & ASKAM HEMATITE IRON COMPANY, LIMITED,
MILLOM, CUMBERLAND.
(Incorporated under the Companies Acts 1862 to 1886

SHARE CAPITAL	£250,000
DIVIDED INTO	
10,000 Seven per Cent. Cumulative Preference Shares of £10 each	100,000
15,000 Ordinary Shares of £10 each	150,000
	£250,000

ALSO

First Mortgage Debentures, at Five per Cent. Interest £150,000

PAYABLE AS FOLLOWS:

	SHARES.	DEBENTURES.
On Application	£0 10 0	£5 0 0 per Cent.
On Allotment	2 0 0	20 0 0 ,,
On 17th Nov., 1890	2 10 0	25 0 0 ,,
On 19th January, 1891	2 10 0	25 0 0 ,,
On 23rd March, 1891	2 10 0	25 0 0 ,,
	£10 0 0	£100 0 0

Or the whole can be paid upon Allotment, entitling the holder to interest at Five per cent. per annum upon the amount paid up in advance.

The Debentures will be charged upon the whole undertaking and assets of the Company, and will also be secured by a Trust Deed conveying to Trustees for the Debenture Holders the Company's freehold, customaryhold, and leasehold property, buildings, fixed plant and machinery, and also the Shares held in other Companies. The Debentures will be issued for sums of £100 each, or multiples thereof, and will be redeemable at the option of the Company on six months' notice after 1st January, 1900, at £105 for each £100. The interest will be payable half-yearly on 1st January and 1st July in each year.

The Preference Shares will rank next to the Debentures and before the Ordinary Shares as regards both capital and dividend.

TRUSTEES FOR DEBENTURES HOLDERS.

THE INSURANCES TRUST AND AGENCY, LIMITED, 120, St. Vincent-street, Glasgow.

DIRECTORS.

The Right Honourable A. J. MUNDELLA, M.P., 16, Elvaston Place, London, S.W., Chairman.

T. BARLOW-MASSICKS, Esq., J.P., Millom, Cumberland, Deputy Chairman and Managing Director.

HERBERT CAMPBELL, Esq., South Hill Road, Liverpool.

HENRY COOK, Esq., J.P., Barrow-in-Furness.

GEORGE EDWARD HOLT, Esq. (of George E. Holt and Son), Orange Court, Liverpool.

WILLIAM JACKS, Esq., J.P., Iron and Steel Merchant, Glasgow and Middlesbrough.

The Honourable GREVILLE RICHARD VERNON, M.P., Auchans, Kilmarnock (Director Caledonian Railway Company).

BANKERS.

Messrs. BARCLAY, BEVAN, TRITTON & Co., 54, Lombard Street, London, E.C.

THE BANK OF LIVERPOOL, LIMITED, Liverpool.

Messrs. WAKEFIELD, CREWDSON & Co., Kendal Bank, Barrow-in-Furness.

THE LANCASTER BANKING COMPANY, Lancaster and Millom.

THE BRITISH LINEN COMPANY BANK, Glasgow, London, and Branches.

SOLICITORS.

THOMAS HOWSON, Esq., Whitehaven.

STEPHEN HART JACKSON, Esq., Ulverston, Lancashire.

Messrs. RITCHIE & GRAHAM, Writers, 123, St. Vincent Street, Glasgow.

BROKERS.

GLASGOW—Messrs. MACKENZIE & AITKEN, 68, St. Vincent Street.

EDINBURGH—Messrs. JOHN ROBERTSON & Co., 31, George Street.

LONDON—J. W. WEIGHT, Esq., 2, Copthall Buildings, E.C.

AUDITORS.

Messrs. R. MACKAY & Co., Chartered Accountants, Middlesbrough-on-Tees, and 3, Lothbury, London, E.C.

WM. D. CAIRNEY, Esq., Chartered Accountant, 24, George Square, Glasgow.

SECRETARY (pro. tem.)

Mr. W. F. MAPLESTON.

TEMPORARY OFFICES.	REGISTERED OFFICES.
3, Lothbury, London, E.C.	Millom, Cumberland.

PROSPECTUS.

This Company is formed to acquire and amalgamate, as going concerns, the Millom Iron Works, of the Cumberland Iron Mining and Smelting Company, Limited; the Askam Iron Works, of the Askam and Mouzell Iron Company, Limited; and also the Hematite Iron Ore Mines, Limestone Quarries, and other assets of both Companies, including the goodwill in the well-known and established brands of pig iron—"Millom Hematite" and "Askam Hematite." Both concerns have hitherto been carried on as private limited Companies, but owing to the recent decease of many of the Shareholders, the present change has become necessary.

ASKAM IRON WORKS AND MINES.

WORKS.—The Askam Iron Works, erected 1866, with all mines belonging thereto, and also additional mines and royalties, were purchased by the Askam and Mouzell Iron Company, Limited, in 1881, after which the works were reconstructed, and an entirely new plant of 15 hot-blast firebrick stoves erected. There are four blast furnaces of the largest type in the district, and seven blowing engines, giving a large reserve of power. The depôt accommodation is of extra capacity, and the works are on a most extensive and substantial scale, having a producing capacity of 145,000 tons per annum. The shipping port for the Askam Works is Barrow-in-Furness, between five and six miles distant. The Cumberland Company now own and will cause its nominees to transfer to the new Company or its nominees all the shares of the Askam and Mouzell Company.

HEMATITE MINES.—Attached and belonging to the Askam Works, but also supplying ore to the Millom Works, are the following Hematite Mines, estimated to produce annually about 130,000 tons of ore :—

Mouzell Mines, Dalton-in-Furness, Lancashire.

Dalton, Tytup, and Crossgates Mines, Dalton-in-Furness, Lancashire.

Martin and Powka Mines, Dalton-in-Furness, Lancashire.

Lindal Mines, Dalton-in-Furness, Lancashire.

Holmes Green Royalty, Dalton-in-Furness, Lancashire.

Askam Mines, Askam-in-Furness, Lancashire.

Goldmire Mine, Askam-in-Furness, Lancashire.

Thwaite Flatt Mine, Askam-in-Furness, Lancashire.

Plumpton Mine, Ulverston, Lancashire.

These mines, along with those of the Elliscales Mining Company, Limited, and those of the Askam and Roanhead Mines, belonging to Messrs. Kennedy Brothers, are connected with the Iron Works by means of private railways recently constructed at a cost of over £15,000. A large portion of the ore supply is therefore delivered at the furnaces free of railway dues. The mineral grants held under lease are very extensive and capable of great development; new pit shafts are now being put down, and active exploration is going on. The Askam Company own the minerals under, as well as the surface of, 56 acres of land adjoining to and on which the Iron Works are partly built. A shaft is sunk here and ore being raised. The leasehold mines are held on terms prevailing in the district, the principal lessors being the Crown, the Duke of Buccleuch, the Duke of Devonshire, the Earl of Derby, and John Clegg, Esq.,—the tonnage rental, in most cases, being fixed by a sliding scale depending upon the prices obtained for iron ore. Full particulars of these leases may be inspected at the offices of the Company's Solicitors.

GOLDMIRE LIMESTONE QUARRIES, about a mile from the works, and on the Furness Railway, are leased from the Duke of Devonshire, and produce an ample supply of excellent limestone for the furnaces.

LAND, BUILDINGS, AND OFFICES.—The freehold estate on which the works are erected extends to 138 acres, including the 56 acres before mentioned. There are four dwelling-houses for foremen at the Iron Works, and freehold and leasehold houses for workmen at the mines; while the offices, fitting, waggon and other shops, stables, &c., are excellent and ample.

RESERVOIRS.—There is a good supply of water, free of charge, and a reservoir capacity of 10 millions of gallons.

The Millom and Askam Works combined are capable of producing annually 365,000 tons of Pig Iron, and the situation of both works for receiving raw material and for despatching pig iron has advantages not surpassed, if equalled, by any similar work in the district. The Pig Iron produced at the furnaces is of high-class quality. The brands, "Millom Hematite" and "Askam Hematite" are well-known in the iron and steel trades, and the customers include H.M. Government and the principal home and foreign consumers of hematite pig iron. The Works, Mines, and Quarries have a full equipment of 18 locomotives and 249 mineral waggons, besides loose plant and tools of every description. There is a large extent of land belonging to the Company at both Millom and Askam available for extensions, or for the erection of Steel or other works.

PROFITS.—The books of the Vendors have been examined by Messrs. R. Mackay and Co., of the Royal Exchange, Middlesbrough, and 3, Lothbury, London, E.C., Chartered Accountants, who report as follows:—

3, Lothbury, London, E.C., 1st Sept. 1890.
To the Directors of the Millom and Askam Hematite Iron Company, Limited.

To the Directors of the Millom and Askam Hematite Iron Company, Limited.

Dear Sirs,—We beg to report that we have examined the Books and Accounts of the Cumberland Iron Mining and Smelting Company, Limited, and the Askam and Mouzell Iron Company, Limited, for the eight years ending 31st December, 1888, and we certify that after deducting all working and business expenses, but exclusive of interest on capital, the annual average profits shown thereby have been £32,975 6s. 10d.

The trading of the year 1889 was seriously disturbed by a strike during a large portion of that year, and the working resulted in a loss of £1,657 3s. 4d.

We have examined the amounts expended on the maintanance and repair of buildings, plant and machinery, and are of an opinion that such expenditure has been ample for the purpose.—We are, dear sirs, your obedient servants.

R. MACKAY & CO.,
Chartered Accountants.

The average Annual Profits of the Millom Company over a period of 20 years have been £27,763, and those of the Askam Company, over 8½ years, £12,960—together £40,723. On account of the protracted strike of the workmen at both Askam and Millom in 1889, lasting for over five months, the results for that year are not given as a basis for estimating the dividend, for although the Companies were successful, the strike seriously interfered with profits. This is the only strike the Companies have had.

The results for the eight years ending 31st December, 1888, during which the iron trade was extremely depressed, and there was no year of good prices or inflated profits (with the exception of 1882, when the profits amounted to £77,875 9s. 6d.), show, according to the Accountants' certificate, average profits of £32,975 6 10

cane, average profits of   £32,975 6 10
Deduct therefrom:
 Interest on £153,000 Debentures, at 5 per cent, per annum............... £7,500 0 0
 Interest on £100,000 Preference Shares, at 7 per cent 7,000 0 0
        ————— 14,500 0 0

  Leaving a sum of ....£18,475 6 10 equal to a dividend upon the Ordinary Shares of fully 12 per cent. It is not intended to pay a larger dividend than 10 per cent. until the present issue of Debentures has been redeemed.

  No account is taken of profits likely to accrue from the further development of the Company's extensive mineral property, or from the saving effected by the amalgamation of the Companies and the centralization of management. It is estimated that these further profits and savings will be ample to cover depreciation.

  VALUATIONS.—The Works, &c., have been valued by Mr. Jeremiah Head, ex-President of the Institution of Mechanical Engineers, as follows, viz:—

	Millom.	Askam.	Total.
Land, Buildings, Fixed Plant, and Machinery	£127,925	£100,706	£228,631
Rolling Stock, loose tools, Stocks, and Stores......	32,173	26,989	59,162
Total	£160,098	£127,695	£287,793

The Mining Properties, including the Iron Ore Mines and Royalties, and the Railway Plant, Freehold Land, and Houses, &c., connected therewith (but exclusive of the Whicham Property), have been valued by Mr. Augustus H. Strongitharm, C.E., J.P., at 116,382

(They have also been valued by Mr. Henry Woolcock, C. & M. E., F.G.S., at £128,171.)

The Share of the Whicham Mines, agreed to be sold to the Company, is valued by Mr. Woolcock at 34,814

Total Valuation of the Properties to be acquired by the Company................ £438,989

The price to be paid for the properties, &c., including goodwill, is £370,000, which, it will be observed, is considerably less than the valuation. This price will leave £30,000 for working capital, which, in addition to the value of the stock-in-trade, pig-iron, and raw material £59,162) in hand, is considered ample.

The goodwill, which is considered of great value, passes with the transfer of the properties, but no sum has been included in the Valuations in respect thereof.

The Shareholders of the existing Companies will, at the option of the new Company, accept £97,500 in Ordinary Shares fully paid up, and £30,000 in Preference Shares fully paid up, in part payment of the purchase money.

The Company will take over the business as at 30th September, 1890, and the existing Companies will pay and receive the debts due by and to them up to that date, but as the Valuations were made prior to that date the Vendor guarantees that the properties taken over at 30th September will not be of less value than the sum contained in the Valuations above referred to, and undertakes to pay to the new Company the sum, if any, which at stocktaking may be found to be deficient. The Vendor will pay all expenses connected with and incidental to the formation of the Company up to the date of allotment.

Mr. Thomas Barlow-Massicks, who has been Managing Director of the Millom Works since their formation, and of the Askam works since their purchase in 1881, has agreed to join the Board and act as Managing Director for five years,

The following Contracts have been entered into, viz.:—An agreement dated 18th September, 1890, between the Cumberland Iron Mining and Smelting Company, Limited, of the one part, and William Barclay Peat, of the Royal Exchange, Middlesbrough, in the County of York, Chartered Accountant, of the other part; an agreement dated 26th September, 1890, between the said William

Two full bars of Askam iron probably from the latter years of the works production, these survived due to being used as ballast in my family's boats (Kevin Alexander Collection)

Barclay Peat, of the one part, and the Millom and Askam Hematite Iron Company, Limited, of the other part; and an agreement dated 26th September, 1890, between the Millom and Askam Hematite Iron Company, Limited, of the one part, and the said Thomas Barlow-Massicks of the other part; and copies thereof, and of the Memorandum and Articles of Association, the Draft Deed of Trust for securing the Debentures, and Engineers' Valuations, may be seen at the offices of the Company's Solicitors.

There are also various trade contracts and agreements too numerous to be specified, and also contracts and agreements in regard to the subscription and issue of capital; but applicants for shares shall be deemed to have notice of all such contracts and agreements, and to waive further specification thereof, whether under Section 38 of the Companies Act, 1867, or otherwise.

Where no allotment is made the deposit will be returned in full, and when the number of shares or debentures allotted is less than the number applied for, the susplus deposit will be credited in reduction of the amount payable on allotment. In case of default in the payment of any instalment when due on either shares or debentures, all amounts previously paid shall be liable to forfeiture and the allotment to cancellation.

Application will forthwith be made for quotations of both debentures and shares on the Stock Exchange.

Prospectuses may be obtained from the Company's Bankers, Solicitors, Brokers, and Auditors.

1st October, 1890.

Millom Gazette, 6th August 1897.

AWFUL SUDDEN DEATH AT ASKAM IRON WORKS.

Quite a sensation was caused in the Askam district on Sunday by the news than an engine cleaner, named Fred Dent, residing at Sawmillfield, and aged 57 years, had been found dead in the engine house. Dent was employed as engine cleaner, and generally was on the day set. As usual, on Saturday evening, he returned to work to prepare the engine for work on Sunday. The deceased had cleaned the greater portion of the engine, and was found with his feet close to the engine, as though he had fallen backwards, while in the act of getting on the step to finish off his work. In his hand he held a large piece of cotton waste, when found by two fellow workmen, named William Grice and John Standing, about 5 a.m. The latter, who is an engine driver, thought "Fred" was late in getting up the steam, and upon approaching the engine house found Dent lying on his back. Information was at once conveyed to Dr. Cook, who was immediately in attendance, as also was P.C. Young, but life was then extinct. Dent had, in all probability been dead four or five hours. The coroner was communicated with but did not deem an inquest necessary.

Millom Gazette, 4th August 1899.

THE ASKAM IRONWORKS DISPUTE.

NOTICES ISSUED.

MEETING OF THE MEN.

The management have issued a notice personally to their workmen. The following is a copy:—" Millom and Askam Hematite Iron Company, Limited.—Askam Ironworks, 29th July, 1899.—We hereby give you notice that we shall not require your services after Saturday, the 5th of August, 1889.—For the Millom and Askam Hematite Iron Co., Ltd., A. SAHLIN.—Applications for reinstatement will be received by your foreman on or before 2nd August."

MEETING OF THE MEN.

A meeting of the men was held in the large room adjoining the Railway Inn on Saturday night, addressed by Mr. P. Walls, the blastfurnacemen's agent for Workington. Mr. Walls, in the course of his address, gave the men advice on the critical point at issue, and exhorted them to accept the masters' terms for the present, in order that they may see what the future might bring forth. The men seemed to favour this view, with one or two exceptions, and the general impression is that the struggle will not be of long duration.

Millom Gazette, 1st September 1899.

WATER FAMINE AT ASKAM

SHUTTING DOWN ASKAM FURNACES.

The continued spell of dry weather has seriously affected Askam. The iron furnaces, which have been working so well, were shut down on Monday for want of water, the supply which they are receiving from Roanhead mines not being sufficient to keep the furnaces in blast. Never, in the history of these works, has such a thing occurred before.

The shutting down of these works will mean a serious loss to the company as well as to the men themselves. We understand that the stopping will be at least a month before a sufficient supply of water is a hand to start the works.

Millom Gazette, 9th November 1900.

MASS MEETING OF FURNESS IRONWORKERS

A mass meeting of the men who have been locked out at the Askam-in-Furness Ironworks, was held on Saturday, when Mr. P. Walls, agent of the Lancashire and Cumberland Blastfurnacemen's Association, delivered an address. The company had declined to recognise Mr. Walls' right to interfere in the dispute. He said that when the men received notice of 10 per cent. reduction he wired them to accept it under protest, as the state of the iron market did not warrant anything so sweeping. The company had announced that they had made a profit of $17\frac{1}{2}$ per cent. Some of this might have been used to pay for increased cost of fuel instead of making the men do it. Such treatment was unfair and un-English.

Millom Gazette, 7th December 1900.

THE MILLOM AND ASKAM IRONWORKS COMPANY SET THEIR FACE AGAINST UNION MEN.

The Millom and Askam Ironworks Company are evidently determined in the future that no man connected with any Trades Union shall be employed at their works. Not only will they not allow any of their men to join the Union in the future, but if any man who had previously been connected with the Union were in their employment, they will have to leave or sever their connection with the Union as the Company agree and pledge themselves not to employ in any position around their furnaces any man who does not sign their agreement. Amongst other things in this agreement the workmen have to solemnly promise and pledge themselves on their personal word of honour not during the time that they remain in the Company's employment to hold membership in or pay any contribution to any Society or Union having for its object, or one of its objects, the interference with or regulating of the direct personal relations between employer and employed, and particularly that they shall not after last week remain or become a member of the National Last Furnacemen's Federation, and also that they will consider and recognise as a proper cause for immediate and disgraceful dismissal the violation on their part of this pledge, and their breaking of their freely given word of honour.

Millom Gazette, 7th June 1901.

ASKAM IRONWORKS.

Very considerable and important additions to the plant are being made, and though the blast furnaces ordinarily in operation had to be damped down until the necessary alterations and extensions have been completed, the staff of men who had decided to accept the Company's terms have been kept employed at labourers' work principally, but at a higher rate of pay. The additional plant includes a new furnace of the self-charging American make, with self-cleansing flues; several new and large blast engines and pumps; new slag pans, turned by hand; a mechanical pig-lifter and breaker, operated by electric power, &c., and other labour-saving devices. In respect of water supply it is anticipated there will be no more stoppages on this account, as took place two years ago, as the Company has opened up a new spring on the Greenscoe Farm estate, which is believed to be an inexhaustible supply, and will come to the works by its own gravitation, though pumps are provided to meet exigencies. No. 2 furnace will be ready during the present month and probably be in working order, but the 6th of July is named as the date for starting the new plant. When all is finished, the works will be as up-to-date and complete as can be met with.

Millom Gazette, 2nd August 1901.

THE ASKAM IRONWORKS.

It is understood that the Millom and Askam Ironworks Company are preparing to start their works at Askam, which have been standing idle for several months. It appears so far as the men who came out on strike are concerned, no satisfactory arrangement has been come to, as bills are posted up throughout the district asking furnacemen to keep away during the dispute. It is very much to be regretted that some amicable settlement cannot be made, not only in the case of this dispute, but so many others throughout the country. Some method whereby the employers and their employees can be imbued with the idea that they are directly interested in the welfare of their own particular company or concern, and ought each to use every effort to promote its welfare will of course, at once do away with all labour trouble such as now exists at Askam. So long, however, as there is a feeling that one side is desirous of taking the advantage of the other whenever the opportunity presents itself so long will there be such **unfortunate disputes, with their corresponding losses to both sides.**

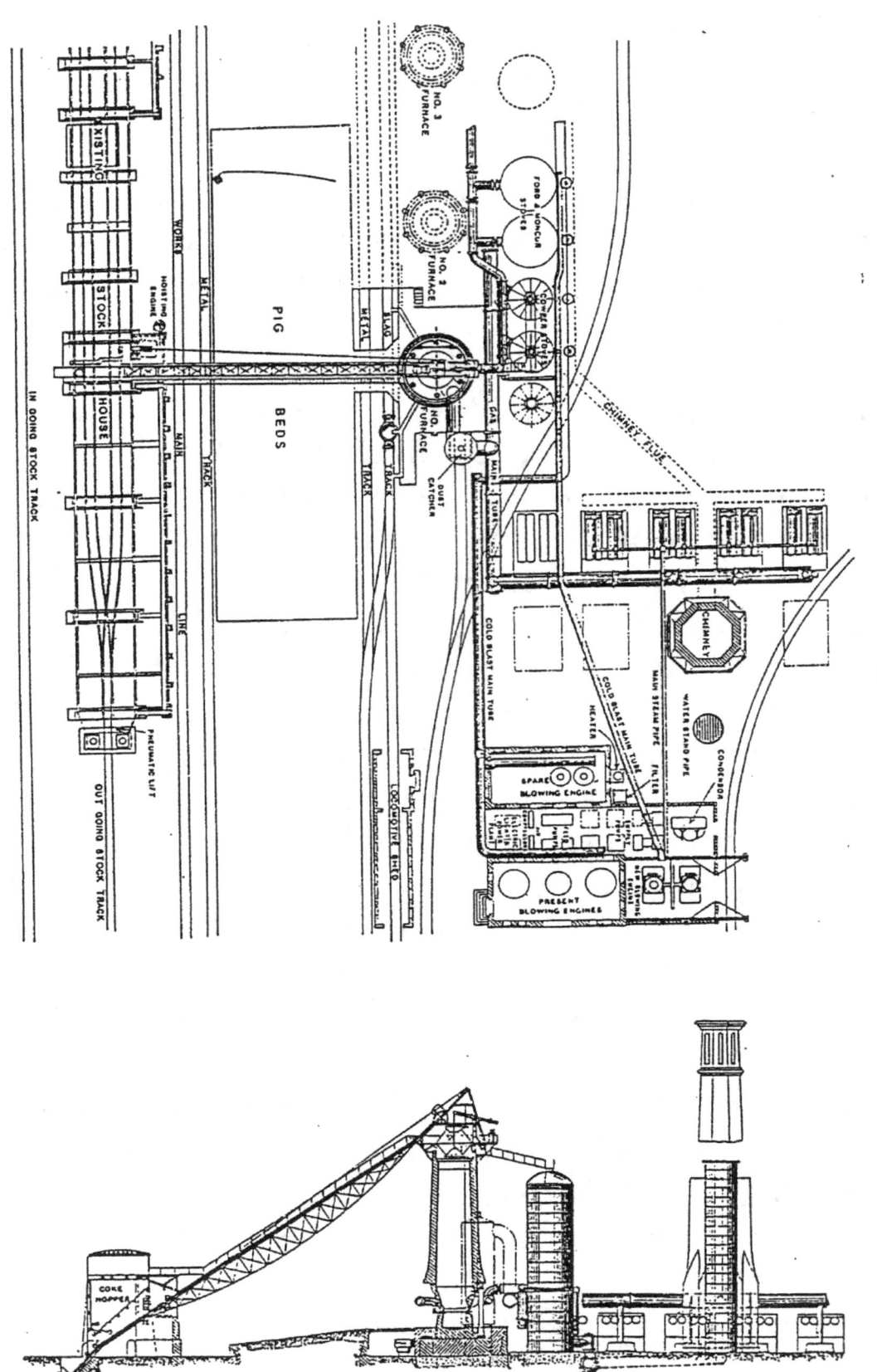

A plan of the ironworks in 1900 showing the new "American furnace," also a railway tunnel for the slag wagons can be seen. I wonder if it's still there under Parklands Drive. (Courtesy of William and Hilda Eccles)

A close-up view of the works. (Courtesy of Jeanette Shepherd)

A view of the ironworks taken from Askam wood. (Courtesy of Jeanette Shepherd)

Soulby's Ulverston Advertiser, 14th July 1904.

BLASTING OPERATIONS: A NUISANCE —The blasting operations introduced at the slag bank of the Askam Iron Works is so noisy in working as to be a nuisance to the neighbourhood during the early hours of the morning, and an effectual destroyer of sleep after 4 a.m. It seems a pity that this sort of thing should be carried on so early, greatly to the annoyance of everybody. Some other time should be allotted says a householder, for the blasting of scrap iron from the slag.

Soulby's Ulverston Advertiser, 26th October 1905.

ASKAM IRONWORKS.

PROBABLE EARLY RESUMPTION.

After being closed over two years, there is every probability of a re-start at the Iron Works at Askam at an early date. For a week or two the hearth of the American furnace has been "aired," and several men are already engaged at the works, including mechanics. Yesterday (Friday) a consignment of coke arrived at the works by rail, and there is much rejoicing at the prospect of seeing the works in full swing again. It will be a few weeks before a full complement of men will be required, and then the Askam men and those whose names are on the books will be given first chance.

Millom Gazette, 10th November 1905.

ASKAM PREPARING FOR THE DAY.

RE-STARTING THE IRONWORKS.

Askam "buzzed" on Wednesday morning when smoke was seen to rise in the early morning from the big chimney which, for so many years now, has been smokeless.

The smoke was looked upon as a token that the putting into blast of the Askam furnaces will soon be an accepted fact, and it will be a welcome day for the Duddonside town, for it will mean increased prosperity for it.

People there are now looking forward to the day which will mean so much for them, and will also enable Askam to join to an even greater extent in work for the war.

The Anglo-Afghan is the war they are referring to.

Millom Gazette, 8th February 1907.

Askam Ironworks Stopped.

On Saturday, the men employed at the Askam Ironworks received notice to leave their employment. Owing to the top part of the lining of the large American furnace falling in the furnace has been put out of blast. A thorough examination will have to be made of the furnace to see what repairs are necessary. It is feared that some time will elapse before the works will be re-started, as the furnace may have to be entirely re-lined.

Barrow News, 19th April 1919.

BAD FOR ASKAM.

IRONWORKS TO CLOSE DOWN.

Restarted in May, 1917, after being closed down for some nine years, owing to German competition, the Askam Ironworks, which have given employment to about 100 men, are again to go out of blast.

Notices have been posted at the works that the plant is to be closed down forthwith. Mr. Linnell, the present manager, leaves at the end of this month, but, as already stated in the "Mail," he resigned some weeks ago in order to take up a more important post at Tipton (Staffs.).

The subsidies that have been granted to makers of iron by the Government and Government control of the trade will come to an end this month. The trade will then return to the old competitive system.

Since the works restarted, the men employed did not reach the number when the works were in full swing many years ago, but hopes were held out that the town would see once again its old-time prosperity as an iron ore centre revived.

The chimney is said to be the tallest but one in the United Kingdom, being beaten by one at Glasgow.

For some time there has been a large stock of ore on hand owing to shortage of railway wagons.

This marked the very end of manufacturing iron at Askam forever.

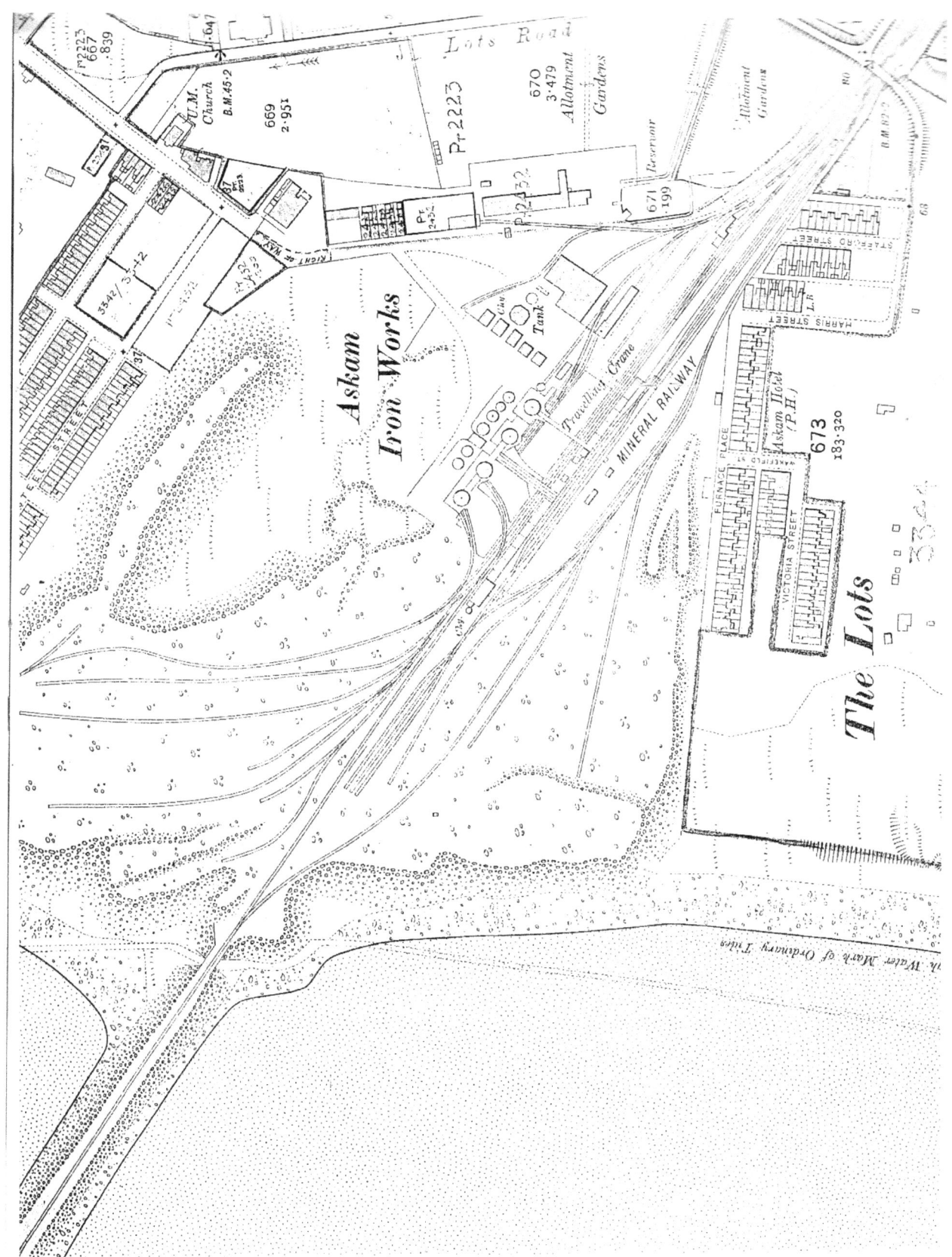

An ordnance survey map of 1913 showing the works and part of the pier. (Kevin Alexander Collection)

After the closure of the works the site became derelict apart from the offices where Mr. A. Lewis the company's caretaker lived, anything of any worth made its way over to Millom. Between 1931 and 1938 the company decided to start selling off the buildings and land, the bricks were reused in other buildings elsewhere in the district, many ending up in peoples pens! any metal found was scrapped, some structures partly survived into the 70s however with the building of the Parklands housing estate only the pier and slagbank survive today. Purchasers of the ironworks land were, Mr. Atkinson, Mr. M. Coward (Greenscoe and reservoirs), Mr. Greenop, Mr. T. D. Dixon, Mr. Gillbanks and Dalton Urban District Council.

Overall, I would say the works had an unlucky run compared to the other furnaces in the area, but how different a place Askam would be today if the ironworks had been more successful than it was, the character of the place no doubt would have been that of a town like E. T. Wakefield and others had intended it to be. Thankfully Askam became a rural industrial village instead, with open land, filled with washing posts and pens scattered all over the place, that's how I know our village as and hopefully it can retain its character into the future.

A brilliant and rare photograph showing the ironworks offices to the right, the end of the slagbank on the left, and Furness Tavern in the centre. (Courtesy of Jeanette Shepherd)

Barrow News, 18th November 1933.

Ironworks Chimney.

Although the furnaces and stoves at the Askam Ironworks have been almost dismantled, the chimney, which is the tallest in the district, is still standing, a buyer not having been found for the massive structure. Bricks from the parts of the works already dismantled are being used in buildings which are being erected.

FELLING THE ASKAM IRON WORKS CHIMNEY.

(Courtesy of Leslie Eveson)

Barrow News, 10th February 1934.

Iron works Chimney.

Several feet deep into its side and overhung by the towering mass above them, a squad of six men have been engaged since Tuesday cutting away the brickwork at the base of Askam Ironwork's 327ft. chimney, and though the huge erection, the second highest in the country will not be felled on Friday, as had been anticipated, it will be some time early next week at least. The depth of the brickwork, in some places 10ft., and its solidarity, is greater than had been anticipated. The men are working on the Barrow side of the chimney, and its million and a half of bricks will fall in a seaward direction. Built in 1865, it was sold to Mr. G. Liddle, of Dalton, for demolition. Squads of men have been engaged for months dismantling the furnaces, engine houses, etc., of the rest of the works.

Barrow News, 17th February 1934.

Chimney Felled.

Askam's big chimney fell at 3.40 p.m. on Sunday. It was unexpected, and the prediction had been confidently made only an hour or so before that it would not collapse till Monday. Since Tuesday six men have been cutting the bricks away at first one of its eight corners and then another. That was how it was done —with hammer and chisel. There was no blasting, no underpinning, and firing. It is the first time a chimney of such tremendous size has been so dealt with, but it is necessary for an accurate fall. That was made on the Barrow or seaward side of the chimney. A man was watching at the other side for the fatal crack to come. It never did. Just as a couple of "shots" sounded from the distant Greenscoe Quarry, where they were blasting, there came a fall of bricks and dust. The crack ran up the Askam side of the huge mass. It trembled and then came straight down upon itself like a concertina. There was no room for the last thirty yards of it to fall, and this toppled slowly over and crashed mightily alongside the old engine house. The whole thing had happened before you could count five. All that is left now is a great heap of bricks, and southward stretches another low mound of bricks and iron bands that once circled the chimney to the top.

THE PIER

Some might think that the pier was built as a way of bridging the Duddon Estuary, this was never the case. And some think it was to set Askam up with a means of shipping the pig iron and iron ore out directly from the works. Well, yes that was an intention but not the direct intention for its construction, you see Askam before the pier and in fact before the slagbank was plagued with sand drifting in and blocking the sewers and roadways - it truly was a problem for a fledgling settlement.

Well before the pier was dreamt up the council and ironworks proposed building an "Embankment" from the iron works along the shoreline towards Marsh farm in 1876. However, due to some of the costs being put on the landowners and the loss of access to the shore the scheme was never to be, although the ironworks did make their part of the embankment which we can see today, it was subsequently heightened later on. Another scheme was to build a wall out of brick at the rear of Steel Street, from Duke Street all the way down to the shore, and again this came to nothing as the iron works had already a wooden fence in place.

An agreement to build the pier between the Duke of Buccleuch and the Millom and Askam Hematite Company was agreed on the 1st January 1895, it was then proposed to the public in September 1895 and approved a month later by the Department of trade. Then on the 2nd April 1898, the Duke of Buccleuch gave a licence to build the pier to the Millom and Askam Hematite Company, on the foreshore of the Duddon Channel for a term of 32 years, the rent being wayleave of 1d per ton shipped from the pier. Construction began soon after and by 1902 the timber wharfs were completed at the end. A further two more licences were granted with similar terms with slight amendments in 1903 and 1907, basically asking the Duke for permission to enlarge the pier.

However with the works being closed for a long time and the realisation that the company would be closing the works for good in the near future they applied to the Duke in 1918 to release the Company from a clause binding them to maintain the pier, they also asked the Duke if they could take away the timber from the pier in return for compensation of £750. (£36,158.39. in 2024 prices)

(Kevin Alexander Collection)

A rare photograph showing the timber at the end of the pier, the Pier Stick can be seen behind the man who might have been a Stevenson, it was used to mark where to tip the slag when the pier was extended - another would have been on the shore on the Lots too, however that has long gone. (Courtesy of Maxine and David Hughes)

Soulby's Ulverston Advertiser, 10th August 1876.

THE PROPOSED EMBANKMENT AT ASKAM.

The Surveyor produced a plan showing the proposed embankment along a portion of the foreshore at Askam, which Mr. Crossley had promised to make by throwing slag along it if the Board would consent to make a road. The surveyor said that the owners would gain about 60 feet of land, that the material to be thrown along the shore would amount to 50,000 cubic yards, and that to place it there at the Board's expense would cost £3,000. Mr. Crossley had offered to do that for nothing if the Board would engage men to make the road. It would probably take two or three men to do that work whilst the road was being made.

The Rev. J. Padley said the question was one of great importance to the public at Askam. The embankment, if made, would stop sand from going on the shore. He thought it would be a great advantage, but the consent of the owners of the adjoining land would be required.

Mr. Fisher thought if these owners get an addition of 60 feet to their land, they ought to bear some portion of the expense.

Mr. Robinson believed some difficulty had arisen as to those owners giving their consent.

The Surveyor understood that seven owners were interested in the adjacent land, and went on to say that certain streets were likely to be made highways in future, and if so, the proposed road and embankment would then be of very great importance.

Mr. Robinson said the embankment would be a great protection to the whole of Askam, and remarked that as some of the fields had been sold in parcels, the number of owners was now about 12 or 14.

Mr. Fargher thought that possibly one man might be able to go on with making the road as fast as the slag was delivered.

Mr. Ashworth expressed as his opinion that unless the owners pay one-half of the expense of making the road, the work be not proceeded with.

Mr. Askew proposed that the owners be written to, and informed that the plan of the proposed work was on view at the Board's offices. That it should be pointed out that they would be gainers of land by the making of the embankment, and that they be asked to contribute something towards the expense of making the road.

The Surveyor remarked that the making of the road was likely also to be of great advantage to the Board in future with respect to certain streets and highways.

Soulby's Ulverston Advertiser, 12th September 1895.

NOTICE.

Proposed Embankment and Pier on the Duddon Estuary at Askam.

NOTICE is hereby given, that the Board of Trade have instructed Vice-Admiral Sir George Nares, K.C.B., F.R.S., to hold a PUBLIC INQUIRY at the Askam Iron Works Offices, at Askam-in-Furness, on Tuesday the 17th day of September, 1895, at 12 noon in the matter of an application of the Millom and Askam Hematite Iron Company, Limited, for the sanction of the Board to the construction of a solid EMBANKMENT and of a PIER in the Duddon Estuary at Askam.

The Works proposed will consist of an embankment for double line of railway formed of blast furnace slag, extending from the Iron works Slag-Bank out into the Estuary, a distance of 666 yards, to a small channel with a wood pier at the end. The Embankment and Pier will be 7 feet above ordinary high water line at ordinary spring tides. An under bridge will be constructed on the foreshore, at ordinary high water line, carrying roadway under railway, of a span of 14 feet and clear head room of 28 feet.

It has been suggested that the construction of the contemplated embankment might affect the main navigable channel of the Duddon River, and lead to an accretion of shore, thus diminishing the tidal capacity of the Estuary.

All persons interested should attend.

T. H. W. PELHAM, Assistant Secretary.
Board of Trade, Harbour Department,
28th August, 1895.

633

Millom Gazette, 2nd May 1902.

ASKAM IRONWORKS PIER.

The new pier at the ironworks is rapidly nearing completion. The pile driving is finished and the workmen are boarding up the interstices between the piles. The work of filling in has already commenced, slag, etc., being tipped to fill the space between the embankment and the piles.

Millom Gazette, 22nd August 1902.

ASKAM IRON-WORKS PIER.

Messrs. W. Gradwell have finished their contract for the erection of the pier. It only remains for the embankment to be levelled and filled in to be quite completed. There is ample accommodation for four vessels. The facilities for shipping iron will no doubt give a good impetus to the trade of the town.

Soulby's Ulverston Advertiser 20th August 1903.

BOATING ACCIDENT.—A young man named Tyson was sailing in Mr. J. Constable's boat, on Thursday when he somehow got between the steam barge "Hobby" and the pier, as the barge was leaving. The strong tide partly swung the Hobby round, and the boat was crushed like an eggshell, the young man just saving himself by leaping on to the Hobby.

Soulby's Ulverston Advertiser, 24th September 1903.

A NEW PORT.—Much interest was caused in Askam on Sunday by the arrival at the Ironworks pier of the S.S. Greta. This is the first vessel to take a cargo from here. She loaded 320 tons of pig-iron for Glasgow. During the afternoon the vessel was visited by scores of people, Captain Marshall kindly allowing the public to look through the vessel. The Greta departed again yesterday.

This was the only boat to use the pier, apart from the ironwork's own boat "Hobby" that collected sand for the pig beds at Millom.

Picture from Barrow News, 20th November 1910, however it states the wrong date of 1905 instead of 1903. (Picture courtesy of Peter Burt)

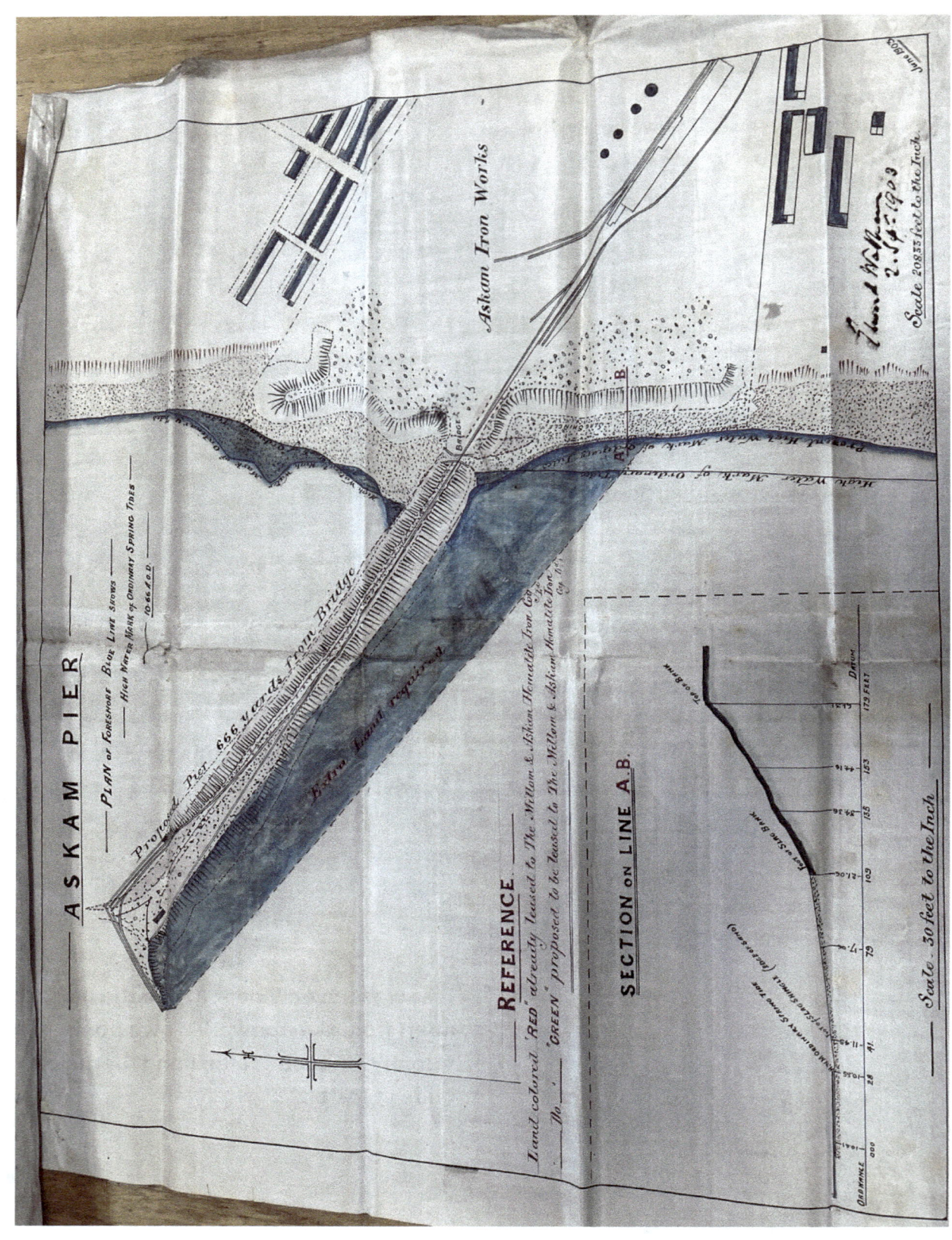

The plan drawn up in 1903 for the pier's extension in blue. (Cumbria Archive Centre, Barrow BDBUC/22/04/13)

One thing I had completely overlooked until it was pointed out to me by Peter Holmes, was that the ironworks had two types of slag wagons. I had only really noticed the round shaped blocks left behind on the pier and slagbank, however if you look closely, you will come across square blocks too!

Here is Peter Holmes brilliant description of slag tipping;

"Slag disposal

Until the 1890s, and in some case through into the early 1900s, it was usual practice at iron smelting works for slag to be moved in 'boxes' or 'pans'. These consisted of an open-bottomed tapered box or pan about six feet across and four feet deep, sitting on a small flat railway wagon. The joint at the bottom would be sealed with fireclay, and the slag from the furnace would be run in. The theory was that the slag would cool to form a solid block, and the tapered shape would allow the box to be lifted off the slag with a crane and put down on an 'empty' wagon coming back from the tip on a parallel line. The block of slag would be run up to the tip head by a locomotive, or in early days by a horse, and dumped off the wagon endways by running the front wheels off the end of the rails, or sideways by having one rail end shorter than the other.

It wasn't always that simple, because there was always pressure to turn the things round as quickly as possible. So, the men sometimes found themselves compelled to lift the box off the slag before it had cooled properly. In 1892 there was a bad accident at Distington Ironworks because of this, aggravated by a stuck box.

As an aside, the slag tipping gang at Distington had repeatedly asked for more boxes because the practice of stripping the blocks while hot was becoming increasingly dangerous. The predictable response had been "if you won't do the job, there's a line of unemployed men at the works gate who will". It's comforting to record that at the inquiry, and this was in 1892 remember, the judge found in favour of the injured man. I wouldn't be surprised if there were similar incidents at Askam, or indeed anywhere else where this remarkably hazardous way of slag disposal was employed.

It's possible that some of the slag blocks, as distinct from 'poured' slag, can still be seen in the older parts of the slag banks at Askam.

When the American Furnace was introduced Askam got some new tipping 'ladle' wagons of American make to shift the slag from it. I think the three older furnaces continued to use the slag boxes. The reason for the new wagons was that the new furnace was designed to run at a higher blast temperature than the old ones, and it produced a more fluid slag. It was therefore possible to take the wagon of slag out to the tip and pour the contents out while they were still fluid.

Ernie Tyson (Of Askam) had occasionally driven the loco on the slag run, and he recalled that tipping from the American ladles could be risky, because if you weren't careful you would get hot slag all over the rails. No doubt it then had to be broken up with hammers and pick axes while still hot. The surface of freshly poured slag cooled from white heat to red to black within a matter of seconds, but still retained sufficient heat beneath to make handling it a risky business.

The photo of the Wiemer ladle shows that it was tipped by hand, by spinning that large wheel. Even though it would be operated with the ladle tilting away from the operator, he would still be uncomfortably close to the hot slag. Later slag ladles, as seen at Millom and Barrow, were tipped remotely by means of the loco backing away while pulling on a light chain."

A box type slag wagon. (Peter Holmes Collection)

The Weimer ladle wagon. (Peter Holmes Collection)

(Kevin Alexander Collection)

An example of the round ladle slag block (foreground), and a square slag block (background) by Pier Gap on Lots shore.

A maker's official photograph of an ironworks train 'ASKAM No.1', this was built by Neilson & Co of Glasgow in 1895. (Peter Holmes Collection)

Marks left behind in the slag of railway sleepers. (Kevin Alexander Collection)

THE MINES

This chapter I won't delve too deep into details regarding every pit or shaft sunk as this has been covered brilliantly already in two books; "THE RED EARTH" by Dave Kelly and "THE RED EARTH REVISITED" by Brian Cubbon, Peter Sandbach and Colin Woollard. I recommend obtaining these books if you are interested in the Furness iron mines.

Mining in Furness is thought to go back before medieval times, and in all probability it did. Well, here we are interested in the Askam area for this book and what we know for sure was that in the 1700s Crossgates iron ore was being carted to Ireleth Marsh and shipped off to Scotland and further up the estuary to the Duddon Bridge Furnace. Some of this this ore can still be seen today on the shore in small piles at the end of Duddon Road as they would dump the ore directly on the shore and then load onto the boats. And again, we know that in the 1700s a mine was opened in the northern part of the Park Estate by either Micheal or George Knott of the Newland Furnace near Ulverston, as this pit took the family's name being known as Knotts Pit, this pit was directly across from where the brickyard is today on the other side of the railway line.

Purple/red pieces of iron ore on the shore at Duddon Road.

(Kevin Alexander Collection)

Some of my Askam mining collection, these include railway shoes and steam train shovel from the Roanhead Line, also seen are various picks and nails, a piece of narrow-gauge rail and a piece of a borehole sample. (Kevin Alexander Collection)

& ASKAM HEMATITE IRON Co., LIMITED

NOTICE.

Not more than Four Persons must Ride on any Cage at one time.
No Person must Ride except against an Empty Cage.
No Person must get on the Cage until he has received the Signal that all is right.
All Tools and Loose Material must be securely placed in an Empty Bogie when sent Up or Down the Shaft.

SIGNALS.
THE FOLLOWING SIGNALS SHALL BE OBSERVED.

1 Knock or Ring to Stop Engine.
2 Knocks or Rings to Reverse Engine and Lower Cage.
3 Knocks or Rings to Start Engine.
4 Knocks or Rings, Precautionary Signal that Men are about to Ride.
5 Knocks or Rings, Precautionary Signal to Stop at some Intermediate Height.
6 Knocks or Rings, Precautionary Signal that Tools or Loose Material are about to be sent
8 Knocks or Rings to Start Pumps.
10 Knocks or Rings to Stop Pumps.

BY ORDER.

(Kevin Alexander Collection)

Askam Hematite Iron ore. (Kevin Alexander Collection)

PARK MINES

It all started off in the Park Royalty the land belonging to the Duke of Devonshire, as already mentioned a pit was first sunk here in the 1700s. Well, a gentleman by the name of Henry Schnieder visited Furness in 1839 and he made sure to visit the local iron mines due to his family's business in owning mines in Cornwall, Wales and Mexico already. After a meeting with the Dukes agent and a visit to Knotts Pit he decided to take on the Park lease and with an investment of £50,000 (£4,321,633.45 in 2024 prices) from his father, London geologists were tasked to do a survey of the district, and they urged the family to sink a mine down the Haggs at Dalton. This proved to be a mistake, and nothing was found, Schnieder then reopened the old Knotts pit coming away with a few hundred tons of ore until it was abandoned. He moved on to Plumpton and then to Whitriggs and Mouzell the latter two producing steady amounts of ore for him.

It wasn't until 1850 when his lease was coming to an end that he was asked to either give it up or search for ore! He decided to make one last attempt and committed £50 (£5,710) to sink a shaft close to the original Park farm that was built by Furness Abbey monks. The money unfortunately ran out and Schnieder turned to his men and told them to abandon the mine, however led by Richard Hosking they offered to carry on unpaid for another week as they were certain they were going to hit ore, which indeed they did. They had discovered the giant body of ore called the Park Sop, which became the second largest deposit of iron ore in Britain with over 15 million tonnes extracted. This mine directly led to Schnieder opening the largest iron and steelworks in the world at that time in Barrow in 1859. He also helped to found the first shipyard on Barrow Island in 1871; the site Bae Systems now occupy.

Park Mine was closed by the Barrow Haemitite Steel Company (Schnieders steelworks) in 1921. The mine was bought by the neighbouring mine owners the Kennedy Brothers in 1922, on account to stop their own mines from flooding out at Roanhead. In 1937 they opened up some old workings in the California Pits, raising some considerable amounts of ore. Unfortunately, this was dirty black ore which needed cleaning before it could be sold. Leading the company to abandon raising anymore. The pumps here were kept going up until 1942.

There is no doubt in my mind that the discovery of the ore at Park was the catalyst for the creation of the town of Barrow and in no doubt the reason why Askam became a planned town with similar ambitions.

Barrow Herald, 24th August 1878.

SHOCKING DEATH AT AN IRON MINE.—On Friday afternoon, a man named Richard Johnson was being lowered down the shaft at the Park Mines, near Dalton, when the cage left the rope, and was precipitated to the bottom of the shaft. Johnson was instantaneously killed. A new rope had been fixed to the cage that morning, and it is supposed that the connecting bolt gave way. The deceased leaves a widow and a family of five children. An inquest was held on Monday last, before John Poole, Esq., coroner, and a jury, of which Mr. William Wilson was foreman, at the Clarence Hotel, Ulverston-road, Dalton, when, after the evidence of Messrs. John Wilson, John Butler, and William Blackwell had been taken, a verdict of "Accidental Death" was returned. Deceased was much esteemed by his fellow-workmen and others.

Soulby's Ulverston Advertiser, 12th June 1879.

FATAL MINING CALAMITY AT PARK MINES.

A sad mining accident, involving the loss of three lives, and the narrow escape of a fourth man, took place at the Park Mines, the property of the Barrow Steel Company, on Monday night last. It appears that about 6-30 p.m., Matthew Walsh, of Askam, aged 60; James Hicks, Dalton, 30; William Cooil, Dalton, 38; and William Hogg, of Dalton, were at work in a drift at the Park Mines. They had put in a blast, and the three former were leaving the drift, Hogg staying to fire the shot. Before he could do so, however, the fore breast fell in, burying the three, and Hogg escaped over the *debris*, and gave the alarm. Vigorous attempts were at once made to dig out the men, but it was not until 8 a.m., on Tuesday morning that the bodies of two were recovered, and the third was reached at 11 a.m. Of course, all were dead, the bodies being sadly crushed. J. Poole, Esq., opened an inquest yesterday, but adjourned it to allow of the presence of the Government Inspector of Mines. All the three deceased were married men, and leave families.

A view from 1879 of Schnieder's famous last attempt to find ore at Park, the original mine with the remains of the original farm in the background. (Cumbria Archive Centre, Barrow. BDP 37)

Dayshift workers, Burlington Pit 1879. (Cumbria Archive Centre, Barrow. BDP 37)

The impressive Burlington Pit in 1879. (Cumbria Archive Centre, Barrow. BDP 37)

Burlington Pit with an old Furness Railway Train in 1879. (Cumbria Archive Centre, Barrow. BDP 37)

Barrow Herald, 2nd October 1880.

PIT ON FIRE AT PARK MINES, NEAR DALTON.—On Monday morning as the miners employed in the Burlington Pit, Park Mines, we proceeding down the shaft to their work they discovered that the pit was on fire somewhere in the workings. The smoke was so dense and suffocating that four or five men were almost overcome in vainly attempting to find out the seat of the fire. Efforts were at once made to subdue the flames, and the strenuous efforts of Captain Lawn and a staff of energetic and experienced miners to put out the fire have been very successful. Although the fire is still smouldering it is confined within very narrow limits.

Barrow Herald, 2nd July 1881.

ACCIDENT AT THE PARK MINES, NEAR DALTON.—On Monday last, a miner, named Thos. Alexander, of Askam, was seriously hurt whilst employed at the above mines. So far as we can learn, it appears a bogey fell upon him and bruised him very much about his head. He was carefully conveyed to his home, and his injuries promptly attended to.

Park North Crossing in 1908 showing the North Pit and the broken ground of the large Park Sop. My great, great grandparents Jack and Charlotte Wells home can be seen in the background hidden by the orchard trees. Jack worked in the Roanhead Mines and was the wash plant foreman. (Kevin Alexander Collection)

Part of the Park Mine Sidings at Park North Crossing. (Kevin Alexander Collection)

A view looking at Park North Crossing in the 1930s. (My great grandparents' home; Doug & Elsie Moore). Doug worked on the railways but in his "spare" time worked at Roanhead too. Burlington pit can be seen along with the deep broken ground. (Kevin Alexander Collection).

A closer view of the broken ground now full of water in the 50s, hard to imagine it was once over **744ft deep.** (Kevin Alexander Collection)

CHAPMAN'S LOT

Mining began here in 1863 when Myles Kennedy leased the right to mine minerals from the Duke of Buccleuch, and a shaft was sunk finding ore. however, in 1865 the land was sold to Edward Thomas Wakefield a London barrister who lodged legal proceedings against the Duke of Buccleuch and Kennedy for mining on land he now owned. The Duke claimed the mineral rights as he was the Lord of the Manor of Plain Furness and with this, he was entitled to the soil of all said moors, commons and wastes, and to all mines, minerals, and quarries of whatever nature or kind soever as which was stated in the enclosure acts. This land was sold by the Duke of Buccleuch in 1831 to Jane Towers to defray the cost of him enclosing it under the acts. Wakefield however took the stance that he bought the property as a freehold and with that the mineral rights passed to him.

After a drawn-out battle in the courts and then in the house of Lords it was decided in the Dukes favour in 1870, even with this decision no mining took place here until 1893, when Wakefield applied to the Duke for permission to mine which was granted and the Wakefield pit was sunk soon after. In 1902 Edward's wife surrendered the mines licence and sold the Lots to Myles Kennedy. Kennedy Brothers then took out a licence here in 1905 and carried on winning ore from the Wakefield Pit, however they began to access the royalty from their No. 3 Pit on the Roanhead Estate and brought the ore out here leaving the Wakefield Pit as an air shaft. Chapman's Lot was worked out by 1910, and the site was used to tip waste from the Roanhead mines. The licence was finally surrendered in 1940. Today the site is known as the "Fishy Pond" where the mine subsided along with Mackinnon Lot.

A rare view of the headgear of the Wakefield Pit to the top left, the street seen is Stafford Street. On a separate note a building can be seen on the incline of Lots Bridge. (Courtesy of Jeanette Shepherd)

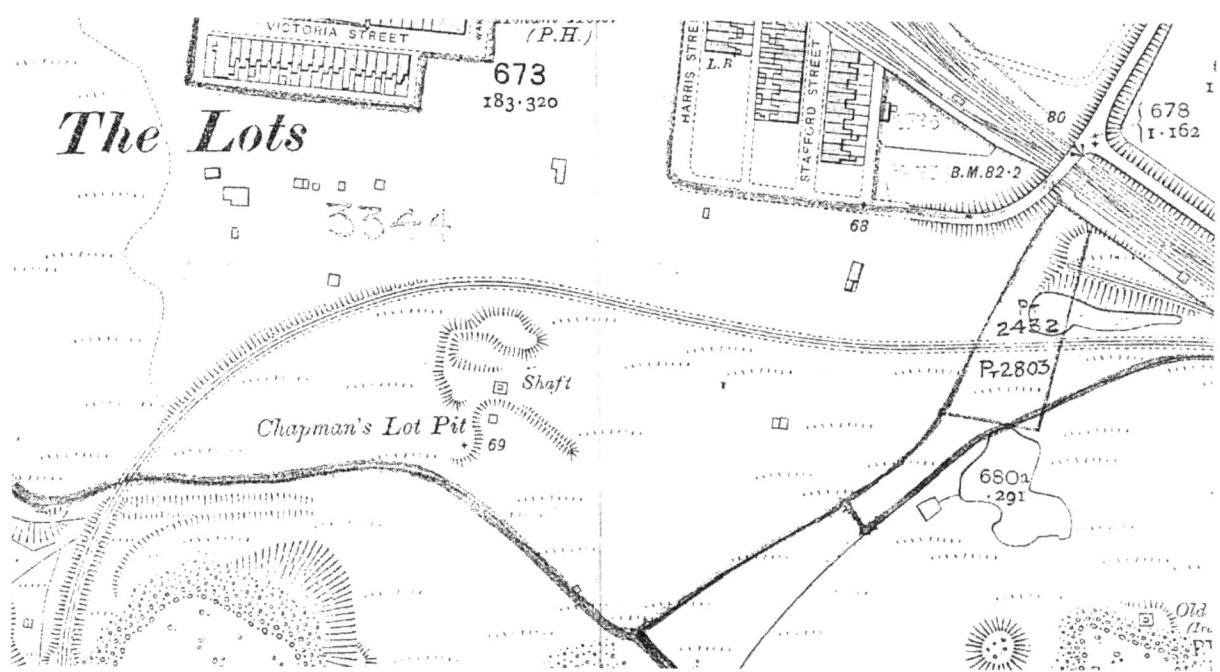

1913 Ordnance Survey showing Chapman's Lot Pit, also known as the Wakefield Pit. (Kevin Alexander Collection)

Soulby's Ulverston Advertiser, 24th September 1903.

IRON MINE RE-OPENED.—Chapman Lot Mine, which was purchased by Messrs. Kennedy Bros., from Mr. Wakefield, is to be opened out again shortly. This is good news for Askam, as it will give employment for some of the men out of work through the stoppage of the Ironworks.

MACKINNON LOT

Also known as the Greenscoe Mine, as it was within the Greenscoe Estate of the MacKinnon family. Mining began here in 1849 when Charles Storr Kennedy took out a lease from the MacKinnon family for a term of 21 years.

When the MacKinnon's invested in the Furness Iron and Steel Company at Askam they took the decision to buy back the licence in 1868 and took control of the mine for themselves including the Kennedy's equipment. Kennedy's later received payment for the seized equipment after legal proceedings. The mine later passed into the possession of the ironworks and in all had 11 shallow shafts which caused the ground to subside even into Chapman's Lot, this mine was worked up until 1909.

This mine was situated south of Lots Road, where Low Greenscoe Farm is now situated and the subsided ground is part of the "Fishy" Pond.

Askam miners 1900, a Richard Kitchen is pictured on the right. (Courtesy of Ted Grayless)

Soulby's Ulverston Advertiser, 28th September 1893.

FALL OF EARTH IN AN IRON MINE AT ASKAM.

Two Men Entombed.

On Monday morning, at the Greenscoe Iron Mine, at Askam, the men working below were greatly startled at a sudden fall of earth, which took place just before noon. There were several men working in the immediate vicinity, and after a search had been made it was found that two men named Thomas Stuart and Edward Cole were entombed. A number of men at once set to work to clear the shaft, but it was only after four hours' hard work that the two entombed men were rescued. Happily they were not injured in the slightest degree, the passage to where they were working only being blocked. Work was resumed immediately after, the place being little the worse.

Millom Gazette, 26th May 1899.

DISCOVERY OF ORE NEAR ASKAM.

There seems to be every liklihood of the Greenscoe Mines, now leased by the Askam and Mouzell Iron Company, proving a source of great benefit to the Company. It appears that extensive boring operations have recently been carried out on this estate, with the result that a fine body of metal has been discovered, equal, if not superior, to any yet found in Furness. The outcome of this is the sinking of a shaft, which exceeded all expectations, and now preparations are in progress for putting down an engine and the fixing of a pit top. The scarcity of iron ore should tend to cause a great revival in the iron trade in this district. The general impression is that there is a large body of workable metal at the present mines and also in the immediate vicinity.

ROANHEAD MINES

This Estate was owned by the Sandys family of Graythwaite Hall near Hawkshead and the mining lease was first taken out by C. S. Kennedy in 1852, he was already busy in the area being a partner in the Ulverston Mining Company in 1837 and he also had a lease at Greenhaume in 1848 and MacKinnon Lot in 1849 too.

The Kennedy family were the most successful local mining families by far and over a long period of time, because of this there are a lot of individual mines, each with their own history to tell which I cannot cover in this book. So please refer to the books mentioned at the beginning of this chapter for a more detailed account. However, I will give a brief breakdown here.

Some of the main Roanhead mines were the Woodhead Pit, no5 pit and no3 Pit at the Askam end of the territory. Other notable pits were the Plunger Pit, no16 Pit, Kathleen, Ethel, Peggy, Betty, Rita and Nigel Pits, the later pit alone gave out 11,000,000 tons.

The Kennedys's later bought the Roanhead Estate that they leased, they took over Sandscale Mine in 1892, Chapman's Lot in 1902 and the Park royalty in 1922, the idea of occupying these mines was to keep them clear of water so that the Roanhead mines wouldn't flood. They did go into all of them to see what was left behind and carried on winning ore in varying amounts. They worked the Roanhead mines until 1941 and the following year equipment was then sold at auction. The mining might have come to an end, but foreign ore was brought in to be crushed for annealing ore using the old wash plant at Nigel Pit, work came to an end in January 1945 when the wash plant was finally dismantled.

Kennedy Brothers company seal. (Kevin Alexander Collection)

My Lads Doug and Bill standing at the remains of the tramline embankment at the Woodhead Pit (Blacks Pond), Built to protect the mine from the sea. This Rail line was connected to the Roanhead Line and had access to the ironworks. To the right, off picture, you can see poured slag on the stone lining and two round slag blocks that cooled to soon and were unable to be poured. (Kevin Alexander Collection)

Barrow Herald, 8th April 1871.

FATAL MINING ACCIDENT AT ASKAM.

An inquest was held at the Bridge Inn, Dalton, on Monday morning, before W. Butler, Esq., coroner, upon the body of Jonathan Inman, a miner, 38 years of age, who was killed while working in the Askam mines on Saturday last. The Rev. J. M. Morgan acted as foreman, the following being the jurymen:—Edward Southward, Robert Watts, Edward Skelton, John Fox, Robert Thornborough, Joseph Shaw, Jonathan Dixon, John Fargher, Joseph Borwick, Samuel Huddleston, and Thomas Towers.

John Jones, Prymbo, Derbyshire, shoemaker, first called, deposed that deceased was his son-in-law.

James Towers, miner, Dalton, working at the Askam mines, deposed: Deceased worked in No. 4 drift at the Askam mines. I worked in No. 35. On Saturday I was at work about half-past four o'clock when I heard a crash in the drift where deceased was. I ran to the spot, and hearing a groan, I said to a companion named Richardson, "there is somebody killed; go for help." I went into No. 4, and found the place broken down and deceased underneath. He was lying on his face, with his head and shoulders visible. A piece of wood was lying across the back of his neck, with 14 or 15 feet of ore and stones, which had fallen, lying upon it. He was quite dead. Either four or five pieces of wood have fallen. There was no one working there at the time but deceased, his mate not having arrived. The working was wooded at the sides and top, the wood supporting the roof. From the manner in which the body had fallen, I think deceased was making his way out. He had not been in the place two minutes. The accident must have been caused by a slip from the side. Deceased had not fired a shot, but they had been shooting all night.

In reply to the Rev. J. M. Morgan, witness said he knew positively that the wood touched the rock roof, but he could not say whether deceased was informed before going into the mine that shots had been recently fired.

William Alexander, miner, Askam, said: I work in No. 4 working, and was in it on Friday night up ts half-past three on Saturday morning. It was a solid rock roof which had never been disturbed at that place. There is no old working over. There is an old working on a higher level, just at one side, running partly in the same direction. There is solid ground between us. We had been shooting, having fired six holes during the night. Where the fall has taken place it was solid wood, and touching the roof. It was a side slip which caused the accident. Our shots were fired in the forebreast, and would have no tendency to shake the ground where the wood fell in. It is wet ground.

By the Rev. J. M. Morgan: I informed deceased when I came out that shots had been fired, and how the work stood.

John Wilson, the third witness, foreman at the Askam Works, saw No. 4 drift on Friday afternoon, and saw no danger in it. They worked none of the mines without timbering, unless it was a solid rock roof. There was no bar upon the quantity of timber to be used. There was a little water at this place in the mine.

This was all the evidence called, and a verdict of "Accidental death" was returned.

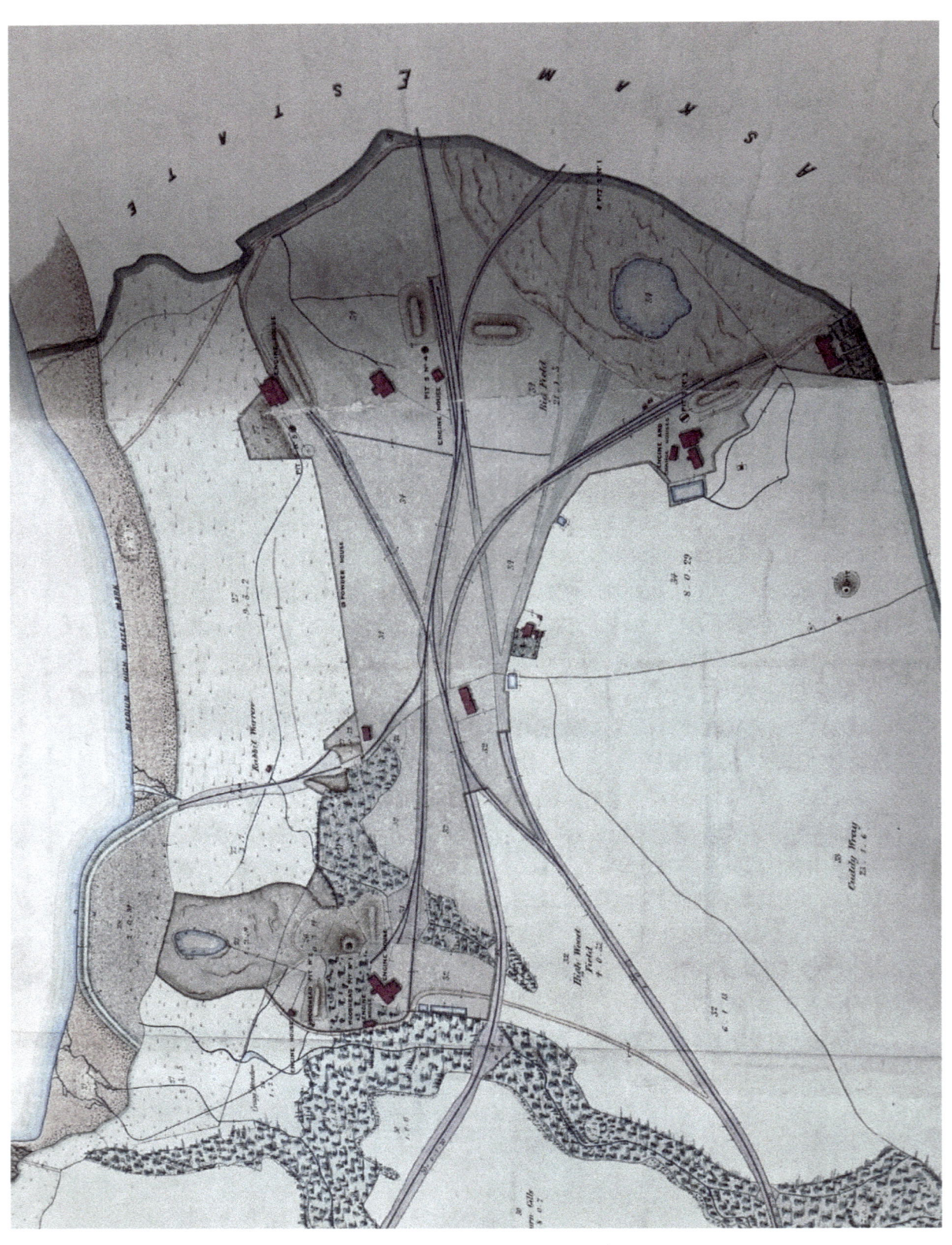

Askam section of the Roanhead Estate in 1877. (Cumbria Archive Centre, Barrow. Z2928)

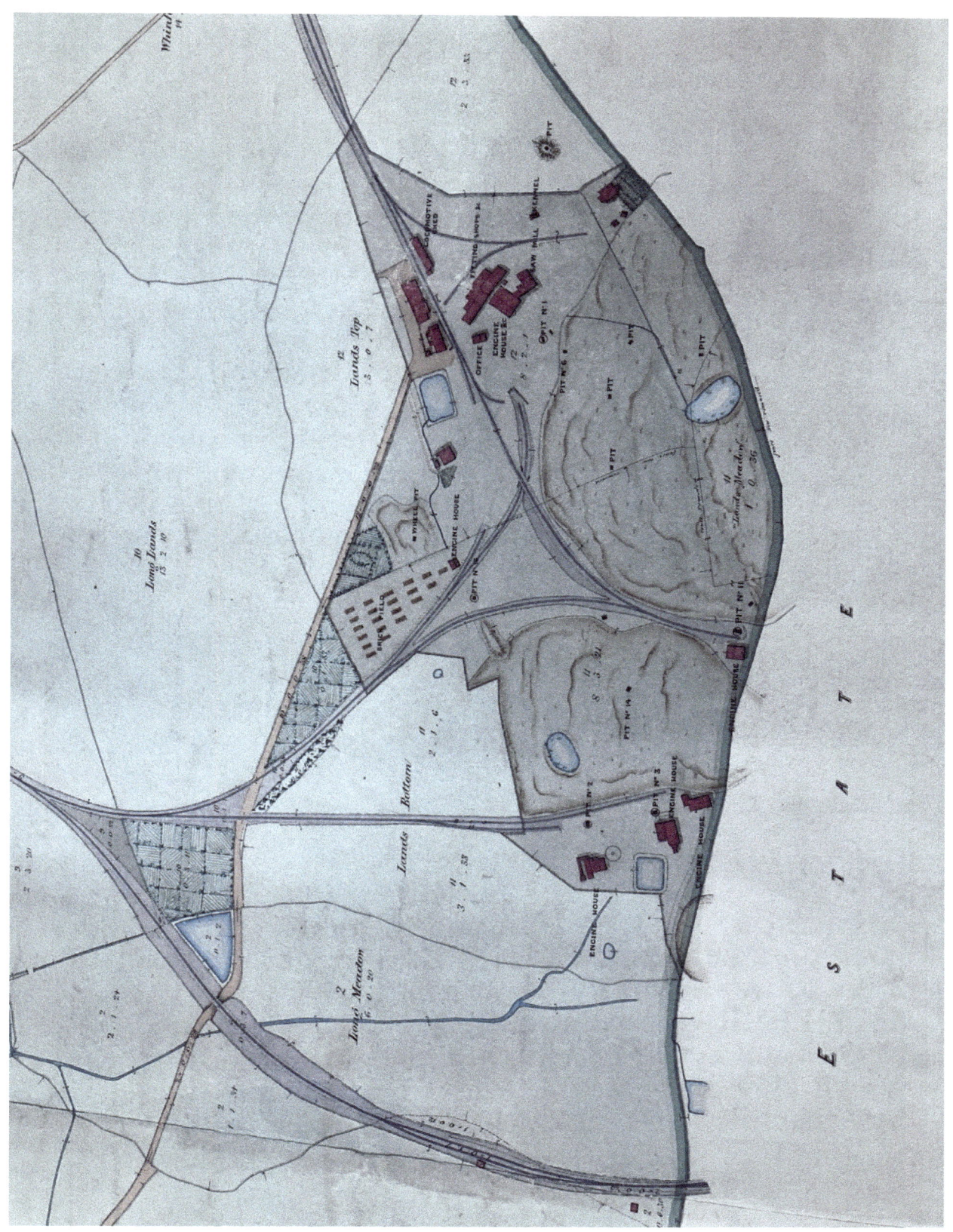

The other Mining section of the Estate in 1877 bordering Park Mine. (Cumbria Archive Centre, Barrow. Z2928)

Barrow Herald, 2nd July 1881.

PILFERINGS AT ROANHEAD MINES.—On Tuesday evening, or early the following morning, the changing house at Paddy Pit, Roanhead, was broken into and a quantity of men's wearing apparel stolen, amounting to over £5 worth. The Askam police have the case in hand and are investigating the matter.

ACCIDENT AT ROANHEAD MINES.—On Saturday last a somewhat serious accident happened to a labourer named Adam Jones, of Askam, at the above mines. It appears he was engaged constructing a new mine floor when a "shudder" of clay fell upon him and broke his leg. He was conveyed to his home, and we have since heard that he is improving rapidly.

Barrow Herald, 3rd September 1881.

STRANGE ACCIDENT TO A MINER.—On Tuesday last, a miner named Edward Barrow, of Steel-street, Askam, was seriously burnt about the face at Woodhead Pit, Ronhead Mines. He was about to ignite a fuse, when a spark of fire dropped into his powder can, which blew up instantaneously into his face, scorching him fearfully and almost blinding him.

Barrow Herald, 26th August 1882.

ACCIDENT AT ASKAM.—On Thursday last a sad accident befel a miner named Edward Cox, of Askam. It appears that he was walking along the railway towards Ronhead Mines (where he is employed) when he was struck by a locomotive belonging to the Askam Iron Company. He fell with one leg across the metals and the train passed over him, cutting the limb completely off. Every effort was made by the engine driver to attract the attention of the poor unfortunate man, but his efforts being unnoticed the sad calamity could not possibly be averted.

Barrow Herald, 31st January 1891

FATAL ACCIDENT AT ROANHEAD MINES.

Whilst Wm. Woodburn, residing in Dale-street, Askam, was engaged with others putting in what is called a "pillar of wood" in S 5 pit, at the above mines, a piece of ore fell and caught Woodburn somewhere about the small of the back. He was extricated as early as possible, but the poor fellow died before he was brought to the surface. Much sympathy is felt for the widow and family. The deceased was a prominent member of the Wesleyan body, by whom he was highly esteemed, and by them and his family will be much missed.

Soulby's Ulverston Advertiser, 15th October 1903.

SERIOUS MINE SUBSIDENCES.—Within the past few days very serious subsidences have taken place at the Roanhead Iron Mines belonging to Messrs. Kennedy Bros. The first indications of something wrong were noticed on Friday, when the watchman on duty at the Woodhead Pit felt the ground shake several times. Towards evening a large piece of land 100 yards long and nearly the same in width suddenly gave way with a tremendous noise, carrying with it thousands of tons of rock and clay into the workings of the mine. Fortunately there were no men in the pit at the time. Portions of rock continued to fall all Saturday and Sunday, making a loud noise. On Sunday there was a further serious subsidence. The whole place has been fenced off. The disaster is attributed to the heavy rains.

This created the Pond we know today as the Woodend Pond, Blacks Pond subsided in 1873.

Nigel Pit 1938. (Courtesy of Walter Jinks)

Workers with a "Windy Pick," Nigel Pit 1938. (Courtesy of Walter Jinks)

Nigel Pit 1938. (Courtesy of Walter Jinks)

Rita Pit, with a stockpile of pit props. Charlie Severs stood for the photo. (Walter Jinks Collection)

Roanhead Miners. The fella with the pipe and Dynamite fuse around his neck in the middle row is Sammy Smith, my great, great, grandad. (Photograph courtesy of Daniel Edwards)

Roanhead Miners. (Courtesy of Daniel Edwards)

The News, 26th December 1969.

Here is an account my great grandad wrote.

ROANHEAD MINES: A WORKER LOOKS BACK 35 YEARS

The last metal heaps to be loaded up at Roanhead Iron Ore Mines reached from Nigel Pit to Billy Pit and were loaded up by conveyors and shovels somewhere around 1934 to 1935. I can't just remember exactly.

There were three men and a metal picker in each gang, and I was one of them. The metal picker was a young lad just left school. His job was to pick the lumps of ore off the conveyor belt as it was being loaded up, which were called grains, the best ore, pencil and kidney ore. This was loaded up separately and went away to special firms.

I can name a lot of men engaged on this job of work; T. Regan, J. Thompson, A. Cowin, T. Windle, W. Smith, D. Moore, D. Wilkinson, A. Kiplin, J. Longmire. Two of the above have recently, J. Thompson and A. Kiplin.

It's hard to believe we were on piece-work and the loading price was 4d. per ton. Eight-hour shift – 20 minutes mealtime. We used to average three 20-ton wagons a day – 6s. 8d. per man.

If you were on a conveyor, you could make more and easier, but if you were on the bogies it was hard work.

We also used to empty the Irish larch for pit props which came in wagon loads from the docks. We received 9d. per ton loading and stocking Coal for the engine house 3d. per ton.

If you could average £3 10s. to £4 per week you thought, you were well off.

Dick Windle and W. Gaiskell used to collar the pit props ready for the miners down the pit.

The engine and pump house at Burlington Pit was a marvellous building. A credit to the men who built it. You don't see buildings put up like that today.

It was a picture to look at inside. Everything was spotless and clean and the large pitch pine beams 20 yards in length and one foot square went down the shaft connecting engine and pump at the bottom of the shaft, quite a few in all I can't remember the depth the same.

And if a beam broke it was a calamity. You soon knew if anything like this happened. The buzzer would blow and if you looked round you would see the pump doctors away as they were called.

W. Coward, D. Myers and W. Hathway (he was the top hand) used to ring the bell for his mates while working in the shaft.

They used to go round and inspect the shafts every day and their hideaway was at Kathleen Pit.

When anything did break down they had to start dipping to keep the water down. Cages were taken off and dips put on as they were called, and they would lift the water up the winding engine.

The beams I mention were stored at the timber pond, Barrow docks.

When you look at the water now in Burlington water hole and Goldmire you can realise what it must of cost Kennedy Bros. to keep the water down to work these pits. It has all come since the pits closed down. That field at Goldmire they used to play football on.

A team from Dalton had it.

Burlington pump house finished when they put the new electric pump house up on Park. Three of the last drivers would be I think D. Woods, W. Heavyside also S. Uren and D. Chorley.

In those days there was a small donkey engine and pump at Roanhead end which kept the water down in Burlington hole. It used to be alive with rabbits and blackberry bushes. Goldmire also had an engine working there which drove a water wheel and it used to lift the water out into the beck which used to flow from Burlington down past Furness Abbey and Roose which is called the Red Waters – no wonder it got that name.

Violet Pit was also pumping 24 hours a day and Rita and Kathleen were also on standby for emergencies.

The engine and pump house (Burlington Pit) was eventually blown down by the soldiers training at Dalton at the beginning of the war and I can remember it took them almost a week to get down to ground level.

So you can well imagine what a fine building it was. Built with large granite blocks.

I have lived besides Burlington water hole 36 years and over the years watched it fill up and when you tell people it is about 200ft. deep in winter they don't believe you.

It has dropped about 12ft. this summer – being a dry summer. But after all the rain lately it is rising again-

T. D. MOORE, ex- Metal Miller, Park North Crossing, near Dalton-in-Furness.

(Courtesy of Dorothy Alexander)

TELEPHONE No. 26.

KENNEDY BROTHERS, LIMITED,
Roanhead & Askam Hematite Mines.

OFFICES: COUNTY SQUARE.

ALL COMMUNICATIONS TO BE ADDRESSED TO THE FIRM

ULVERSTON.

24th Decr 1941.

Dear Wells,

      You will, no doubt have heard that the Mines are closing. I enclose a cheque for £50 as an appreciation of services rendered, and I earnestly hope that with its aid you will be able to take such steps that will help you to regain normal health.

      I enclose a form for Buxton Hospital in case you desire to make use of it.

      Wishing you the very best, under the circumstances for Xmas and New Year.

      Yours faithfully

      Hugh Kennedy

Park North Cottage
Dalton in Furness

My great, great grandpa Jack Wells's letter informing him of the mines closing and to seek help for his hands as he had bad arthritis. He was the wash plant foreman and had served under Kennedy in the first world war as a sergeant.

(Kevin Alexander Collection)

SCHOOL

Soulby's Ulverston Advertiser, 31st July 1873.

OPENING OF NEW SCHOOLS AT ASKAM.

Yesterday there were opened by the Bishop of the Diocese New Schools at Askam. The schools, which are situate near the railway station, are built of brick and pointed with cement, well lighted, fitted up with modern educational appliances, have a very cheerful appearance are estimated to hold upwards of 500 scholars and, we believe, so built that should an enlargement be required it can easily be made. The plans were, we understand, made at the offices of the Furness Iron and Steel Co., and the contractors were Messrs. Mandell, of Askam.

The ceremony commenced with service at Ireleth Church, the prayers being read by the Rev. J. Padley, the incumbent, the first lesson by the Rev. J. M. Morgan, vicar of Dalton, and the second by the Ven. Archdeacon Cooper, of Kendal. The sermon was preached by the Bishop, who took as his text Ephesians vi., 1-4, and after some admirable remarks on the relative duties of children and parents, and tracing the progress of teaching from the earliest periods when parents taught their own children, to more civilized times when the duty was delegated first to the clergymen and then to the schoolmaster and schoolmistress, remarked there was some danger in these latter days of the parental and filial relationship degenerating. He then alluded to the recent agitation in reference to education, the distinction between secular and religious, and urged the necessity of acting from principle, even at the expense of present advantages which might be anticipated from a contrary course. He advocated the union of secular and religious education, and laid great stress upon the benefits which would result from bringing up children in the nurture and admonition of the Lord and a knowledge of the truths of Christianity, quoting in conclusion the text that the fear of the Lord is the beginning of wisdom.

A procession was afterwards formed which, headed by the Park Mines Band, proceeded to the new school, where the chair was taken by the Rev. J. Padley, who in his prefatory remarks noticed that owing to the rapid development, mainly owing to the establishment of iron works, &c., the population of the place had risen from about 400 in 1865 to about 3,000 now, including the adjoining villages of Ireleth and Askam: this increase required additional school accommodation, and had attracted the attention of the speaker, but it was not until Mr. Crossley, the present manager of the Furness Iron Company, also exerted himself in the matter assisted also by Mr. Wadham that any successful movement was taken. The schools would cost about £2,500, and, had being aided largely by the Furness Iron Company, also by the Dukes of Devonshire and Buccleuch, the Barrow Hematite Company, Captain Sandys, and from other sources, and if the schools answered their proposed beneficial ends, he was sure none of the donors would regret in having rendered assistance.

The Lord Bishop after briefly adverting to the remarks he had previously made in the course of his sermon, said from considerable experience extending over a long period he was tolerably familiar with the subject of education. He observed that he had no fear of over-education amongst those who had to earn their livelihood by the labour of their hands or the sweat of their brow, many of whom had to leave school at the time when the serious education of others might be said to be only beginning. He was not favorable to making a hard and fast line between secular and religious education. He was glad to see the part taken in the matter by the clergyman of the parish and that course, though it might be difficult in large towns, he thought it might be adopted in 99 out of every 100 parishes in his diocese. Though Mr. Padley might consider he had done much when he got those handsome schools built, he would find that the easiest part of the work had only been done, and he hoped all the people in the parish would render every assistance they could to the teachers. The work of education was very much like that at the iron works: they had to take the raw material and fit it according to quality for the various uses to which it could be best applied; and so it was with the children who had to be educated according to their different capabilities—some inferior, some better, and some qualified to become, as Bessemer steel, pre-eminent. He he then formally declared the schools opened and congratulated them on the successful result achieved and trusted that God's blessing might rest upon it. Before concluding, he noticed that there were two defects connected with the church in which he had preached—first that it was a long way off a large portion of the inhabitants, and, secondly, that it was not big enough. He hoped the same energy would be exerted to erect a church at Askam as had been displayed in relation to the schools and he would have great pleasure in opening it.

The Rev. J. Padley stated that half of the compliments he had received were due to Mr. Crossley, without whose exertions the schools never could have been built.

The Hon. F. Stanley, M.P., next addressed the meeting, and said he was desirous of seeing education extended as widely as possible. All education should rest upon a good foundation. In nine cases out of ten a man had a great advantage in early learning his trade, so in education he would derive similar benefits in his after life from the advantages of education, but there was such a thing as getting a mere smattering of knowledge, instead of thoroughly and efficiently, and that would be of comparatively little avail. He heartily congratulated all interested in the schools that their exertions had been so successful.

John Fell, Esq., Flan How, was next called upon, and thought those at Askam had done well to look a-head and make provision for the future educational requirements of the district. He was in favour of combining religious and secular education, and hoped that the difficulties in the way of doing so would be overcome. He did not see why the Protestant denominations of England should not agree upon some satisfactory course, and agreed with his lordship that it was possible by the removal of children at an early age to affect parental duties but hoped it would not be so. He also offered his congratulations and said if further extension was required he had no doubt but shoulders would be put to the wheel and that a development would be made to the extent required.

The Ven. Archdeacon Cooper said he was connected with the Kendal School Board, and was glad the duties of that board mainly consisted in getting children to attend the schools, where he was glad to say sound religious principles were taught. He thought there was a danger of missing the real object of national education, which he conceived was not so much to make the masses seek to rise above labour—for the masses must labour—as to seek to make them contented, and by enlarging, expanding, and cultivating their higher and nobler faculties, provide sources of enjoyment apart from pecuniary considerations. He was glad to see attention had been paid to æsthetics in those schools.

The Bishop again rose, and said that he had alluded to the clergyman of a parish taking a part in the educational movements of it, if possible, but he could not be successful unless supported by one or two of the leading people, who would also earnestly put their shoulders to the wheel. Now in relation to that school one name had been mentioned several times—it had been said over and over again that those schools could never have been built but for the kind co-operation, hard work, and sympathy of Mr. Crossley—(cheers); and it was not one of the smallest pleasures he had had that day in meeting with him, and to whom he subsequently proposed a vote of thanks, which was heartily carried.

Mr. Crossley, in returning thanks, said he was somewhat selfish in what he had done, because he was of opinion that attention to the education of the workmen and others would indirectly benefit the Company; but that Mr. Padley's exertions were unselfish. He himself was in favour of a School Board, though he deemed it advisable not to wait till one was established there, but to take more prompt action. He thought education ennobled men's work to them, and made them more satisfied with it, and noticed that in the recent evidence on the coal question there was a remark to the effect that by education men were enabled to do the same amount of work with less manual labour, thus benefitting the people without impoverishing the country, or making the results less. He considered education would be the means of enabling them to get better men, and of giving many a child an opening towards making his way in the world.

Edward Wadham, Esq. then proposed a vote of thanks to the Chairman, and was of opinion that the basis of all sound education was religion; and that such an 'education' would do far more than penal laws to diminish drunkenness and other evils.

The vote of thanks to the Chairman having been carried amidst great applause, he returned thanks, and subsequently, along with the Bishop and a number of others, proceeded to the works of the Furness Iron Co., where luncheon was provided. The school children were, at the conclusion of the meeting, treated to tea, &c., at the schools, where a public tea-meeting was held afterwards.

This was Askam's first school, and was situated on the corner of Duke Street and School Street - later it became the Askam Senior School when the Askam Victoria Board School was built on Lots Road and now half of it survives as a community centre.

Barrow Herald, 20th March 1888.

The ordinary monthly meeting of the Board was held on Monday afternoon. There were present the Rev J. M. Morgan in the chair. Messrs R. Blake, G. Nelson, Lloyd Evans, and the Rev. J. G. Anderson.

The attendance returns for the month ending March 16th, were presented as follows:—

	Present last school year.	av'ge 3 months.	present on day of return	no. on books
Senior Boys	210	228	235	297
„ Girls	182	189	163	271
Mixed	511	215	172	273
Infants	250	281	196	443
Newton	74	69	59	100

The Askam New School was opened that day, the accommodation being for 238 children. A telegram was received from the head master, Mr. Wilson, stating that the number present was 119 boys, 62 girls, and 56 infants, thus showing that the school was already full. Mr. Wilson was also desirous of having extra help, as his staff was not sufficiently large for the number in the school.

Mr. Blake said Mr. Wilson had sent word to him, as living the most convenient, asking for extra help. He (Mr. Blake) had seen Mr. Gundry, who informed him that he could spare a teacher out of his school. They straighway sent one over to Askam to help Mr. Wilson. He would move that Bateman be transferred from the Nelson-street School to that at Askam.

The Chairman said they must consider the fact that Bateman had resigned. He also stated that they had 1,008 children in their schools and had a staff for 1940, and thought that the staff ought to be lowered. It was clear that Askam School was insufficiently staffed, and he thought they should appoint a certificated teacher. In fact, they would require both a male and female certificated teacher.

Mr. Anderson said he pointed out at the time the Askam School was being staffed that they would require a certificated teacher, but they would not support his argument. They would have to appoint a certificated teacher for the girls, that was certain.

Mr. Blake: Have we no transfers?

Mr. Anderson: No certificated teachers!

Mr. Nelson asked had they none that could fill the positions as well.

It was stated that the attendance at the Dalton Schools had been much affected by the severe weather and the prevalence of measles in the town.

The Finance Committee reported the expenditure for the month to have been £872 9s. 6d., receipts £81 16s. 8d.

CORRESPONDENCE.

A letter was read from Mr. John Tyson, clerk to the Local Board, desiring that instruction be given to the teachers to take precaution by means of enquiry against the spreading of measles in the town, and to keep the children at home where measles are prevalent.

The Clerk intimated that this matter had already been attended to.

USE OF ASKAM SCHOOL.

A letter was read from Mr. J. Coulton, the secretary of I.O.G.T. Lodge No. 2,564, asking for the use of one of the class rooms in which to hold their meetings, every Tuesday evening, from six to nine o'clock.

Mr. Lloyd-Evans: I suppose we must stick to the usual rules that the figure be 10s.?

The Chairman said it was for a good object, it was partly for public benefit.

Mr. Anderson said it would have to be a rental of so much a year or so much a quarter, and not weekly.

The Chairman thought they had better give it their consideration.

SHORTHAND CLASS.

A letter from the promoters of the shorthand class at Askam, which was read at last Board meeting was again held over.

A letter received from Miss E. Rain, thanking the Board for her appointment to the Newton School together with an increase of salary.

This was the opening of the Lots Road School for the juniors and infants the original school on Duke Street became home to the seniors.

Askam Victoria School also known as the Board School, Lots Road. (Barrow & Low Furness, Past & Present by John Garbutt)

Never absent children 1900-1901. (Courtesy of George Henry)

First Prize Choir 1915. (Courtesy of George Henry)

Prize Choir 1907. (Courtesy of Askam Village School)

PUNISHMENT BOOK

Year 1900-3

Date: Month & Day	Name of Scholar	Std. or Class	Nature of Offence	Punishment	Signature (or Initials) of Teacher who administered the Punishment
Nov. 7	Will'm Milligan; Jas. & Rd. Crossman	III & I	Abusing Rd. Tippett	5, 3 & 1 respectively on hands	W. E. Brown
" 26	Jas. Ruthers; Joe Lowe	II. II	" Rd. James	3 + 2 " "	W.B.
Dec. 4	Evan Lewis	VI.	Truanting & Falsehoods	Across bench	W.B.
Jan. 30th 1901	Jno. W. Carter	I.	Falsehoods	2 on hands	W.B.
Sept. May 1	Robt. Quail	I.	Truanting & Falsehoods	Across bench	W.B.
Aug. 27th	Jno. W. Needham; Ernest Tippett	I	Truanting	2 on hands	W.B.
Oct. 7	Albert Speight	II	Annoyance to another class at drill	3 " "	W.B.
" 9 1902	Stephen Cottier; Arthur Chapman	III	Insulting N.S. Teacher	3 " "	W.B.
Jan'y 27	Christopher Coulter	I.	Truanting	4 Hands & Bench	W.B.
" 29	Bowfield Albert	Inf.	"	2 " 2 "	W.B.
July 16	Mailes Chas	"	"	3 " 3 "	W.B.
Sep. 1	Needham Joseph	IV	Inattention & insubordination	2 " 3 "	W.B.
Nov. 20	Trenwith Mildred	III	Taking ribbon off hat	3 on hands	W.B.

(Cumbria Archive Centre, Barrow. BDS 17/28)

(Courtesy Askam Village School)

ASKAM BAND

The earliest mentions of bands in the area are that of the Park Mines Band and the Askam Ironworks Temperance Band both in 1873. The Askam Ironworks Band lasted until 1889, the year of the ironworks strike and lock out. It would seem that the workers/band members decided to reform and drop any connection to the ironworks forming the Askam Town Silver Band.

The following is a history of the band by Andrew J. Cain.

The Askam Town Silver Band was formed in 1889 when the Conductor was George Andrew Cain. He was only 17 years of age but capable of taking over from scratch. In those days times were bad and anyone who wanted to join had to buy their own instruments – one can imagine the struggle they had to keep going. Anyway they kept going until 1906-08 when the committee decided to invest in some new instruments. A 'Monster Bazaar' was arranged and a princely sum of £100 (a lot of money in those days) was raised and the new instruments were bought.

Although the Band was largely looked upon as a Town Organisation, it was, and is to this day, a private organisation maintained by members subscriptions and voluntary workers in and on the Band Committee.

From the purchase of new instruments in 1907 the Band decided it was time a uniform was introduced so that they could go out and play at functions around the district. This was achieved in 1911 when they purchased their 'first ever' uniform.

During 1907-11 the bandmaster – George Cain – emigrated to Canada, in 1909 to be correct. Times were hard and work was scarce and a few members were lost through immigration but the Band still carried on and Stanley Cain (George's brother) took over as bandmaster at the age of 19 yrs. At that time Mr. Thomas Satterthwaite was secretary and Mr. J. Woodrow treasurer. The Band seemed to be organising most of the events in Askam and children's sports were held annually. The biggest effort as yet was in 1913 when the Band organised the 1st Hospital Parade. The 1st Askam Rose Queen was Miss Doris Brocklebank (1913) followed by Alice Bloyd (1914) Edna Ward (1915). All proceeds were equally divided between the two local hospitals at that time.

The people of Askam supported the Band up to the hilt and made all the efforts a huge success. The Band struggled on during the First World War and raised £400 which was distributed to the Red Cross and comrades in the Forces.

After the war in 1918 work was in short supply and some of the members had to leave Askam to find work elsewhere but in 1925 the Band started contesting. Tuition was by the renowned conductor, Mr. W. Halliwell, who conducted five or six Bands at Belle Vue

Contest, including Foden's Motor Works etc. Askam Band came 5th out of nine at Maryport but at Bentham they redeemed themselves by taking 2nd place in Selection and March, out of 12 Bands highly rated too. Mr. Halliwell promised to send us a top Cornet player to Bentham and everyone was delighted when Mr. Harry Mortimor of Foden's turned up; He was at his best and only in his twenties.

The greatest project of the Band commenced in 1925 when it was decided to build a Band Hall. The barrier was money but our President and Vice President at the time were Mr. Myles Kennedy and Capt. J. Challinor, who were guarantors at the Bank and were able to arrange finance to carry out the building of the hall, but without voluntary financial help and willing helpers from the village this goal would never of been achieved. Prominent members who supervised the work were Mr. R. Gibson (Builder), Mr. R. Thexton (Joiner), although with other tradesmen who laid the floor – Messers. H. Langhorn, George Woods, Myles Satterthwaite, John Mason – and of course various other tradesmen.

Mr. F. Webster was secretary at the time and all credit must go to him for his untiring work during the building of the Hall. The new Hall was opened on the 29th January 1927 by Capt. and Mrs. J. M. Challinor. The Band then carried on playing at concerts, fetes, sports parades etc., in the late Twenties and into the Thirties.

In 1932 Harry Mortimor (Cornet) and Alec Mortimor (Euphonium) visited Askam to keep a promise they made to Mr. S. C. Cain – they played at concert on Sunday before a packed audience and the only cost to the Band was for petrol for their car with Mr. & Mrs S. C. Cain providing them with accommodation for the weekend. The Mortimor brothers were so delighted with the reception they received that the full Foden Works Band came and gave a concert in Askam Band Hall before going to Scotland to play Glasgow Park for a week. Incidentally, Harry Mortimor played "Alpine Echoes" and "Somewhere a Voice is calling" for an encore. Second half he played "Rule Britannia" and "Love's Old Song". Alec Mortimor played "Lucy Long" and "The Trumpeter", also "Robin Aair" and "Mary of Argyle" to the delight of the audience.

During this time the Band were still working hard to pay off the debt for the new Hall, there were packed dances every Saturday night and the dance of the year, the New Years Ball.

3rd September 1939 – tragedy struck everyone when World War II was declared. The Band Hall was taken over by the Army and the Band was disbanded until 1944. However with the second front on its way and victory in sight the Government relinquished the Band Hall but the only grant received was £46. The President of the Band at the time, Sir Robert Rankin (Conservative member for Liverpool) fought hard for a better grant but to no avail, so the position regarding finance was back to square one.

After the war the Band began to form again and 14 players were raised.

Mr. A. J. Cain took over as Conductor for nearly two years and in 1946 Mr. S. C. Cain resumed as Conductor when he built the Band back up again for contesting once more, introducing a few good players from Dalton, including Mr. G.H. Jackson, the brothers Jones, Robert, Tom and Bill.

To this day Askam Band are going strong and remain a strong presence at local events.

Ulverston Advertiser, 22nd November 1873.

> The Askam Ironworks Temperance Band, under the direction of their able leader, Mr. B. Evans, played a fine selection of music, in a style which speaks volumes for the progress made by this band, which has been in existence less than three months. The four Miss Parkinson's sang "Do the Best"; Mr. Ed. Prescott sang "The Bottle and Glass"; Mr. J. Walker recited "The Poor Drunkard's Child"; and Miss Jackson and Miss Parkinson gave a dialogue in an effective manner.

The Band at the National Schools, Duke Street. (Courtesy of Askam History Club)

Askam Town Silver Brass Band 1911, Showing their first uniform at the Vicarage, Ireleth. (Courtesy of Askam History Club)

Barrow Herald, 10th August 1912.

ASKAM TOWN BAND

FIELD DAY AND SPORTS

The committee of the Askam Town Brass Band entered upon a more ambitious scheme for their annual Children's Field Day and Sport's on Saturday. The venture was amply justified by the success attained. The usual sports programme was preceded by a procession round the town in aid of the Old Folk's Treat Fund.

The pageant was commenced from the National Schools; Duke-Street, and was certainly one of the most attractive and picturesque ever seen in Askam; and seeing that its inauguration was the work of but a few days, the result was distinctly creditable to all concerned. In addition to their own personal efforts, the band, officials and committee, had the able assistance of the Day and Sunday School teachers, and of many willing outside helpers notable amongst whom were the residents of the Lots who instead of holding their own usual annual parade, decided to throw in their lot with the band in this laudable effort to swell the fund which provides annually a treat for the old folk's.

About 200 children in all took part in the procession and in their summer dresses and artistic adornments of artificial flowers, etc., they presented a very pretty spectacle. Following the banner came the Town Band, under the Conductorship of Mr. Stanley Cain, and then followed the splendid turn-out produced by the people living on the Lots, which was the subject of general and well-merited admiration from the crowds which assembled en route.

Conspicuous amongst these units was, of course, the prettily decorated car conveying the King and Queen. Miss Violet Steele made a charming Queen, and Master Fred Newby looked "every inch a King" in the role of "his Majesty." The Queen had two pretty maids of honour in Dora Turford and Everlyn Crossley. The lorry for this pleasing feature was provided by Mr. Jno. O'Connor, and there was a second lorry containing a bright group of children with Mr. T. Mason in the costume of a knight in armour, in charge.

The King and Queen it must be mentioned were accompanied by the local company of the Boy Scouts as a guard of honour.

Another highly interesting feature of the pageant was the Dalton Fire Brigade (under Capt. Comber) and their engine, gleaming in the sunshine and drawn by three horses in the able hands of Mr. T. Wellstead. They were followed by the members of the Askam Fire Brigade, and the rear was brought up by an excellent turn-out of scholars from the local Sunday schools in charge of their respective teachers. The general attractiveness of the procession as a whole was considerably enhanced by a number of youths and young men in comic costume.

A collection was taken on the route and in this the members of the two fire brigades rendered valuable assistance. The arrangements were ably carried out by the band officials and committee and for the excellent display provided, from the Lots the greatest praise is due to the ladies of that district and especially to Mrs. Dickinson, Mrs. Nicholl, Mrs. Foster, Miss Dunn, Miss. Waters, and Miss. Crossley. The procession was broken up in Duddon-Road, after which a capital sports programme commenced on the Askam Football Field, for which a good crowd assembled.

Unfortunately, rain fell shortly after five o'clock, and the events could not be completed. Tea was served on the field to the children who took part in the procession, this having been provided from a fund kindly collected for the purpose by Councillor A. Jackson.

The following were the sports officials: Judges, Messers. Lishman, Bell, and Greetham; starter, Mr. G. Mackereth; bellman, Mr. T. Bell, Kirkby; linesmen, Messers. Sewell and Antliff; clerks, Messers. Spray and Olliver; secretary. Mr. J. Atkinson.

Finals:-

Boys' Sack Race (10 to 13 years), 100 Yards. -1, Wm. Cole; 2, Thos. Robinson; 3, Wm. Hargreaves.

Girls' Flat Race (7 to 9 years), 100 Yards. -1, Ada Robinson; 2, Maggie Burrows; 3, Ellie Park.

Boys' Flat Race (10 to 13 years), 880 Yards. – 1, W. Smith; 2, H. Woodrow; 3, R. Alexander.

Girls' Thread Needle Race (10 to 13 years), 100 Yards. – 1, D. Smith; 2, A. Walker; 3, M. Greaves.

Boys' Sack Race (7 to 9 years), 100 Yards. -1, E. Crawley; 2, T. Webster; 3, Langhorn.

Girls' Flat Race (10 to 13 years), 100 Yards. – 1, H. Marshall; 2, G. Park; 3, S. Lawley.

Boys' Shoe Race (7 to 9 years), 100 Yards. -1, W. Bettany; 2, J. Mossop; 3, E. Chaplin.

Girls' Thread Needle Race (7 to 9 years), 100 Yards. – 1, Mary Robinson; 2, Ada Robinson; 3, Agnes Fallows.

Boys' Flat Race (7 to 9 years), 100 Yards. – 1, Edwin Crawley; 2, Norman Wharton; 3, Norman Bettany.

Barrow Herald, 17th August 1912.

ASKAM TOWN BAND CHILDREN'S GALA.—A GROUP OF PROCESSIONISTS.

PUBS, HOTELS AND OFF-LICENCES

As was the case with many settlements in the 19th century the inhabitants tended to drink beer instead of ordinary water due to the fact that water wasn't always the safest option at that time, and also the settlement needed hotels to house the influx of new workers coming in.

Interestingly it seems that the ironworks along with commissioning houses to be built they also had two hotels and a pub built, these were the Victoria Hotel (named after the Queen at that time) this hotel changed its name soon after opening to the Vulcan Hotel (named after the roman god for metalworking), Temperance Hotel (for those opposed to drinking alcohol) and the Furness Tavern (named after the ironworks company), all built on the Furness Iron Company's land.

Here's a list of Askam establishments;

ASKAM HOTEL, 1 & 3 Victoria Street.

ASKAM TEMPERENCE HOTEL, 64 & 66 Duke Street.

FARMERS ARMS, 34 & 36 Ireleth Road.

FURNESS TAVERN, 140 Duke Street.

GREY HORSE, 27 Duddon Road.

LONDON HOUSE, 90 Duddon Road. (STILL TRADING 2025).

RAILWAY INN / (WHITTLE SPRINGS 1890-1899), 24 Ireleth Road.

VICTORIA VAULTS, John Street. (nick-named the stumps)

VULCAN HOTEL / (VICTORIA HOTEL 1867-1867) 94 Duke Street.

Off-licences;

33 Beach Street.

112 Beach Street.

121 Crossley Street formally 76 & 78 Steel Street.

4 Harris Street.

19 Stafford Street.

75 Duke Street. (STILL TRADING 2025 – ASKAM POST OFFICE).

There could be more that I have missed as anyone could apply and they may of only had a licence for a year, but these were the main off- licences that I have found.

The Vulcan from Beach Street, the present building was remodelled in the 1930s however a portion of the original survives as the hairdressers. (Courtesy of Jeanette Shepherd)

A picture of the London house when James Allanson was the landlord. (Courtesy of Jeanette Shepherd)

Barrow Herald, 24 November 1877.

ASKAM SPORTS.—On Saturday last Mr Jones, of the Askam Hotel, held his annual sports. The 200 yards handicap open to all miners of Askam was won by J. Huartson, to whom was awarded the 1st prize, a leg of mutton; 2nd F. Woodend, a couple of rabbits; 3rd J. Seaward, a pound of tobacco. 200 yards handicap for men working at the Askam Iron and Steel Works. Entrance 1s First prize a piece of beef, B. Hutchinson; second prize, a couple of chickens, F. Ennis; third, a pound of tea, F. Humphreys. 100 yards handicap for boys not over 16 years:—1st prize 5s. J. Brown; 2nd, 3s. R. Walker; 3rd 2s. J. Lewis. There was a consolation stake, but the hour being so late it did not come off.

The Furness Tavern. (Kevin Alexander Collection)

Barrow and Furness District Directory 1887.

VULCAN HOTEL, ASKAM.

EDWIN CLIFFE

(Late of the Ram's Head, Barrow),

Begs to inform his friends and the public that he has taken the above Hotel, which has been thoroughly beautified, and many improvements have also been made for the better accommodation of visitors.

THE VERY BEST QUALITIES OF

IRISH & SCOTCH WHISKIES, BRANDIES, WINES, &c.,

Will always be found in stock at ordinary prices.

BURTON ALES AND GUINNESS'S STOUT

IN BOTTLE AND ON DRAUGHT.

CIGARS OF THE FINEST BRANDS.

AN EXCELLENT BILLIARD TABLE

IN GOOD CONDITION.

LONDON ARMS, ASKAM.

JOHN WILLIE SMITH,

PROPRIETOR.

In announcing that he has taken the above Old Established Inn, Mr. Smith desires to inform his friends and the public that the house has been thoroughly renovated and made much more suitable for a good business.

HE HAS IN STOCK THE VERY FINEST QUALITIES OF

WHISKIES, BRANDIES, WINES, CIGARS, &c.

DUBLIN STOUT AND BURTON MILD

AND

BITTER ALES.

Barrow Herald, 9th June 1891.

A BREWERY CLAIM.—This was an action brought by the Brunswick Brewery Co., of Leeds, against Joseph Simpson, of Askam, for the recovery of £10 10s. 11d. for beer supplied.—Mr. Bradshaw represented the company, and Mr. Poole defendant.—Mr. Woods, a representative of the firm, swore that he received orders from the defendant at the London House, Askam. Defendant had paid nothing for five years, and the company had not sued him before because of the respect they held for the man.—Mr. Poole, for defendant, argued that he was the *factotum* of a Mrs. Smith, who in 1887 sold her goods at Askam, and made a composition to her creditors, of which claimants were one. Defendant had never contracted any debts whatever with the company in his own name.—The defendant Simpson, examined, said he was Mrs. Smith's brother. She formerly lived at the London House, and then went to the Vulcan. He managed the house for her, and never, on any occasion, ordered a barrel of beer on his own account. What orders he gave were given on his sister's instructions. He recollected a traveller calling after his sister had left Askam, and he told him at that time that he had nothing whatever to do with the debt. He left the London House when his sister quitted the Vulcan.—Mr. Poole put in invoices from other breweries in the name of Mrs. Smith, with instructions on those invoices that the beer should be delivered to Simpson.—Mr. Bradshaw said before their firm could be liable in the same respect, invoices must be produced showing identical instructions from them.—Mr. Johnson, traveller for the firm, swore that he called upon defendant for orders, and in respect of the debt in 1886-7 and into 1888. It was afterwards proved, however, that defendant did not occupy the hotel at that time.—His Honour said there were facts against claimants' which he could not get over. They had got a witness to swear in the box that he had called upon defendant at a certain date, and it was proved the man was not there at the time alleged.—Mr. Bradshaw: He is wrong so far as 1888 is concerned.—His Honour said 1887 was also against them, and in addition to that, they had allowed nearly six years to elapse before bringing that action. On those two facts he should give a verdict for the defendant, and he thought if they had summoned the man sooner they would have made him their debtor.—Mr. Bradshaw: Of course we cannot appeal without your honour's leave.—His Honour made no response.

BANKRUPTCY MATTERS.—Mr. Pearson applied for an adjournment in respect of the Dawson, Gradwell, and Patterson bankruptcy matters. He said it appeared no one was instructed on their part to ask for an adjournment, but had written to ask him (Mr. Pearson) to consent, and under the circumstances he would take upon himself to apply for a months' adjournment.—Mr. Taylor said he appeared on behalf of Mr. Dawson. They had held a meeting last Friday and came to terms subject to the approval of the court, and matters would probably be arranged.—The application was granted.

Barrow Herald, 12th November 1895.

Fire at the Vulcan Hotel.—On Saturday afternoon, between three and four o'clock, smoke was seen issuing through the floor of the billiard-room of the Vulcan Hotel, and an alarm was immediately given to Mr. Edwin Goad, the proprietor, who was at the time busy in his office. The smoke was first seen by a man named William Johnson, and Mr. Goad, with a few willing helpers, was soon on the scene. Proceeding to the cellar under the billiard-room, and after knocking some plaster from the ceiling, the fire was discovered smouldering away. As soon as a current of air got to the seat of the fire it livened up, and burned like a furnace. Mr. Goad applied several pailsful of water, but this took little or no effect on the burning mass. He then applied the yard hose pipe, which soon had effect, and it was thought the fire was got under, but on Mr. Goad going to the place between eight and nine o'clock it was seen the fire was kindling up again, but this was soon got under, and after examination of the place it was found no trace of the fire was observable. How long the fire had been burning is a mystery. It seems that between the billiard-room floor and the ceiling of the cellar a large quantity of dust had accumulated, as well as a quantity of cinders. It is thought that some live cinders had fallen behind the fire-place, thus causing the fire. A disagreeable smell was observed some time before the fire was really found out, but it was thought some men had emptied beer on the fire. It was not thought in the least there was any danger of fire. Had the fire broken out during the night time, the consequence would have been serious.

Over twenty years ago I came across an article of the Vulcan blowing up due to a gas leak from a lamp, the windows blew out, and a couple of people got minor injuries. However, I cannot seem to rediscover this unfortunately.

Barrow Herald, 17th November 1900.

ASKAM LANDLORD IN TROUBLE.

At the Ulverston Magistrates' Court on Thursday, William Roots, landlord of the Victoria Vaults, John-street, Askam, was charged with supplying drink to a drunken person on his licensed premises, and Henry Proctor was charged with being drunk on licensed premises.

P.S Carr said P.S Hudson and himself were near the Victoria at 9-15 on Saturday night, November 3rd. Upon hearing a noise inside they entered, and saw Proctor sat in the tap-room in a very drunken condition, and witness drew the landlady's attention to it. At 10-30 the same evening they again heard a disturbance in the vaults, and, going in, saw Proctor with a pint glass containing beer before him. He then ordered Proctor out, and he was taken home by P.C Hudson and a friend. His language was most disgusting all the time. When he was put in the house he came out again and challenged all three to fight; he was put in again. Witness went back to the landlady, and she expressed her regret. Near 12 o'clock the landlord came in a drunken condition to the police station and asked witness to look over it, as his wife was very much upset about it and could not sleep. Witness said it must be reported.

By Mr Poole: Witness said to Mrs Roots in the front room that they were quiet, as there were few in that room. The defendant and Greaves were quarrelling in another room. Roots had summoned two lots for refusing to quit his house. One lot he settled for 50s. and the other £3.

P.C.'s Hudson and King corroborated.

For the defence, Mr Poole contended that the house was difficult to keep on account of the neighbourhood, and the language used there was not of the drawing-room order, and the landlord had done his best to keep the house orderly.

Agnes Roots, the landlady, said Proctor entered the house quite sober between seven and eight o'clock. He had one pint of beer and two pints of cider and beer mixed. When the police ordered him out, he walked out quite straight and was perfectly sober. He and Greaves were not quarrelling, but were having a few high words.

By Supt. Whiteside: Her husband was sober when he came home. He was not a drunken man. She admitted that she had been to the police to complain of his conduct.

George Fallows, a furnaceman, said he was with Proctor all the evening. Witness had three times as much drink as Proctor, who was not drunk. The constables did not assist Proctor, or put him into his house. At 11-30 they went to look at Proctor's nets, walking across the sands to within 300 yards of the Millom Pier, and Proctor carried witness on his back over one channel.

Thomas Mawson, furnaceman, Jas Heather, grocer, John Duncan, furnaceman, the defendants Proctor and Roots, and Amelia Wheeling, servant, gave evidence for the defence, denying the drunkenness.

Roots was fined 20s and costs for permitting drunkenness, the other charge being dismissed, and Proctor was fined 10s and costs for being drunk on licensed premises.

The Railway Inn and Farmers Arms. (Courtesy of Walter Jinks)

Barrow Herald, 19th September 1907.

The 14th annual vegetable, flower and sweet pea show promoted by Mr John Fleet, of the Furness Tavern, took place on Saturday at Askam. Never before has the exhibition attracted such an excellent display, and this despite the unfavourable season. The cut flowers, especially sweet peas and cactus dahlias, were exceedingly fine. The onions, potatoes, cabbage, and cauliflowers were a very good show, and the prize exhibit of celery weighed no less than 12lbs, or an average of 4lbs a stick. Mr Fleet has done much to promote the popularity of allotment gardens in Askam. Great interest was centred in this year's show owing to the fact that Mr John Fleet, jun., presented a magnificent silver medal to the exhibitor securing the greatest number of points. It was a keen race with Mr J. Cartmel, of Kirkby, and Mr J. T. Townson, Ireleth. The former, however, gained the trophy by one point. The figures were 18 to 17. Mr Fleet imposed one condition on the exhibitors, viz., that they had to be holders of cottage gardens. The judge made is awards as follows:—

Best six and heaviest onions, grown from plants supplied by Mr John T. Townson: 1, Tom Martin, Kirkby; 2, Chas. Fleet. Best six and heaviest onions open to all comers: 1, J. T. Townson; 2, J. Cartmel, Kirkby; 3, Ed. Walker, Kirkby. Best eight onions, not to exceed 6lbs: 1 and 2, J. T. Townson; 3, J. Cartmel. Best three and heaviest sticks of celery: 1, J. T. Townson; 2, J. Newton; 3, Geo. Holmes. Best two and heaviest cauliflowers: 1, J. Cartmel; 2, J. T. Townson. Best two and heaviest white cabbages: 1 J. Cartmel; 2, J. T. Townson. Best two and heaviest red cabbage: 1, Ed. Walker; 2, J. Cartmel. Best six kidney potatoes: 1 E. Walker; 2, Chas. Fleet; special 3 (equal), J. Chester, Kirkby and J. Laybourne, Kirkby. Best six potatoes (any variety): 1, John Walker, Askam; 2, J. Cartmel. Best six bunches of sweet peas, not less than six pikes in each: 1, G. Georgetimer; 2, J. Cartmel; 3, Tom Martin. Best six cut flowers, any variety: 1 J. Cartmel; 2, J. T. Townson. Mr J. Cartmel, of Kirkby, also won the silver medal for most points gained in the show which was given by Mr John Fleet, jun. The annual supper takes place on Saturday evening, September 28th.

Soulby's Advertiser, 6th March 1913.

NORTH LONSDALE LICENSES

SEVEN LICENCES REFERRED FOR COMPENSATION.

OBJECTIONS TO BEERHOUSES.

The adjourned Licensing Sessions for the Petty Sessional Division of North Lonsdale were held on Thursday in the magistrates' retiring-room at Ulverston, the court being engaged for the ordinary police business. Mr. W. F. Egerton presided, the other justices present being: Messrs. F. M. Dickson, Jno. Coward, Jno. Hutchinson, J. L. Altham. The court proceeded to consider the objections to seven beerhouses at Askam, Ireleth, Pennington, and Urswick, this being the first of the batch of 20 licences in the division objected to on the ground of redundancy.

The Grey Horse. (Courtesy of Askam History Club)

VICTORIA VAULTS, ASKAM.

Mr. F. W. Poole, who appeared for the owner and tenant, formally applied for a renewal of the licence.

Inspector Hume stated that the Victoria Vaults were situate in John-street, Askam. The registered owners were Messrs. R. and P. Hartley, brewers; tenant, Jane Wilson; poor rate assessment, gross £19 5s.; rateable value, £16 10s.; annual value for the purpose of publican's licence duty, £24. The facilities for police supervision were good. The rent payable per annum was £18. It was a labouring class trade. He considered if the licence were taken away there were ample drinking facilities in the neighbourhood. By Mr. Poole: The nearest licensed house was the Vulcan Hotel, fully licensed, 173 yards away, which catered for a different trade. In reply to the Chairman, he said the population of Askam and Ireleth was about 3,000, and of Askam alone 2,799. Askam had eight licensed houses, an average of one licence to every 350 of the population.

Mr. Poole submitted this was a licence that ought not to be taken. It was situate on the extreme edge of the population. It was on the sands, and the houses round about were served by the licence. If it was considered necessary to reduce the number of licences in Askam he suggested that it would be fairer to deal with one of those in the more congested part. The fact that Mrs. Wilson had been making a good living showed that the house was required.

The Chairman: The Bench will hold over their decision until they have had the other cases.

GREY HORSE, ASKAM.

Inspector Hume stated that this house was situate in Duddon-road, Askam; registered owners, R. and P. Hartley; Elizabeth Wilson, tenant; poor rate assessment, £22 5s.; rateable value, £19; annual value for publican's licence duty, £27; rent payable, £20 per annum; facilities for police supervision not satisfactory, there being three entrances. The nearest licensed house was the London House, 200 yards away. He was of opinion the licence was not required.

Mr. Poole, who represented the owners and tenant, put in a statement of the trade and asked for a renewal of the licence. The house, structurally speaking, was one of the best beerhouses in the district. If the furnaces were restarted this was the part of the district where new houses would be built, and the licence they were now asked to take away would be an absolute necessity for that particular neighbourhood.

FARMERS' ARMS, IRELETH.

Inspector Hume testified that this was an ante-1869 beerhouse; registered owners, R. F. Case and Co.; tenant, Wm. Twyname; poor rate assessment, £20; rateable value, £17; annual value for licence duty £25; facilities for police supervision, good; and state of repair, good. It was a labouring class trade. The nearest house was the Railway Hotel, fully licensed, 40 yards away.

Mr. Poole, for the owners and tenant, applied for the renewal of the licence.

After a private deliberation, the Chairman said: The licences of the Victoria Vaults, Askam, the Grey Horse, Askam, the Travellers' Rest, Hare and Hounds, and Farmers' Arms, Ireleth, will be provisionally renewed; but will be referred to the licensing authority at Lancaster for compensation.

Barrow News, 22ND August 1925.

John Bodley, of Askam, was summoned for assaulting James Allanson, the licensee of the London House Hotel, Askam, on the 8th inst. Mr. F. W. Poole appeared for the complainant, and Mr. C. J. Chapman for the defendant, who pleaded not guilty.

Complainant stated that he had held the licence of the London House for 13 weeks, having come from Burnley. August 8th was Hospital Parade day at Askam, and in the evening the house was crowded with customers. Having occasion to complain of the bad language used by the defendant he went to him and told him that if he did not desist he would be ejected, whereupon defendant struck him a violent blow in the mouth with his fist, driving his false teeth up into his gums. The police were sent for, and with assistance defendant was put out.

By Mr. Chapman: I don't think I have got hold of the wrong man.—By Mr. Poole: I have no doubt whatever that the defendant was the man who struck me.

Robert Hatton, brother-in-law of complainant, corroborated.

Mr. Chapman submitted it was a case of mistaken identity, and called as witnesses Charles Wilson, John Holmes, and the defendant.

The Bench considered the case proved. Defendant was fined 20s and the advocate's fee and witness' expenses were allowed, the total amount being £2 13s.

Beach Street Off-Licence. (Cumbria Archive Centre, Barrow. BLC/P/160.2/VB/BEA 1)

Barrow News, 18th August 1934.

ASKAM LICENSEE FINED.

SUNDAY MORNING DRINKS.

GLASSES UNDER A SEAT.

FORMER PILOT AND THE LAW.

At Ulverston Magistrates' Court on Thursday William H. Mandall, the licensee of the Vulcan Hotel, Askam, was summoned for selling and supplying intoxicating liquor on licensed premises during non-permitted hours to Leonard Wurdle, Walter Woodend, and John Duncan, all of Askam, and the three last named were summoned for consuming. Mandall was also summoned for aiding and abetting the consumption.

Mr. J. Pickavance appeared to prosecute on behalf of the police, and defendants who were represented by Mr. F. W. Poole, each pleaded not guilty.

Mr. Pickavance said the permitted hours in this district commenced at 12.30 p.m. on Sundays, and the offences were said to have been committed on Sunday July 22nd at 11.45 a.m. On that date P.C. Bannister (acting sergeant), and P.C. McMechan were on duty near Duke-street, Askam, when they saw defendant standing at the door of his house. When he saw the officers, who were in plain clothes, he went quickly into the house and they followed.

As they entered a room on the right they saw the licensee remove three pint glasses containing beer from the table where the three other defendants were sitting and place the glasses under a form near the fireplace. P.C. Bannister asked Mandall if he knew what the time was, and he replied: "It is a quarter to twelve."

The police officers then asked how the glasses of beer came to be on the table and Mandall said: "These three men have been doing a bit of work for me washing the floors, and I gave them a drink each," the other men confirming this statement.

If these men had washed the floors for the licensee, Mr. Pickavance said, it would still be within his submission that there was a sale, because instead of paying the men for the services rendered if the licensee liked to give them beer in lieu thereof, the liquor was in exchange, and was, in effect, a sale.

Evidence was given by P.C. Bannister and P.C. McMechan, and the witnesses were cross-examined at length by Mr. F. W. Poole.

Mr. Poole, addressing the bench, said the case was a very simple one. The licensee had served through the war as a pilot with very great honour, and had taken over the licence of the Vulcan Hotel some two and a half years ago. It was quite reasonable to say that he could not be well conversant with the licensing laws. Two of the men had been in the habit for some time of going down to the hotel on Sunday morning to give a helping hand. Woodend, who was a plumber, was asked to come in to work at a beer pump which had gone wrong. Mr. Mandall had no idea he was doing anything wrong in giving the men a pint of beer each. It was only on the spur of the moment that he took the glasses and put them under the seat, and if he had not done that foolish act but had relied on his own behalf that he was not doing anything wrong, there would have been no difficulty at all in asking the bench to believe he was perfectly right and justified in serving the drinks. It might be a technical offence, but he simply gave them a pint of beer each because they had helped him.

The defendants gave evidence on their own behalf, but the bench found the cases against the licensee of supplying intoxicating liquor proved, and imposed a fine of £1 in each case, plus costs and advocate's fees, and the charges of aiding and abetting the consumption were dismissed on payment of costs, making a total of £6 1s. 6d., the other charges being dismissed.

On Mr. Poole's application, the bench granted a certificate that the conviction would not affect the licence.

The other defendants, Windle, Woodend, and Duncan were each fined £1, but asked for time in which to pay, but Mandall said, "I will pay for these gentlemen, as I am responsible."

DIRECTORIES

POST OFFICE DIRECTORY

Lancashire

1873

ASKAM.

Crossley William, Greenscoe House

Harrison James, Victoria Street

Postlethwaite James, Alexandra Place

Askam Bonded Stores Co. Limited, grocers (John Quarmby, manager)

Askam Brick Co. (R. Pearson)

Atkinson Thomas Henry, shopkeeper

Bell Richard, draper

Brocklebank Joseph, *Askam inn*

Chapman Arthur Atkinson, draper

Cook William, shopkeeper

Davis William Henry, shopkeeper

Fuller Charles, shopkeeper

Furness Iron & Steel Co. Limited, manufacturers of iron & steel (Bessemer), & iron ore proprietors & merchants (William Crossley, managing director; James Postlethwaite, cashier; James Harrison, engineer).

Hinds Henry, shopkeeper

Hinds Joseph, farmer

Huston James, boot & shoe maker

Huston Robert, boot & shoe maker

Jones Adam, shopkeeper &c

Kennedy Bros. iron ore proprietors & farmers. Ronhead mines; offices; Ulverston

Kennedy Miles, farmer, Ronhead farm

Kendall David, *Vulcan hotel*

Lamb John, boot & shoe maker

Lyne Richard, shopkeeper

Mandall Nicholas, tin plate worker &c

Mandall William, shopkeeper & builder

Mason Robert, draper

Parry Robert, shopkeeper

Roberts Ishmael, beer retailer

Smith Hezekiah Cook, shopkeeper

Smith John, beer retailer

Askam Bonded Store. (Courtesy of Brenda Jefferson)

Stephenson George, coal dealer

Warwick Robert, joiner

Woodburne Thomas, farmer, Sandscale

IRELETH.

Padley Rev. James Sandby, M. A

Sharpe Joseph, Bankfield house

Walton Mrs

Atkinson John, beer retailer

Benson Thomas, beer retailer

Brocklebank Jas. Blacksmith & at Lindal

Chapman James Bainbridge, yeoman

Chapman John, yeoman

Chapman Richard, yeoman

Clark Thomas, farmer, Holmes green

Edmondson Thomas, farmer

Hodgson William, farmer, Old Park

Holme Betty (Mrs.), *Railway inn*

Huddleston John, farmer

Johnson William, farmer

Kirkby Ann (Mrs.), miller & shopkeeper

Longhorn Jackson, Farmer, Old Park

Lowther Andrew, farmer

Martin Agnes (Mrs.), shopkeeper

Mason Robert, farmer, Marsh grange

Mason Samuel, yeoman

Mellon Henry, mining engineer

Mitchell William, shopkeeper

Newby Nicholas, yeoman

Parker Robert, tailor

Pearson Robert, yeoman

Riley Thomas, shopkeeper

Sharpe Joseph, yeoman

Silver Thomas, beer retailer, Holmes green

Spencer Peter, inspector of reservoirs for Barrow Corporation

Turner Robert, *Bay Horse*

History and Directory of Barrow-in-Furness, and the whole of North Lonsdale.

Mannex & Co 1876.

ASKAM DIRECTORY.

Post Office at William Cook's, Sandy road

ANDERSON William, M.R.C.S., surgeon, King's row

Askam Bonded Stores Co., grocers and provision dealers, Sandy road;

Robert Weston, manager

Askam & Ronhead, iron mines, Kennedy Bros., proprietors; Henry Kendall, manager

Atkinson William, shopkeeper, Beach street

BAINES Richard, vict., Askam Hotel; Robert Baines, manager

Barrow Francis Clark, chemist and druggist, Sharp street and Barrow

Barrow Iron and Steel Co., mine proprietors, Park Mines; Richard Hoskin, manager

Bell Richard, draper and hosier, Askam House, Sandy road

Brockbank Mr. Joseph, Sea View House

Bryning Alice, schoolmistress (National), Duddon road

COOK William, Post-master and mining agent, Sandy road

Crossley William, manager of iron works, Green Scow House

DALTON Co-operative Stores, (Branch), grocers and provision dealers, Duddon road; William R. Kellet, manager

Dixon Jonathan, ironmonger, Sandy road

FALLOWFIELD Samual, joiner, Huddleston row

Fleming William, station-master

Foot James, assistant schoolmaster (National), Duddon road

Forsyth Thomas, beerhouse, Beach street

Fry Thomas, shopkeeper, Sharp street

Fuller Charles, shopkeeper, King's row

Furnell William, Horse keeper, Iron Works Cottages

GARDNER Jonathan, store keeper, Park Cottages

HALL Hannah, schoolmistress (National) infants, Duddon road

Harrison James, engineer, Dutton terrace

Hawkins William, shopkeeper, Sharp street

Hewett Peter, boot and shoemaker, Stafford street

Heywood Bernard, engineer's assistant, Alexandra place

Hinds Joseph, farmer, Green Scow

Hinds Mary A., shopkeeper, Harris street

Holmes George, beerhouse, Steel street

Huston Robert, boot and shoemaker, Sharp street

JACKSON Alfred, porter, Alexandra place

Jenkins John, schoolmaster (National), Sandy road

Jones Adam, grocer and coal dealer, Beech street

KELLET William R., manager of co-operative stores, Duddon street

Kennedy Bros., mine proprietors, Ronhead; h. *Ulverston*

Kennedy Henry, (Kennedy Bros.), managing partner

Kitchen John Newby, beerhouse, Duddon road

Knowles John, butcher, Sharp street

LAMB Edward, draper and hosier, Sharp street

Lamb John, boot and shoemaker, stationer, tobacconist, and coal dealer, Sandy road

MACDONALD Hugh, furnace manager, King's row

Mc.Calpin Edward, confectioner and Temperance Hotel, Sandy road

Mandall & Hesketh, joiners and horticultural builders and hot water engineers, Newcombe street

Mandall & Simpson, bricklayers and builders, Duddon road

Mandall Nicholas, (Mandall &Simpson); h. Ireleth

Mandall William (Mandall & Hesketh); h. Sandy road

Mason Robert, draper and farmer, Sandy road

Mattews John, constable of police, Station, King's row

NATIONAL Schools, Sandy road; John Jenkins (Boys); Alice Bryning (Girls); Hannah Hall (Infants)

Naylor Robert R., Duddon View

Nutter Eli, bookseller, stationer, and newsagent, Duddon road

PARKER Robert, tailor and draper, Duddon road

Pickering Edward, earthenware and smallware dealer, Steel street

Postlethwaite James, cashier of ironworks, Alexandra place

RICHARDSON Edwin, watchmaker, Steel street and *Barrow*

Rigg John, butcher, Steel street

Riley John, beerhouse, Back Beach street

Riley Thomas, shopkeeper, Sharp street

SIMPSON Joseph, builder (Mandall & Simpson) and vict., Vulcan Hotel, Sandy road

Slater William, farmer Park Farm

Smith George, beerhouse, Back Beach street

Smith H.C., vict., London House, Duddon road

Smith John, beerhouse, Sandy road

Spencer George, grocer and provision dealer, Sandy road

WALTON Nelson, weighing clerk, Ironworks Cottages

Warwick Robert, joiner, builder, and saw mill proprietor, 1 Harris street

Weston Robert, manager of bonded stores, Sandy road

Williamson John, foreman, Duddon road

Wilson James, foreman fitter, 2 Stafford street

Wilson M. & Co., shopkeepers, King's row

31 Duddon Road. (Courtesy of Mark MacLean)

HISTORY AND DIRECTORY OF FURNESS AND CARTMEL

MANNEX P. 1882

IRELETH-CUM-ASKAM

Askam Assembly Rooms; Dixon Bros., proprietors

Askam and Mouzell Iron Co., Limited; Horace Massicks. Manager

Askam and Roanhead Iron Mines; Kennedy Bros., proprietors; Joseph Neale, manager

Atkinson Joseph, coal dealer and carrier

Atkinson Wm., coal dealer and beerhouse, Victoria vaults

Backhouse James, Foreman joiner

Barrow Haematite Steel Co., Limited, Park mines; William Kellet, Esq., general manager; h. *Southport*

Barton Hugh, shopkeeper and painter

Bell Richard, linen draper, Duke street

Bell Samual, miner, Saw Mill Field

Birkett Thomas, butcher, Duke street

Brockbank Mr. Joseph, Sea View house

Bush George, contractor

Burt Harry, miner, Beach street

Butcher James Kirby, book agent, 14 Sharpe street

Calvert Thomas, joiner, Sharpe street

Carson John, out-door ale and porter license

Challinor Samuel MacMillan, surgeon, Duke street

Chapman Arthur Atkinson, draper

Chapman Law. Parker, chemist, Duke street

Clark John, station master, Park station

Cook Willaim, postmaster, Duke street

Cooper John, miner, Duddon road

Cross Hugh, bellman and billposter, 41 Sharpe street

*Dalton Co-operative Stores (*branch*),* grocers and provision dealers, Duke street

Dawson John, miner, Duke street

Dixon Benjamin, miner, Duddon road

Dixon Bros., grocers and ironmongers, Duke street

Dixon Isabella, out-door license

Fell William, shopkeeper, Steel street

Fleet John, grocer, Sharpe street

Fleming William, station master, Askam

Forsyth Isaac, carter and cow keeper, Sharpe street

Hall Anthony, shopkeeper, Victoria street

Hamer James, cashier, Moor house

Hamer Robert, shopkeeper, Harris street

Harrison John, earthenware and general dealer and newsagent, Sharpe street

Haworth William, linen draper, Duke street

Higgins Ann, shopkeeper, Duddon road

Hodgson William, police sergeant, Police station, Duke street

Holden James, watchman, Roanhead

Jackson Alfred, clerk, Iron works

Jervis William Stelfox, grocer and provision dealer, Duke street

Jones Adam, shopkeeper, Steel street

Kelly James, miner, Duddon road

Kennedy Bros,. mine proprietors, Roanhead

Kennedy Myles, (Kennedy Bros.), managing partner; h. Stone Cross, *Ulverston*

Kitchen John Newby, grocer, Duke street

Lamb James, boot and shoemaker, tobacconist and toy dealer, Duke street

Lehr Frederick, pork butcher, Duke street

Lindsay Richard, miner, Sharpe street

Lishman Joseph, beerhouse, Grey Horse

Lewis Alex., store and timekeeper, Duddon road

McGarrity John, police constable, Duke street

McLeain Wm., shopkeeper, Sharpe street

Mandall William, builder, plumber, and painter

Millican Watson, clogger, Sharpe street

Milner R. A., tailer, draper, and hatter, Duke street; Henry Edmondson, manager

National Schools, Duke street; Matthew Wilson (boys); Elizabeth Vile (girls); Margaret Troughton (infants)

Nicholas Thomas, lodgings, Crossley street

Nicholson Henry Johnson, engineer, Alexandra place

Noble John, agent for prudential Assurance Co., Sharpe street

Oliver Lewis, grocer, Sharpe street

Park Thomas, fruit, fish, and potato dealer, Duke street; h, Marsh street

Parker Robert, tailor, &c., Duddon road

Pennington William, shopkeeper

Riley Richard, hind, Roanhead farm

Sandscale Mining Co., Limited; P. Wurtzburger, manager

Scott - , miner, Low house

Sharp Matthew, engine driver, Duke street

Simpson Joseph, builder, Duddon road

Smith Hannah, vict., Vulcan Hotel

Smith Mary, beerhouse, Furness Tavern

Stables Mary Ann, shopkeeper

Stephenson George, coal dealer

Suart George, boot and shoemaker, Duke street

Towers John, mining agent, Duddon road

Troughton Mrs. Mary, Duke street

Walton Nelson, weighing clerk, Alexandra place

Ward John, furnace foreman, Alexandra place

Warwick Robert, joiner and builder, Furness place

Waterhouse John, shopkeeper

Watkins George, vict., London House

Watson Joseph, draper, Sharpe street

Wearing William, miner, Duddon road

Welch John, miner, Marsh cottages

Welch William, miner, Marsh cottages

Whitehead Jonathan, pork dealer

Wills James, farmer, Green Haume

Wilson Edward, miner, Marsh cottages

Wilson John, fisherman &c.

Wilson William, farmer, Marsh farm

Winder John, baker and confectioner, Duke street

BARROW AND FURNESS DISTRICT

DIRECTORY.

1887.

Post Office, Askam.

William Cook, Post Master. -Letters arrive (from Carnforth) at 5-50 a.m. and 2-54 p.m. and are despatched thereto at 7-36 and 8-36 p.m. Money Order and Telegraph Office and Savings Bank.

Gentry, Clergy, and Private Residents.

Carruthers, Mr Benjamin, Old Parsonage, Ireleth

Challinor, Mr Samual Macmillan, Duke street, Askam

Douglas, Rev Thos., B.A., Ireleth

Hamer, Mr Jas., Moor House, Sandscales

Johnson, Mr Sydney, Old Park, Ireleth

Metcalf, Rev Thomas, Ireleth

Sharp, Mrs M., Ireleth

Academies and Schools.

National school

Askam Post office. (Courtesy of Askam History Club)

Askam- Matthew Wilson, master; Elizabeth Vile, mistress; Margaret Troughton, infants' mistress

Blacksmiths.

Dixon, John, Ireleth

Boot and Shoe Makers.

Riley, George, Ireleth

Stuart, George, Duke street, Askam

Builders and Contractors.

Simpson, Joseph, Duddon road, Askam

Butchers.

Wetherald, Thomas, Duke street, Askam

Chemists and Druggists.

Chapman, L. P., Duke street, Askam

Clog and Patten makers.

Watson, Milligan, Sharp street, Askam

Coal Dealers.

Stephenson, George, Duddon road, Askam

Confectioners.

Cox, John, Duke street, Askam

Troughton, Stephen, Duke street, Askam

Conveyance by Railway on the Furness lines.

Station, Askam – William Fleming, station master

Dentists.

Chapman, L.P., Duke street, Askam

Farmers.

Bell, William, Old Park, Ireleth

Butler, John, Ireleth

Chapman, John, Ireleth

Clark, Anthony, Stewner bank

Clegg, John, Park Farm

Hinds, Joseph, Greenscow Farm, Askam

Kennedy, Myles, Roanhead

Langhorn, Jackson, Scale bank

Lowther, Andrew, Ireleth

Lowther, Thomas (trustees of), Standish Cote

Mason, Robert, Marsh Grange

Slater, William, High Haum

Stephenson, John, Ireleth

Tyson, James, Stewner bank

Woodburn, Thomas, Sandscales

Grocers and Provision Dealers.

Carson, John Sharp, Askam

Cook, William, Duke street, Askam

Dalton-in-Furness Co-operative Society, Limited, Askam

Dixon Bros., Duke Street, Askam

Hall, Anthony, Victoria street, Askam

Harrison, John, 1, Sharp street, Askam

Jervis, William S., Duke street

Kirkby, Elizabeth, Ireleth

Oliver, Lewis, Sharp street, Askam

Pennington, William, Stafford street, Askam

Hotels.

Vulcan, Edwin Cliffe, Duke street, Askam

Iron Manufacturers.

Askam and Mouzell Iron Co., Limited, Askam-in-Furness – Thos. Barlow-Massiscks, managing director

Iron Ore Masters.

Askam and Mouzell Iron Co., Limited, Askam-in-Furness – Thos. Barlow-Massiscks, managing director

Barrow Hematite Steel Co., Limited; Park mine, offices, Dalton – William Kellet, manager

Kennedy, Brothers, Roanhead Hematite Mines; office, Ulverston

Sandscale Mining Co., Limited, Dalton – Horatio H. Strongitharm, manager

Ironmongers.

Dixon Bros., Duke street, Askam, and at Millom

Linen and Woolen Drapers.

Forsyth, William, Duke street, Askam

Gadie, Charles, Duke street, Askam

Haworth, William, Duke street, Askam

Dixon Bros., Duke street, Askam

Newsagents.

Fell, Mary Ann, Ireleth

Public Buildings, Offices, &c.

Ireleth Church – Rev. T. Douglas, vicar; Rev. Thomas Metcalfe, curate

Methodist (Wesleyan) Askam

Methodist (United Free Church), Askam

DALTON-IN-FURNESS DISTRICT LOCAL BOARD.

Chairman, John Walton, Ireleth; Robert Wilson, Roanhead Farm; James Hamer, The Moors; Horace Barlow-Massicks, Greenscoe House, Askam; Samual M. Challinor, Askam; John Towers, Duddon Road, Askam;

Assembly Rooms, Askam – Dixon Bros., proprietors

Police Station, Askam – Robert Allen, sergeant

Quarry owners.

Widdows, Frank Arthur, Greenhaume Quarries, Askam

BARROW AND DISTRICT

YEAR BOOK

1905

Askam and District.

Local Information.

Askam School: Master, W. E. Brown; Infants, Miss Hind.

Askam National Schools: Master, W. Ward; Infants, Head Mistress, Miss Sharp.

Askam Unionist Club: R. Noble, Secretary.

Askam Football Club: W. E. Benjamin, Secretary.

Askam Cricket Club: F. Carruthers, Secretary.

Askam Prize Brass Band: Thos. Satterthwaite, Secretary.

Askam Poultry and Pigeon Society: J. Barton, Secretary.

Ireleth Schools: Mistress, Miss Wright.

Dnnerholme Golf Club. – A new 10-hole course, about 5 minutes' walk from Askam Station. Subscription £1. 1s. per annum. Ladies 10s. 6d. ;1s. per day. First year will commence in March 1905. Secretary, John Mason, Marsh Grange, Kirkby-in-furness.

Askam Foresters, Mark Backhouse, secretary.

Askam-in-Furness

Alexander Place.

Kemsley, George
Hutchinson, Robert
Tyson, William
Tyson, John

Askam View.

1 Wilson, Thomas
3 Wildman, William
5 Welsh, William
7 Ormandy, Joseph

Beech Street.

19 Small, Enoch
21 Latham, William
23 Fallow, Wm.
25 Kidd, Henry
26 Blackburn, Wm.
27 Ferguson, Samuel
28 Crawley, James
29 Fallows, Thomas

33 Carson, John
61 Kirkby, John
63 Bennison, Joseph
67 Spry, R.
69 Williams, Charles
71 Edmondson, Mrs.
75 Edmondson, Robert
84 Coulston, J. J.
86 Lewis, Daniel
90 Shuttleworth, R.
91 Satterthwaite, M.
92 Seward, Richard
93 Newton, John
94 Benson, W.
95 Walker, Elizabeth
98 Coward, Richard
100 Myers, William
102 Mylrea, Thomas
106 Spry, Charles

108 Newton, W.
110 Crawley, David
112 Forsyth, Mrs., beerhouse.

Crossley Street.

91 Kidd, John

Dalton Road.

1 Williams, John
3 Stevenson, Robert
5 Cole, J. H.
7 Wildman, Henry
9 Swainson, William N.
11 Noble, John
13 Longstaff, William
15 Knipe, Thomas
17 Smith, Mrs.
19 Dixon, Joseph
21 Berry, Thomas
23 Barr, A.
25 Hind, Walter

27 Noble, Richard
29 Woodhall, William
31 Walker, W. E.
33 Foster, Robert
35 Norman, J.
37 Myers, Amos
39 Sutcliffe, Joseph
41 Wilson, William

Dale Street.

Martin, Isaac
1 Marshall, George
3 Woodburn, Mrs.
4 Mason, Thomas
5 Rawlinson, Thos.
6 Mossop, F.
8 Dickinson, Thomas
9 Nanson, Henry

Duddon.

Hutton, Thomas
4 Wilson, Edward
6 Morris, Wm.
8 Todd, T.

Duddon Road.

Sharp, William
3 Sharp, Matthew
5 Bell, James
7 Mingins, John
9 Dawson, Thomas
11 Lewis, Alexander
13 Marshall, James
15 Dewhurst, R.
17 Chaplain, J.
21 Atkinson, John
23 Thome, E.
25 Kitchen, Mrs.
27 Benson, E.

29 Coward, William
48 Fell, Thomas, K.
? Edmondson, Mark
61 Nicholls, C.
65 Mackereth, Wm.
67 Buxton, William
69 Mylchreest, D. T.
71 Lloyd, John
73 Riley, William
75 Dixon, Wm.
77 Shakley, John
79 Brown, William
81 Lishman, J
83 Woodend, Issac
85 Storey, James
87 Sharp, E.
89 Wetherald, Thomas
90 Smith, William
91 Jones, G
92 Dixon, John
94 Park, Thomas
96 Ormandy, Joseph
98 Crawley, R.
100 Chapman, Robert
102 Taylor, Wm.
108 Hutchinson, Edward
110 Walker, Richard
112 Kellet, Thomas
114 Higgins, Mrs.
Wharton, James
Dixon, Wm.

Duddon View.

1 Smith, G.
2 Hill, Thomas
3 Birkett, Robert
4 Picthall, Thomas

5 Davies, David
6 Berry, Ephraim
7 Birkett, Joshua
8 Postlethwaite, John
9 Leece, Thomas
11 Birkett, Wm.

Duke Street.

1 Jervis, William, grocer
3 Greetham, Robert
5 Mason, William
7 Chapman, Arthur
9 Co-operative Stores
11 Cook, Samual, M.D.
13 Post Office, Miss Cook, postmistress
15 Police Station, Sergt. H. Dunn. Roberts, E.E., P.C.
National Schools.
Unionist Club.
Anderson, Joseph
Stephenson, John
Strickland, Clark
Chaplin, John
Smith, Jas. Warriner
Salvation Army Hall.
71 Shuttleworth, R., Fruiterer.
73 Braithwaite, J., Joiner.
75 Fell, Mrs., Newsagent.
77 Greenup, J., Fruiterer.
79 Cross, B., Boot & Shoe Maker.
81 Leach, J., and Son, Drapers.
83 Jackson, A., Chemist.
85 Forsyth, Miss, Draper.
87 Ormandy, W., Grocer.
89 Atkinson, Wm., Butcher.
91 Jackson, Miss, Confectioner.
93 Dixon J., Grocer.

Assembly Rooms.

131 Millican, Watson

133 Woodrow, Fred

135 Sheridan, J., Tobacconist.

Graham, Allan

Trenwith, John

Fleet, John, *Furness Tavern*.

Goad, Mrs. *Vulcan Hotel*.

Lancaster Bank, Branch.

Parker, R., Tailor.

Olliver, L., Boot Maker.

Dunnerholme.

Oversbury, Myles

Wood, Edward

Proctor, John

Brocklebank, William, Railway Line.

Atkinson, Thomas

Knight, Wm.

Furnace Place.

McGivon, John

1 Millar, J.

2 Brocklebank, Edward

3 Lynham, James

4 Swainson, John

5 Carter, John

8 Nicoll, Henry

9 Price, James

10 Duke, Edwin

11 Robinson, William

12 Pelter, J.

13 Bell, Richard

16 Wallace, Mrs.

18 Pedan, David

19 Cree, Mrs.

20 Higgins, James

21 Fulton, Hugh

22 Cowperthwaite, Robert

23 Smith, William

24 Pendlebury, Samual

25 Holmes, Lancelot

26 Sawrey, William

27 Kellett, George

28 Newby, James

29 Murphy, William

30 Gilbanks, James

32 Crossley, John

33 Emms, Mrs.

34 Wilson, Mary A

35 Tebay, John

36 Quayle, John

37 Eccleston, Thos

Greenscoe

Hind, Joseph

Thompson, T.

Mooney, Wm.

Riley, J.

Leece, Henry

Green Haume.

Clark, James

1 Sticks, John

2 Courtney, Michael

3 Courtney, Michael

4 Dolan, Mrs.

5 Eccles, Mrs.

6 Eccles, Joseph

7 Uren, Emanuel

8 Cavanagh, James

9 Yates, Micheal

10 Brockbank, George

11 Farnon, Owen

12 Parker, Thomas

13 Clark, John

14 Wilkinson, Thos.

Harris Street.

Quirk, Thomas

2 Dunn, Mrs.

6 Walters, William

10 Cross, John

12 Tyson, James

14 Cloudsdale, Robert

16 Hull, Anthony

Hollowgate.

2 Townson, Mrs.

6 Fox, William

8 Postlethwaite, J.

10 Wilson, W. H.

12 Kellett, George

14 Towers, Mrs.

16 Dickinson, Henry

17 Crowford, John

19 Ashburner, James

Ireleth.

Langhorn, William, Old Park Farm.

Bell, William, Old Park.

Slater, Wm. Jun., High Haume.

Carruthers, Mrs.

Sharpe, Joseph, Bankfield, Barrister-at-Law.

Kitchen, William

Wilson, Robert

Parker, Thomas

Garth, Edward

Mellon, Henry, Brooklea.

Jackson, John

Spencer, Peter, Beulah House.

Butler, Mrs. Moor Side.

4 Hughes, Mrs.

5 Baxter, David

6 Tyson, John

7 Atkinson, Mrs.
8 Chapman, J.
10 Chapman, John
11 Ainsworth, James
12 Gill, Daniel
13 Sanderson, Mark
15 17 Thompson, E. J.
18 Kitchen, William
20 Tyson, Mrs.
21 Hunter, John
22 Burns, John
23 Ormandy, Thomas
24 Danson, George
25 Smith, James
27 Barrow, John
Leonard, Rev. J. G.
28 Jackson, Benjamin
29 Atkinson, A.
30 Wood, Robert
31 Stables, Thomas
14 Nuttall, R. R.

Ireleth Brow.

1 Knight, Mrs.
3 Williams, R.
4 Dixon, Thomas
5 Swainson, Jas.
6 Bell, Thomas
7 Riley, John B.
8 Shaw, Geo.

Ireleth Road

Clayton, George
Danson, Andrew
Stewart, John
Knight, William
22 and 24 Nicholls, Charles
26 Edmondson, Myles

28 Coward, Mrs.
30 Slater, John
32 Towers, Wm.
34 and 36, Turname, Wm. (Twiname)
38 Townson, James
40 Johnson, William
192 Atkinson, Stephen
230 Challinor, Dr. T. P.
232 Marr, Frederick
234 Beck, Henry
238 Airey, William
250 Proctor, Richard

James Street.

Dickenson, John
Chapman, Richard
Askew, Joseph
5 Bird, William
11 Kitchen, Adam
13 Myers, Cristopher
15 Routledge, William
17 Hall, Robert, John
19 Park, James Mason
21 Walker, James
23, Brown, Thomas
25 Chapman, Robert
27 Dixon, Mrs.
29 Blezard, James
31 Forsyth, William
1 Houghton, J. B.
3 Chapman, J. J.

John Street.

20 Fallows, Jas.
28 Lowther, Mrs.
30 Burt, Harry
32 and 34 Wilson, John. Higgins, Thos.
27 Glover, Thos.

29 Brown, James
31 Shepherd, Thos.

Lord Street.

11 Tyson, Nathaniel
13 Seward, Jas.
15 Quayle, George
17 Askew, Charles
19 Williams, Edward

Marsh Grange.

Mason, Robert
Wilson, John
Newton, William

Marsh Street.

Simpson, Joseph
1 Rigg, Mrs.
2 Jefferson, Jos.
4 Kellet, William
5 Woodburn, John
6 Twiname, John
7 Parrington, James
8 Dixon, Mrs.
9 Webster, F.
10 Cowley, George W.
11 Lawley, David
12 Boyd, Robert
13 Huddleston, Hannah
14 Hall, Mary A.
15 Atkinson, R.
16 Kellett, William
17 Atkinson, William
18 Raven, James
19 Sandham, William
20 Constable, John G.
21 Kitchen, Jas.
22 Pickthall, Henry
23 Proctor, James

25 Seward, John
26 Black, Richard
27 Wilson, W.

Moor Road.

Hoole, William, Moor Farm
Hutton, Myles, Stewner Park
Lowther, John, Standish Cote
Hutchinson, Henry, Standish Cote
Spencer, E. E., Powka Reservoir
Butler, John, Moor Side
1 Walker, Edward
2 Walker, William
3 Walker, Richard

Park.

Barton, Joseph
Clark, William
Woods, Richard
Etherington, Alf.

Paradise.

1 Riley, John
3 Robinson, Thomas
5 Knowles, Robert
7 King, Joseph
9 Knight, John
11 Gardener, James
13 Atkinson, Nicholas
15 Atkinson, Joseph

Ronhead.

Bird, Micheal
Hamer, James, The Moors
Duke, John
Duckett, John
Ormandy, Thomas
Burns, John
McNevin, John junr.
Greenup, Richard, Thwaite Flat

Sandscales.

Allonby, Thomas
Lloyd, Edgar
1 Jackson, Emanual
2 Nelson, John
3 Nicholson, William
4 McNevin, Nicholas
5 Hunter, Thos.

School Street.

Ward, William
Simpson, Richard
Buncle, Mrs.

Sharp Street.

2 Upham, Robert
4 Price, Mrs.
6 Dawson, Thomas
8 Wilson, John
10 Chaplin, James
12 Milligan, Barnard
14 Cottier, William
16 Park, Mrs.
20 Stephenson, Arthur
24 Cottier, Archie
22 Beckett, J. W.
26 Walker, Robert
30 Ingram, John
34 Metcalf, George
35 Cox, John
36 Cain, Andrew John
37 Wadeson, Thomas
38 Oliver, Lewis
39 Lewis, Samuel
40 Cain, George Andrew
41 Walker, William
42 Alexander, Mrs.
43 Carson, Thos.

44 Chapman, James
45 Webster, John
46 Marshall, Mrs.
47 Lewis, R.
48 Parry, Thomas
50 Windle, Edward
51 Benjamin, William
52 Woodburn, Thos.
53 Wilson, John
55 Atkinson, John
56 Benson, Robert
57 Sharp, A.
58 Pope, James
59 Riley, Albert, Edward
63 Bettany, Edward
65 Chappell, John
67 Chapman, John
69 Wilson, T. E.
71 Kissick, R.
72 Venables, John
73 Greaves, Wm. Hy.
74 Atkinson, John W.
75 Hoggarth, William
76 Richards, Thos.
77 Stevenson, Jos.
78 Watson, Joseph
79 Brockbank, Mrs.
80 Calvert, Thomas
82 Quine, Joseph
84 Millican, Jacob
86 Millican, Joseph
88 Venables, John
90 Crawley, Thos.
117 Leybourne, Mrs.
119 Oliver, Charles L.
123 McDougall, Duncan

127 Coward, Matthew
129 Hannah, John Jas.
131 Kirkby, Henry
133 Berry, John
137 Duncan, John
139 Workmaster, Paul
141 Duncan, David, Jas. P.
143 Milburn, Jacob
145 Mawson, Joseph
147 Sandham, William
149 Baldwin, H.
151 Turner, Henry

Stafford Street.

2 Bourland, Benson
4 Dixon, Mrs.
7 Barnes, John
9 Brown, John
10 Stables, Thomas
12 Trenwith, Stephen
13 Johnson, John
14 Floods, Arthur
15 Grice, William
18 Sandham, Joseph
19 Sharp, John
20 Walker, John

Steel Street.

33 Rigg, Margaret
35 Hoggarth, William
36 Kaggan, Thomas
38 Cox, Edward
39 Bundy, William
41 Butcher, James Kirkby
42 Barr, Mrs.
43 Proctor, George G.
44 Jones, Esau
45 Benjamin, George

46 Flinn, Charles
47 Wearing, William
48 Cole, Mrs.
49 Roberts, Thomas
52 Hughes, John
54 Blamire, Edward
55 Mailes, Francis
57 Webb, Charles
65 Absolom, Francis
68 Millican, Thomas
69 Strickland, John Thos.
71 Millburn, Thos.
72 Leek, Jesse
73 Heley, John
74 Clarkson, Thomas
77 Martin, Henry
78 Waterhouse, John
81 Mawson, Mrs.
84 Knibbs, John
85 Fell, Thomas
86 Quayle, Wm. Hy.
87 Riley, Samuel
88 Robinson, Robert
89 Rawes, Thomas
90 Tyson, Thomas
91 Fry, J. R.
92 Atkinson, Jos.
93 Townson, William
94 Strickland, George
96 Gess, James
97 Standing, John
98 Butcher, James
99 Knibbs, William
100 Fell, James
101 Peutherer, Robert
102 Lowe, Thomas

103 Postlethwaite, Roger
105 Pearson, J.
107 Jackson, Ann
108 Jackson, Henry
106 Carter, William
109 Holmes, William
110 Sewell, William
111 Whitehead, Jonathan
112 Wood, Alexander
117 Stockton, Mrs.
123 Wilson, Cristopher
129 Proctor, Mrs.
131 Storer, James
133 Tyson, Kate
139 Birbeck, John

Sun Street.

1 Hunter, John
3 Postlethwaite, James
5 Medcalf, Thomas
7 Medcalf, Thomas, junr.

Victoria Street.

Brockbank, Mrs
1 and 3 Stuart, Thomas
7 Foster, John
9 Johnson, Edward
11 Turford, Jesse
12 Backhouse, Enoch
13 O'Connor, William
15 O'Connor, James
16 Watson, George
22 Greaves, Richard
24 Harris, Alexander
28 Henley, William
30 Leigh, Mrs.
32 Smith, William
40 Myers, William

42 Furness, Thomas

44 Brockbank, William

Walker Street.

Sanders, Thomas

2 Woodend, Joseph

4 Marr, Mrs.

8 Satterthwaite, Thomas

6 Dacre, Matthew

10 Woodrow, James

12 Woodrow, John Alfred

20 Bland, Joseph

22 Martin, Mrs.

FURNESS AND DISTRICT YEAR BOOK 1926

ASKAM WITH IRELETH

St Peters Church, Ireleth. Sunday Services; Holy Communion, 1st Sunday in month after Matins, 2nd Sunday in month at 8 a.m., 3rd Sunday in month at 10.30 p.m..; Children's Service, third Sunday, 2 p.m. The Benefice is of the annual value of £350. The present vicar, who has held the living since 1905, is the Rev. E. W. Ridley, St. Bees Theological Collage. Churchwardens, Mr. E. W. Brown (vicar's), Mr. R. Knowles (people's); Organist and Choirmaster, Mr. W. Williams; Parish Clerk, Mr. H. Riley; Sexton, Mr. J. B. Riley; Superintendent of Sunday School, Mr. Walter Williams; Diocesan Reader, Mr. Woodcock.

Wesleyan Church. Duddon Road.- Minister, Rev. F. Taylor, Wesley Manse, Dalton. Sunday Services, 10.45 a.m. and 6 p.m.; Week-night Services, alternate Thursdays at 7 p.m. Caretaker, Mrs. Park, 94, Duddon Road.

Primitive Methodist Church. Beach Street.- Sunday Services, 10.45 a.m. and 5.45 p.m. Sunday School, 10 a.m. and 1.45 p.m. C.C., Wednesday 7.15 p.m. Ministers; Rev. E. P Sellers, Dalton; Rev J. L. Stafford, Millom.

United Methodist Church, Duke Street.- Minister, Rev. S. Wilding, 42 Storey Square, Barrow. Sunday Services, 6 p.m.; Tuesday, 7 p.m.

Church of Christ. Duddon Road.

Gospel Hall. Assembly Rooms, Duke Street.

Schools.- Askam Senior School: Headmaster. Mr. W. E. Brown.

Juniors and Infants: Miss. Shaw. Ireleth School: Headmistress, Mrs. Postlethwaite.

Post Office, Duke Street.- Deliveries , 7 a.m., 10.15 a.m. (parcels), 3.30 p.m. Despatches, Box cleared 11.30 a.m. and 6.30 p.m.; parcels for same despatches, 11.30 a.m. and 6.30 p.m. Telephone Call Office, Askam 1. Mr C. H. Blakeman. Postmaster.

Unionist Club. Duke Street.- President, Myles Kennedy, Esq., J.P.., D.L. Steward, Mr. W. P. Kellet; Secretary, John Lishman, 81, Duddon Road.

Y.M.C.A.- Secretary, W. E. Brown, School House.

Police Station.- Duke Street. Sergt. R. W. Greenhalgh.

Askam Advertising Committee.- Chairman, Coun. Joseph Gill; Secretary, Coun. R. Noble, Duke Street, Askam; Treasurer, Mr. C. H. Blakeman. Committee : Messers. R. Noble, D. Riley, T. F. Massicks, Geo. Mason, Coun. W. H. Buxton, Wm. Atkinson, A. Goodman, J. Newton.

Furness Flying Club.- Headquarters, Furness Tavern. Secretary, W. Walsh, John Street.

Askam Tennis Club.- Hon. Secretary, Miss D. Birch, Duddon Road.

Askam Cricket Club.- Ground, Duddon Road. Hon. Secretary, John Myers, Post Office, Ireleth.

Askam Rugby Football Club.- Ground, Duke Street. Headquarters, Railway Inn. Hon. Secretary. Fred Jackson, 57, Steel Street.

I.O.G.T.- Lily of Askam Lodge, No. 2564; Lodge Room, P.M. School, Beach Street; Meetings, Thursday at 7.30 p.m.; Secretary, Miss Ida Taylor.

R.A.O.B., Duddon Lodge.-Club Room, Furness Tavern. Meetings, Fridays, at 7 p.m. Hon. Secretary, Joseph Gill.

A.O.F. – Hon. Secretary, W. Wilson, Duddon Road.

Prize Brass Band.-Secretary, Frank Webster, James Street. Conductor, Stanley Cain.

Manchester District Banking Co., Ltd.- Tuesday s and Friday, 9.30 to 11.15

Dunnerholme Golf Club.- Secretary, G. B. Rogerson, 38, Athol Street, Barrow. Treasurer, J. T. Parker, District Bank, Ltd., Dalton-in-Furness.

Bank of Liverpool.- Days: Mondays and Fridays. Hours 9.45 to 11.15.

R.S.P.C.A., Askam and Kirkby.- Hon. Secretary, Mrs Ridley; Committee;

Miss Cook, Mr. Marriott. Mr Taylor, Miss Trenwith, Rev. E. W. Ridley.

MEDICAL LIST.

COOK, SAMUEL BIRD, Duke Street, Askam-in-Furness. B.A., Cape of Good Hope, 1881; M.D. London, 1892; M.D., 1889; M.R.C.S., L.R.C.P., London, 1887; (St Thomas's); Late Assistant House Surgeon; Clinical Assistant Skin Department, and Assistant House Physician, St. Thomas Hospital, London.

ALEXANDER PLACE.

1 Twiname, W.

2 Airey, Thos.

Vickers, Geo.

3 Hutchinson, Mrs.

4 Richards, Charles.

5 Kirkby, t.

BEACH STREET.

(Right Side.)

2 Anderson, J., Builder

24 Williams, Agnes.

26 Coward, Richard.

28 Myers, R.

30 Walker, J.

84 Coulson, J. J.

86 Procter, Mrs.

90 Newton, John.

92 Satterthwaite, R.H.

94 Gillfillan, J. J.

96 Crawley, Mrs. M.

98 Edmondson, R.

100 Myers, William.

102 Fry, Ed. E.

104 Butcher, Jas. K., Jr.

106 Houghton, C.

108 Newton, William.

110 Thexton, R.

112 Forsyth, Jane.

(Left Side.)

Phifer, J., Hairdresser.

19 Thompson, Lancelot.

21 Kitchen, William P.

23 Noble, J.

25 Fallows, Thomas.

27 Noble, William T.

29 Wearing, Isaac.

31 Burrows, J.

33 Carson, Mrs.

61 Morley, W.

63 Walker, W.

65 Quirk, J. T.

67 McCurdy, Mrs.

69 Shepherd, Thomas.

71 Kershaw, R.

73 Dixon, Mrs.

75 Burrows, Mrs.

Primitive Methodist Chapel.

91 Walker, Mrs. E.

93 Bath, G.

95 Holmes, W.

97 Windle, E.

CROSSLEY STREET.

(Right side.)

1 Fidler, L.

2 Cain, Mrs. E. J.

4 Tyson, A. j.

28 Myers, R.

84 Coulson, J.

86 Procter, Mrs.

116 Calvert, T.

(Left Side.)

Fleet, J., Ivy Cottage

Duckworth, M. Ivy House.

Christian Meeting House.

91 Cain, J. W.

93 Marshall, J.

95 Tyson, Miss. Kate.

97 McDait, P.

121 Holmes, Mrs. (Out-door Licence).

DUDDON.

2 Hutton, Mary.

4 Hutton, Jno. J.

6 Crawford, J.

8 Shaw, W.

DUDDON ROAD.

(Left side.)

1 & 3 Satterthwaite, G.

5 Chaplin, Charles E.

7 Seward, R. W.

9 Crawley, Mrs.

11 Martin, Isaac.

13 Constable, J. G.

15 Sandham, Jos.

17 Norman, James.

19 Pickthall, W.

21 Thompson, J., Tyson, Mrs.

23 Chaplin, J. H.

25 Robinson, T.

27 Mason, T.

27a Duckworth, M.

29 Coward, Ellen.

31 Cain, S.

Askam Gas Works.

61 Todd, F.

63 Brocklebank, Mrs.

65 Mackereth, Mrs.

67 Buxton, William H.

69 Rawlinson, B. R.

71 Butcher, Mrs.

75 Swindle, F. J.

77 Shackley, Edwin.

79 Mason, Mrs.

81 Lishman, J.

83 Woodend, H.

85 Hayes, Mary Ann.

87 Sandham, James.

89 Wetherald, Mrs.

91 Brown, Ruth.

Wilson, W. E, Bungalow.

(Right Side.)

48 Stephenson, John.

50 Elwell, Mrs.

Wesleyan Church.

52 Wharton, James.

54 Goodman, A.

Shackley, J., "Bungalow."

82 Copeland, H. S.

90 Allanson, J. "London House."

92 Dixon, John.

94 Park, Elizabeth.

96 Ormandy, Joseph.

98 Tyson, E. F.

100 Williams, A. E.

Greyhound Racing. (Courtesy of Jeanette Shepherd)

102 Wilson, R.

104 Park, George.

106 Warden, T.

108 Wilson, W. H.

110 Fleming, Mrs.

112 Kellett, Hannah.

114 Kellet, Wm.

Wilson, W. E., The Shelter.

DUKE STREET.

(Left Side.)

1 Jervis, W. S., Grocer, Richardson, J. P.

3 Langhorn, D.

5 Greetham, R.

Co-operative Stores.

7 Lewis, J. W.

11 Cook, Dr. Samuel Bird, M.D.

13 Cook, Margaret B.

15 Police Station. Sergeant R. W. Greenhalgh.

15 Newton, J. Police Constable

Senior Council Schools. Brown, W. E., Headmaster (School House).

Unionist Club. Kellet, W. J.

19 Noble, Richard.

21 Thompson, Mrs.

23 Edmondson, Mark.

25 Seward, F.

27 Walker, W. J.

67 Post Office. Charles Blakeman. Postmaster. Barr, A.

71 Duckworth, M. Anderson, E. A.

73 Williams, Walter H.

75 Gill, Joseph, Newsagent. Etc. Public Telephone Call Office.

77 Greenop, J., Fruiterer

79 Laycock, T.

81 Martin, J. T.

83 Martin and Briscoe.

85 Shaw, C. S.

87 Ormandy, W., Grocer.

Taylor, J. A. (House)

89 Atkinson, William. Butcher.

91 Lawden, T.

93 Dixon, Mrs. Grocer, Birkett, M. Cross, B., Boot and Shoe Repairer.

129 Stables, J.

131 Boydes, Miss.

133 Pope, J.

137, Wood, J. J.

139 Quirk, F.

141 Lewis, A., Iron Works Office.

(Right Side.)

64 Buxton, Miss.

66 Y.M.C.A. Mawson, F. Manchester & Liverpool Bank (Tuesday & Fridays)

94 McGivern, W. J., *Vulcan Hotel.*

United Methodist Chapel.

140 White, Alfred. *Furness Tavern.*

DUNNERHOLME.

2 Johnson, R. H. C.

4 Conlin, J. Soutergate Crossing. Kirkby.

8 Brocklebank, S. B.

Steel, S. T., Railway Crossing.

FURNACE PLACE.

1 Flood, A.

2 Pedan, E.

3 Barnes. Walter.

4 Wilson, W.

5 Jopson, J. J.

6 Lytham, J.

7 Woodall, W. Burt, W.

8 Nicholl, Mrs.

9 Dickinson, W.

10 Wallace, J.

11 Coulson, D.

12 Johnson, W.

13 Wallace, J.

14 Nelson, Mrs.

15 Pelter, J.

15a Clark, Jos.

16 Windle, L.

17 Seward, W.

18 O'Connor. L. A.

19 Flood, A. (Senr.)

20 Airey, J.

21 Hutchinson, T.

22 Cowperthwaite, E.

23 Smith, William

24 Wilson, S.

25 Irwin, W.

26 Stebbins, J.

27 Gillbanks, M.

28 Newby, James.

29 Newby, John.

30 Gilbanks, Mrs.

31 Townson, R.

32 Robinson, F. H.

33 Turner, Mrs.

34 Alexander, W.

35 Wood, W.

36 Crossley, M.

37 Eccleston, J.

GREENSCOE.

1 Stables, J. E., The Farm.

Barnsley, J. The Mansion.

2 Woodburn, M.

3 Grundy, M. J.

4 Kellett, G.

5 Wearing, G. E.

GREEN HAUME.

Knowles, F., The Farm.

Troughton, A. B.

1 Lister, J.

2 Wilson, T.

3 Quayle, R.

4 Dolan, Mrs.

5 Yates, M.

6 Eccles, J. R.

7 Uren, E. Meadows, A.

8 Kavanagh, Mrs.

9 Dunn, E.

10 Wood, R.

11 Yates, T.

12 Wilkinson, Thos.

13 Wilkinson, Mrs.

14 Townson, W.

HARRIS STREET.

(Right Side.)

1 Webster, F.

(Left Side.)

2 Hutchinson, R.

4 Price, Edwin.

6 Waters, C. W.

8 Parker, A.

10 Cross, W. D.

12 Tyson, James.

14 Cloudsdale, I. Latham, A.

16 Hull, A.

JAMES STREET.

1 Barwick, J.

2 Tomlinson, T.

3 Robinson, E. Scott, H.

3a Thompson, J.

4 Twiname, D.

5 Jackson, J.

7 Webster, F.

9 Watson, David.

11 Millican, J.

13 Brooks, R.

75 Dickinson, Mrs.

17 Hall, Isabel. Woodburn, J.

19 Woodrow, A. J.

21 Wilson, W.

23 Chapman, R.

25 Webster, J.

27 Dixon, Miss.

29 Nansen, H.

31 Welch, Hannah J.

JAMES STREET (EAST).

1 Windle, R. H. Hardy, F.

5a Askew, J.

JOHN STREET.

(Right Side.)

22 Fallows, W.

24 Brown, James. C.

26 Kemp, W.

28 Coulson, R.

30 O'Donnell, R. H.

32 Wilson, Mrs. E.

34 Burt, H., Barker, H.

(Left Side.)

20 Thurgood, D., Mawson, Hannah.

27 Neave, A. J.

29 Robinson. J.

31 Jackson, A.

61 Walsh, R.

63 Thackeray, T.

65 Windle, W.

67 Higgins, T.

LORD STREET.

9 Atkinson, T. Tobacco, Sweets. Etc.

11 Woodburn, E. Twiname, J.

13 Knibbs, G.

15 Stables, R. B.

17 Stables, J. F.

19 Rawlinson, Thomas.

MARSH COTTAGES.

4 Hutton, John, James. Marsh Farm.

6 Crawford, J.

8 Shaw, W.

Massicks, T. F., Near Marsh Bungalow.

Wardle, S. J., Cumbria View.

MARSH STREET.

1 Black, J.

2 Smith, Wm.

3 Woodrow, J.

4 Wilson, John.

5 Waddington, J.

6 Twiname, T. R.

7 Parrington, James.

8 Agnell, W. E.

9 Dixon, William.

10 Cowley, George, W.

11 Dodd, J.

12 Helling, John

13 Rawlinson, J.

14 Huddleston, Mrs. Hall, W.

15 Hendley, John.

16 Kellett, William.

17 Simpson, Mary A.

18 Wilson, Robinson.

19 Sandham, Mrs. Fell, Geo.

20 Constable, Agnes.

21 Hutton, S., Crook, W.

22 Pickthall, H.

23 Parkes, Alfred.

24 Martin, H.

25 Woodend, Mrs.

26 Woodend, W.

27 Sandham, W.

28 Burns, Mrs, F.

PARK.

Greenhalgh, S.

1 Wells, J. P.

2 Hunter, Miss, Park Farm.

3 Woods, Mrs. Thwaites, P.

4 Jackson, J. J.

5 Carter, T.

Chapman, A. A.

Ashburner, Martin.

Sarginson, Wm., St Helens Farm.

ROANHEAD.

1 Johnson, R.

2 Mawson, J.

3 Coward, W. J.

4 Myers, J. W.

5 Hunter, T.

7 Duke, E.

8 McNevin, J.

Duke, J., Thwaite Flat.

Severs, C., The Moors.

Longrigg, T., Roanhead Farm.

SANDSCALE.

Hayton, E., The Farm.

1 Brown, William.

2 Buckley, D.

3 Nicholson, William.

4 Walker, J.

5 Morris, T.

7 Molyneux, John, Sandscale Cottage.

SCHOOL STREET.

1 Newton, G., Police Constable

3 Brown, W. E. School House.

5 Simpson, R. T.

7 Tyson, W.

SHARP STREET.

(Left Side.)

35 Tyson, T.

37 Marsden, Sarah

39 Hill, W. H.

41 Tubman, T.

43 Armstrong, Mary

45 Wharton, T.

47 Hornby, R. C.

49 Hargreaves, Wm. J.

51 Gaskell, J.

53 Wales, Mrs. Fanny

57 Wales, F.

59 Bodley, Mrs.

61 Kirkby, T.

63 Barnes, Thomas

65 Trelore, E.

67 Parkes, B. W.

69 Sawrey, Robert

71 Allonby, A. E.

73 Whiteside, Mrs.

75 Hutchinson, E.

77 Price, Mrs.

79 Townson, J.

117 Thompson, W. H.

119 Berry, J.

121 Sandham, Annie

123 Adams, C.

125 Stephenson, B.

127 Woodend, C.

129 Olliver, T. J.

131 Huddleston, J.

133 Quayle, Mrs.

135 Cloudsdale, W. H.

137 Pearson, W. J.

139 Cross, R. W.

141 Duncan, John
143 Wilson, Jas.
145 Hannah, A.
147 Standing, Jas.
149 Stephenson, A.
151 Houghton, J. B.
153 Houghton, A.

(Right Side.)

2 Upham, Robert
4 Berry, J.
6 Singleton, R. d.
8 Dawson, G.
10 Benson, W.
12 Milligan, Mrs.
14 Cottier, Mrs. Nancy
16 Millican, Wesley
18 Nutter, Mrs.
20 Fitzsimmons, Wm.
22 Smith, E.
24 Kirkby, W.
26 Boow, W.
28 Kirkby, Mrs. M.
30 Mailes, Wm.
32 Cross, B. M.
34 Sharp, Joseph
36 – 38 Hoggarth, W. H.
40 Cain, George, Andrew
42 Kewley, W.
44 Atkinson, Mrs.
46 Marshall, Mrs., Flinn, R. J.
48 Pendlebury, John
50 Wadeson, Mrs.
52 Windle, Mrs.
54 Cannon, A., Parkinson, T.
56 Benson, A.
58 Jackson, A.

66 Lewis, J.
68 Chester, T.
70 Boyd, J.
72 Shaw, S.
74 Robinson, R.
76 Wadeson, W. J.
82 Atkinson, J.
84 Quine, Joseph
86 Olliver, Charles
88 Venables, Mrs.
88 Sunderland, J.
90 Coward, W,

STAFFORD STREET.

(Right Side.)

1 Leece, J.
3 Johnson, R.
5 Pearson, Elizabeth M
7 Barnes, M.
9 Brown, Mary
11 Riley, J.
13 Johnson, John
15 Grice, Jane
17 Twiname, J. H.
19 Sharp, John

(Left Side.)

2 Byrne, J.
4 Dixon, Mrs.
6 Wilson, H.
8 Cornthwaite, John
10 Coats, Mary J.
12 Trenwith, Stephen P.
14 Barnes, J. H.
16 Dockeray, Jas. Henry
18 Bell, Richard
20 Jackson, Harrison
22 Sewell, H.

STEEL STREET.

(Left Side.)

33 Riley, J.

35 Kellet, J.

39 Atkinson, R.

41 Whitehead, Adam

43 Sharp, Mrs.

45 Curtis, William John

47 Roberts, W. T.

49 Keggin, T.

51 Marshall, Mrs., Webb, C.

53 Taylor, Margt.

55 Hawton, R.

57 Jackson, F.

59 Dent, F.

61 Woolcock, J. H.

63 Myers, W.

65 Collister, R.

67 Brownlee, F.

69 Chappels, J. A.

71 Phifer, J.

73 Carter, J.

75 Quayle, W. H.

77 Williams, T.

79 Jackson, Mrs.

81 King, W. H.

83 Peutherer, Mrs., Peutherer, W. G.

85 Ward, J.

87 Myers, J. J.

89 White, F.

91 Kellet, William.

93 Brown, Oswald.

95 Stephenson, Joseph.

97 Standing, J.

99 Knibbs, Mrs.

101 Allonby, Robert.

103 Postlethwaite, Roger.

105 Carter, Wm.

107 Quayle, J.

109 Holmes, William.

111 Askew, James.

113 Burbeck, S.

115 Woodend, Mary A.

117 Bodley, J.

119 Clinton, Daniel.

121 Standing, H.

123 Carter, J. W.

125 Shepherd, William L.

127 Procter, James T.

129 Procter, Hy.

131 Stephenson, E.

133 Rose, T.

135 Allonby, Victor.

137 Pattinson, J. H.

139 Burns, Andrew.

(Right Side.)

38 Cox, Mrs. B. A.

40 Wilson, W.

42 Hanna, Mrs., Hanna, J. J.

44 Boulton, Thomas.

46 Flynn, Mrs A. M.

48 Wilson, W. E.

50 Neild, J.

52 Trelore, Robert.

54 Blamire, Mary A.

56 Hoggarth, W.

58 Dent, F.

60 Dunkley, J.

62 Speight, Isabella.

64 Carlton, H.

66 Peutherer, J.

68 Robbie, D.

70 Trelore, T. W.

72 Whitehead, Mrs.

74 Smith, R.

78 Fell, W.

80 Holmes, T.

82 Peutherer, R., Willis, Mrs.

84 Birbeck, Mrs.

86 Askew, John., Askew, W. H.

88 Butcher, J.

90 Walker, T.

94 Hewitson, William.

96 Jess, James., Vinicombe, Mrs.

98 Woods, T.

100 Cussons, A.

102 Walker, E.

104 Tyson, J. J.

106 Rawlinson, F.

108 Jackson, E and F.

110 Askew, W.

112 Kitchen, Mrs.

114 Coward, M.

VICTORIA STREET.

(Right Side.)

1 and 3 Carter, Emily, *Askam Hotel*.

5 Barlow, C. J.

7 Foster, John.

9 Johnson, Mrs.

11 Coates, W.

13 Tyson, J. J.

15 O'Connor, Mary.

(Left Side.)

12 Jackson, W. P.

14 Dickinson, A.

16 Watson, Mrs.

18 Taylor, J.

20 Graves, J. J.

22 Crossley, J.

24 Atkinson, Wm. B.

26 Alexander, W.

28 Alexander, R.

30 Leigh, John.

32 Smith, William.

34 Pelter, J.

36 Backhouse, F.

38 Cornthwaite, E.

40 Hartley, E, H.

42 O'Connor, John.

44 Backhouse, E., Brockbank, W. Sea View.

WAKEFIELD STREET.

1 Clarke, J.

WALKER STREET.

2 Woodend, S.

4 Jones, George.

6 Wilson, E. A.

8 Satterthwaite, Thos.

10 Todd, G., Nanson, Frances A.

12 Edmondson, W.

16 Oldfield, F.

18 Blyton, W.

20 Clayton, G.

22 Brown, T.

ASKAM VIEW.

1 Walker, Edward.

3 Burton, A.

5 Venables, J.

7 Noble, J.

Ormandy, J., Underdale.

Sharpe, Jos., Bankfield.

Sharpe, Mary Agnes., Bankfield.

DALTON ROAD.

1 Dobson, J. H.

3 Walker, H.

5 Atkinson, J. P.

7 Millican, H. P.

9 Jones, N., Sugden, A.

11 Noble, John.

13 Christopherson, Miss., Smith, Misses.

15 Knipe, Mrs.

17 Brocklebank, H.

19 Brocklebank, J. B.

21 Rawlinson, G.

23 Stuart, Ellen.

25 Dixon, T. E.

27 Vickers, R.

29 Preston, H.

31 Walker, W. C.

33 Foster, Robert.

35 Martin, J.

37 Marshall, J. Thomas.

39 Hartshorn, J.

41 Leece, Henry E.

DALE STREET.

(Left Side.)

1 Marshall, George., Kitchen, F.

3 Nanson, J.

5 Nanson, A.

7 Wilson, W. H.

9 Lloyd, J.

(Right Side.)

2 Webster, E.

4 Brown, H.

6 Walker, Mrs.

8 Newton, D.

10 Birchall, E.

12 Martin, T.

DUDDON VIEW.

1 Kelly, Mrs.

3 Birkett, Mrs.

4 Pickthall, Mrs. Simpson, Mrs.

5 Hunter, J. J.

6 Beaver, Arthur.

7 McNevin, J.

8 Ellis, A. R.

9 Kitchen, W.

11 Shaw, Miss.

Spencer, E., Glenwood.

HOLLOWGATE.

Carruthers, A., Cliff Cottage.

1 Chester, J. N.

4 Preston, Mrs, A.

6 Shaw, J.

8 Stables, W. H.

10 Sanderson, J.

12 Kellet, Mrs. Shipton, B.

14 Fox, Agnes Jane.

16 Sanderson, J.

17 Trenwith, C. H.

19 Blezard, J.

IRELETH

1 Jeffrey, A.

3 Smith, G., Post Office Cottage. Croft Cottage, Parker, Margaret.

4 Chapman, J.

5 Bird, J. W.

6 Postlethwaite, G.

7 Johnston, T.

8 Holdsworth, S. L.

Chapman, Mrs. Airey, W., Brookside Farm.

Mellon, H., J. P., Brook Lea.

Jackson, Mrs., Low Brook Farm.

10 Chapman, J. K.

11 Postlethwaite, J.

12 Smith, E.

13 Dalton, W.

14 Storrer, T.

18 Jones, H.

20a Garforth, A.

21 Kitchin, Mrs.

22 Askew, J.

23 Thompson, T. P.

24 Picthall, I.

25 Lewis, H.

27 Daniells, J. B., Anvil House.

27a Stables, T.

(Ever's Cottages.)

28 Tyson, M.

29 McKeever, D.

30 Stables, J.

31 Johnston, S. H. C.

Slater, W., High Haume.

Carruthers, A., Cliffe Cottages.

Ireleth Schools.

Spencer, Miss. Beulah House.

IRELETH BROW.

(Left side.)

Barker, Henry. *Bay Horse Inn*.

2 Mackereth, W.

3 Chapman, M.

4 Hunter, G. A.

5 Swainson, Mrs.

6 Bell, Thomas.

7 Mossop, A.

8 Inman, J. M.

9 Riley, J. B.

(Right Side.)

St. Peter's Church.

IRELETH ROAD.

(Right Side.)

Baxter, D., Ashdene.

22-24 Constable, Ed. A., *Railway Inn*.

26 Gibson, R.

28 Palmer, G. F.

30 Dixon, G.

32 Towers, William.

34 Scott, E. A.

36 Massicks, J., Rock Lea.

38 Townson, John Tyson.

40 Johnstone, Mrs. E., Johnston, Miss.

178 Wilson, J. W., *Ship Inn*.

192 Hodgeson, P.

230 Ridley, Mrs.

232 Beck, Henry.

234 Beck, Henry C.

236 Warwick, J.

238 Millburn, W.

Watson, Mrs., Croft House.

238a Askew, R.

248 Atkinson, Mrs., Rogerson, Mrs.

250 Atkinson, E.

252 Clark, Annie, Post Office and Grocer.

(Left Side.)

Ridley, Rev. E. W., The Vicarage.

MOOR ROAD.

Berry, E., *Traveller's Rest*.

Hayes, C.

1 Webster, J.

3 Helm, R. P.

5 Strickland, Miss.

7 McGuire, T.

Hool, John Thomas. Keay, W. H., Moor Farm.

Thompson, J., Moor Cottage.

Parker, J., Stewner Park.

Smith, F., Stewner Bank.

Lowther, John., Standish Cote.

Ormandy, Thomas, Powka Reservoir.

Barker, Mrs., Round Hill.

KIRKBY ROAD.

Butler, John. Moorside.

Sharpe, Joseph,. Barrister-at-Law, Bankfield House.

Gilchrist, J., Sharpe's Cottages.

Woods. R.

Challinor, Capt. J., Nether close.

Henderson, W., Old Parsonage.

Langhorn, W., Far Old Park.

Bell, F., Old Park.

PARADISE.

1 Newton, E.

3 Casson, T. M.

5 Knowles, Robert.

7 King, Mrs.

9 Atkinson, Abram.

11 Gardner, James.

13 Atkinson, N.

15 Atkinson, J.

17 Cookson, J. H.

19 Griffin, H.

SUN STREET.

1 Hunter, W.

3 Jackson, Issac.

5 Medcalfe, T. Chappels, W. C.

7 Hodson, W.

9 Mackereth, G. A. Henderson, W.

MARSH GRANGE.

King, J., Marsh Grange Cottage.

Penny, A., Marsh Grange Farm.

An Askam Parade on Duke Street. The building on the right was the Temperance Hotel, latterly the YMCA (Courtesy of Mark MacLean)

FURNESS AND DISTRICT YEAR BOOK 1939

ASKAM with IRELETH.

St Peters Church.- Sunday Services; Holy Communion every Sunday at 8 a.m., and every Sunday at 10.30 a.m. (choral); Evensong, 6.30 p.m.; Children's Service, third Sunday, 2 p.m. The Benefice is of the annual value of £350. The present Vicar is the Rev, W. A. Chare. Churchwardens, G. Fell (Vicar's), and A. Burton (People's); Organist and Choirmaster, W. H. Williams; Parish Clerk, Mrs. I. Pickthall. Superintendent of Askam Sunday School, Walter Williams; Ireleth Sunday School, Miss Watson. Parochial Church Council Secretary, Miss B. Robinson, Sharp Street, Askam.

The Askam Mission.- Holy Communion, 9 a.m. (1st and 3rd Sundays); Evensong and Sermon, 6.30 p.m. (During Winter Months 1st and 3rd Sundays).

Duddon Road Methodist Church.- Minister, Rev. A. U. L. Powell, Wesley Manse, Dalton. Sunday Services, 10.45 a.m. and 6 p.m.; Weeknight Services alternate Thursdays at 7 p.m. Sunday School, 10.15 a.m. and 1.30 p.m. Caretaker, M. Todd, 1 James Street (East).

Beach Street Methodist Church.- Sunday Services 10.45 a.m. and 6.15 p.m. Sunday School, 10 a.m. and 1.45 p.m. Sisterhood, every other Wednesday, 3 p.m. C.E., Wednesday 7.15 p.m.

Church of Christ, Duddon Road.

Gospel Hall, Rankin Hall, Duke Street; Secretary, D. Davis, Coniston Road, Barrow.

Schools.- Askam Senior School; Headmaster, Vacant; Askam Junior and Infants; Miss D. Birch. Ireleth School; Headmistress, Mrs Postlethwaite.

Post Office, Duke Street.- Deliveries, 7.20 a.m., 10.15 a.m. (parcels), 3.15 p.m. Despatches, Box cleared 11 a.m. and 6.30 p.m.; parcels for same despatches, 11 a.m. and 6.30 p.m. Telephone Call Office, Askam 109. J. Moore, Postmaster.

Ireleth P.O. Boxes cleared 10.50 a.m. and 6 p.m. Sub-postmistress, Mrs Cotton.

Unionist Club, Duke Street.- President, Capt. Rankin, M.P.; Steward, W. Picthall; Secretary, R. Noble, Duke Street; Games Secretary, H. Robinson, Sharp Street.

Askam W.U.A.- President, Mrs. Mellon; Chairman, Mrs. T. B. Grice; Secretary, Mrs. Benson, 81, Duddon Road.

Police Station.- Duke Street. Sergeant E. K. Skitt.

Askam and Ireleth Homing Society.- Headquarters, Vulcan Hotel; Secretary, E. Walker, Walker Street, Askam.

Askam Rugby Football Club.- Ground, Duke Street; Headquarters, Railway Hotel.

Askam Tennis Club.- Secretary, Miss Satterthwaite, Walker Street, Askam.

R.O.A.B Duddon Lodge.- Club Room, Furness Tavern.

A.O.F.- Hon. Secretary, W. Wilson, Dale Street, Askam.

Prize Brass Band.- Secretary, Frank Webster, James Street. Conductor, G. A. Cain.

Manchester District Banking Co., Ltd.- Tuesday and Friday, 9.0 to 11.0.

Dunnerholme Golf Club.- Secretary, G. B. Rogerson, 38, Athol Street, Barrow.

Martins Bank Ltd.- Days; Mondays and Friday 10 a.m. to 11.15 a.m.

R.S.P.C.A., Askam and Kirkby.- Hon. Secretary, Mrs. Grice "Netherclose", Ireleth; Committee, Miss Lewis and Mrs. Dickinson.

Mechanics' Loyal Duddon Lodge, Askam.- Secretary (pro. Tem.), Mrs. Borwick, Duke Street.

R.S.P.C.C. Askam and Ireleth.- Secretary, Mrs Pyne, Ashdene, Ireleth.

Askam and Ireleth Community Service Centre, Old Foundry, James Street.- Warden D. Twiname; Corresponding Secretary, Rev. W. A. Chare, The Vicarage, Askam.

MEDICAL LIST.

DOOLEY, JOHN LAWRENCE, Duke Street, Askam-in-Furness, B.Sc., M.B., B.A.O. (Dublin); Late Surgeon, Minister of Pensions Hospital, Drogheda; late Clinical Assistant, Coombe Maternity Hospital, and Maternity Hospital, Dublin.

ALEXANDER PLACE.

1 Twiname, J.

2 Greenop, J.

3 Parkinson, L. T.

4 Storer, T.

5 Lawden, M. J.

BEACH STREET.

(Right Side.)

2 Coward, J., *Wood Merchant.*

24 Kewley, B.

26 Coward, R.

28 Windle, E.

30 Walker, E.

90 Barker, H.

92 Sandham, W.

94 Gaskell, N.

96 Conlin, J. P.

98 Bath, G.

100 Myers, W.

102 Barker, F.

104 Walker, E.

106 Houghton, C.

108 Newton, W.

110 Thexton, R.

112 Forsyth, D.

(Left Side.)

19 Nanson, M.

21 Kitchen, W. P.

23 Noble, M.

25 Kitchen, N. C.

27 Noble, F.

29 Wearing, I.

31 Edmondson, E.

33 Duke, E.

61 Benson, H.

63 Walker, W.

65 Fallows, T.

67 Tyson, W. T.

69 Shepherd, T.

71 Quirk, J. T.

73 Penny, S. S.

75 Gordon, M. E.

Beach Street Methodist Chapel.

91 Walker, J.

93 Postlethwaite, E.

95 Holmes, W.

97 Lewis, G.

CROSSLEY STREET.

(Left Side.)

1 Willerton, E. H.

2 Cain, B. S.

4 Burt, A.

84 Coulson, H.

86 Procter, M.

116 Hardy, A.

(Left Side.)

Fleet, J., *Ivy House.*

Christian Meeting House.

91 Morley, W.

93 Fallows, H.

95 Raven, H.

97 Orrell, T.

121 Quayle, J.

121a Quayle, H.

DUDDON.

2 Johnson, J.

4 Hutton, J. J.

6 Crawford, J.

8 Shaw, W.

DUDDON ROAD.

(Left Side.)

1 & 3 Constable, J. G.

5 Benson, W.

7 Rawlinson, W.

9 Brown, E.

11 Mason, G.

13 Hawley, W. J.

15 Sandham, Jos.

17 Norman, E. A.

19 Townson, W, N.

21 Coupland, E.

23 Smith, W.

25 Wales, W. H.

27 Seddon, J.

27a Stables, R.

29 Pope, A.

31 Cain, S.

61 Myers, J.

63 Mason, H.

65 Mackereth, J.

67 Buxton, W. H.

69 Cross, G.

71 Butcher, E.

73 Taylor, J.

75 Swindle, F. J.

77 Shakley, E.

79 Barker, H.

81 Benson, E.

83 Woodend, H.

85 Fitzsimmons, W.

87 Millican, H. F.

89 Wetherald, E. A.

91 Brown, R.

(Right Side.)

48 Graham, T.

50 Brown, H.

Duddon Road Methodist Church.

52 Wharton, J.

54 Bleazard, C.

Shackley, M. J., *Bungalow.*

Askam Gas Works.

82 Taylor, J. L.

90 Atkinson, D. A., *London House.*

92 Dixon, J.

94 Park, E.

96 Watson, D.

98 Tyson, E. P.

100 Williams, M.

102 Vickers, J. T.

104 Park, J.

106 Brown, T.

108 Wilson, W. H.

110 Crawford, J. T.

112 Kellet, H.

114 Phifer, J.

DUKE STREET.

(Left Side.)

1 Seward, R. W. (Shop).   (Kevin Alexander Collection)

3 Barwick, J. H.

5 Fell, W.

Co-operative Stores.

7 Lewis, J. W.

11 Dooley, Dr. J. L.

13 Vickers, R.

15 Police Station. *Sergt,*

Senior Council Schools.

Unionist Club. Pickthall, W.

19 Noble, R.

21 Woodburn, J.

23 Moore, M.

25 Nixon, T.

27 Evans, C. W.

67 Post Office. Telegraph Office. Moores, J.

71 Duckworth, N.

73 Williams, W. H.

75 Gill, J., *Newsagent etc.*

77 Greenop, J., *Fruiterer.*

79

81 Templeton, W. G., Ormandy, M.

83 Gill and Briscoe, *Confectioners.*

85 Lumsden, B.

87 Ormandy, W., *Grocer*. Burrow, T. C. (house)

89 Atkinson, W., *Butcher.*

91 Stables, R. B. Cross, B., *Boot and Shoe Repairer.*

Blakeman, C. H., *Bungalow.*

Stables, W., *Bungalow.*

129 Stables, J.

131 Shaw, J.

133 McGivern, W. J.

135 Roberts, A.

137 Tyson, H.

139 Constable, E.

141 Lewis, H., *Iron Works Office.*

(Right side.)

56 Trelore, R. S.

58 Houghton, R.

60 Houghton, R.

62 Trelore, E.

64 Rawlinson, W.

64a Smith, R.

66 Jones, W. S.

Manchester and Liverpool District Bank (Tuesday s and Fridays)

94 Mandall, S., *Vulcan Hotel.*

St. John Ambulance Brigade Quarters.

140 White, A., *Furness Tavern*.

DUNNERHOLME.

2 Brocklebank, W. H.

4 Johnson, R. H. *Soutergate Crossing, Kirkby*.

6-8 Steel, I.

Westbury, T., *Railway Crossing*.

FURNACE PLACE.

1 Flood, A.

2 Smith, W.

3 Barnes, W.

4 Wilson, W.

5 Jopson, J. J.

6 Cornthwaite, J.

7 Woodhall, W.

8 Brocklebank, E. H.

9 Robinson, P. H.

10 Alexander, R.

11 Allanson, J.

12 Harvey, J.

13 Armistead, G.

14 Nelson, M. A.

15 Moffatt, F.

15a Fletcher, T.

16 Seward, W.

17 Caine, A.

18 Preston, R.

19 Livesey, B.

20 Eccleston, T.

21 Hutchinson, T.

22 Christie, J.

23 Smith, W.

24 Johnson, W. J.

25 Carter, J. H.

26 Pelter, J.

27 Tyson, H.

28 Newby, J.

29 Newby, J. R.
30 Gillbanks, A.
31 Townson, P. M.
32 Backhouse, F.
33 Turner, L. A.
34 Alexander, E.
35 Woods, W.
36 Hannah, A.
37 Price, E.

GREENSCOE.

Stables, J. E., *Farm.*

1 Miners, I. B., *The Mansion.*
2 Fleet, J. H.
3 Grundy, M. J.
4 Hutton, W.
5 Johnson, N.

Marsden, D., *Byways.*

Phillipson, W., *Greenscoe Lodge.*

Ellwood, H., *Greenhaume Farm.*

GREENHAUME.

Ellwood, H., *The Farm.*

1 Rigg, J. J.
2 Bell, W.
3 Quayle, R.
4 Kavanagh, E.
5 Yates, M.
6 Knowles, A.
7 Chester, W.
8 Webb, R.
9 Kavanagh, John.
10 Wood, R.
11 Kenrick, S.
12 Keen, A.
13 Richardson, W.
14 Hodgson, W.

HARRIS STREET.

(Left Side.)

1 Blackley, A. H.
2 Wilson, J. J.
4 Tyson, A.
6 Waters, C. W.
8 Parker, E. A.
10 Wilson, E. W.
12 Tyson, J.
14 Hulston, W.
16 Rigg, J. B.

JAMES STREET.

1 Barwick, J.
3 Dixon, F.
5 Twiname, E.
7 Webster, F.
9 Dowker, G.
11 Millican, M.
13 Brooks, R.
15 Irving, R. P.
17 Gillbanks, J.
19 Windle, R. H.
21 Wilson, W.
23 Chapman, A.
25 Woodburn, J.
27 Dixon, A.
29 Twiname, D.
31 Wilson, J. H.

JAMES STREET (EAST).

1 Todd, M.
3 Atkinson, J.
5 Askew, J.

(WEST)

2 Crook, J. T.
3 Banks, A. J.
4 Fry, E.

JOHN STREET.

(Right Side.)

20 Kirkby, F. J.

22 Fallows, W.

24 Thompson, J.

26 Hutton, S.

28 Robinson, W. E.

30 McConnell, T.

32 Thurgood, D.

34 Burt, I.

(Left Side.)

29 Hodgson, J.

31 Parromore, S. A.

61 Postlethwaite, J.

63 Thackeray, A.

65 McDaid, P.

67 Windle, W.

LORD STREET.

2 Hewartson, T.

4 Currie, J.

6 Parkes, B. W.

8 Lowe, T.

9 Blezard, T. R., *Tobacco, Sweets, etc.*

10 Woodend, C.

11 Park, W.

Olliver, T. J.

13 Knibbs, G.

15 Kitchen, S.

17 Woodrow, A. J.

19 Rawlinson, T.

MARSH COTTAGES.

Johnson, J., *Marsh Farm.*

4 Hutton, J.

6 Crawford, J.

8 Shaw, w.

Stevens, E., *Near Marsh Bungalow.*

Wardle, S. J., *Cumbria View.*

Wharton, S. J., *Cross Lea.*

Bowness, M. G., *Stavely Bungalow.*

McCormick, O., *Marsh Bungalow.*

Peden, S., *Gosforth Bungalow.*

Everett, W. R., *Langley Marsh.*

MARSH STREET.

1 Kellett, G. H.

2 Hickey, A.

3 Park, A. J.

4 Quine, H.

5 Waddington, J.

6 Twiname, I.

7 Parrington, J.

8 Sawrey, R.

9 Dixon, W.

10 Fryer,

11 Pickthall, H.

12 Olliver, L.

13 Bleasdale, J.

14 Hall, W.

15 Hendley, J.

16 Coward, W. E.

17 Rawlinson, J.

18 Wilson, R.

19 Fell, G.

20 Burgin, W.

21 Twiname, T. L.

22 Bradley, J.

23 Robinson, E.

24 Martin, W. H.

25 Woodend, M.

26 Woodend, E.

27 Hendley, S.

28 Banyard, F. O.

PARK.

Greenhalgh, S.

1 Wells, J. P.

2 Hunter, P. B.

3 Abraham, E. J.

4 Moore, T. D.

5 Riley, J. H.

6 Chapman, A. A.

PARK AVENUE.

(Off Duke Street.)

1 Trenwith, C.

2 Ormand, T. W.

3 Sanderson, H. R.

4 Chester, J.

5 Smith, E.

6 McGuire, T.

7 Bleasdale, J.

8 Alexander, W.

9 Allonby, V. W.

POWKA BECK HOUSE.

Spencer, H. W.

ROANHEAD.

2 Mawson, J.

3 Coward, W. J.

4 Myers, E.

5 Newton, J.

7 Molyneaux, J.

8 Myers, R.

Severs, C., *The Moors*

Gunson, C. E., *Roanhead Farm*.

SANDSCALE.

Hayton, J., *The Farm*.

1 Brown, M. J.

2 Morris, T. R.

3 Nicholson, J. T.

4 Walker, E.

5 Morris, T.

7 Hardman, F.

SCHOOL STREET.

3 Higgin, R., *School House*.

5 Neild, J.

7 Kensley, G.

SHARP STREET.

(Left Side.)

35 Tyson, T.

37 Marsden, S.

39 Hill, W. H.

41 Tubman, T.

43 Fitzjohn, J.

45 Cannon, A.

47 Hornby, R. C.

49 Hargreaves, W. J.

51 Irwin, W.

53 Robinson, G. J.

55 Boulton, R. R.

57 Gaskell, W.

59 Barnes, T. L.

61 Williams, T.

63 Bodley, M. J.

65 Painford, J. W.

67 Garnett, A.

69 Stonehouse, J.

71 Marston, J.

73 Whiteside, P.

75 Logie, G.

77 Price, M. A.

79 Atkinson, W.

117 Thompson, W. H.

119 Berry, J.

121 Askew, H.

123 Cannon, R. H.

125 Stevenson, E.

127 Scuddamore, J.

129 Hutton, J. T.

131 Bowes, T.

133 Robertson, C. E.

135 Cloudsdale, W. H.

137 Stables, N.

139 Cross, R. W.

141 Duncan, J.

143 Wilson, J.

145 Windle, L.

147 Standing, J.

149 Stephenson, A.

151 Houghton, E.

153 Fallows, G.

(Right Side.)

2 Smith, J.

4 Berry, J.

6 Richards, C.

8 Dawson, G.

10 Boyers, E.

12 Smith, B. C.

14 Vickers, W. T.

16 Preston. J.

18 Varcoe, H.

20 Sharp, J.

22 Fell, G. H.

24 Relph, R.

26 Wearing, W.

28 Kirkby, J.

30 Mailes, F.

32 Cross, B.

34 Morris, E.

36 Peakman, J. E.

38 Atkinson, J.

40 Cain, M.

42 Kewley, W.

44 Atkinson, E.

46 Flinn, M. A.

48 Pendlebury, R. A.

50 Barnes, J.

52 Windle, A. B.

54 Bodley, E.

56 Stephenson, J.

58 Gaskell, A.

66 Lewis, J.

68 Chester, T.

70 Kellett, T.

72 Shaw, S.

74 Robinson, R.

76 Wadeson, J. W.

78 Smith, H., *Fish Shop*.

82 Atkinson, J.

84 Quine, D.

86 Oliver, C.

88 Black, J.

90 Coward, W.

STAFFORD STREET.

(Right Side.)

1 Leece, J.

3 Heeling, J.

5 Twiname, I.

7 Barnes, M.

11 Riley, J.

13 Newby, M. A.

15 Grice, W. F.

17 Stott, T.

19 Sharp, J.

(Left Side.)

2 Nelson, M.

4 Alexander, J.

6 Brown, F.

8 O'Conner, M. R.

(Courtesy of David Robinson)

10 Coats, M. J.

12 Wilson, S.

14 Barnes, J. H.

16 Dockeray, E.

18 Hornby, W. A.

20 Jackson, H.

22 Rigg, B.

STEEL STREET.

(Left Side.)

33 New, R. J.

35 Hoggarth, W. H.

37 Rigg, J.M.

39 Parrington, H.

41 Pharo, S.

43 Leece, J.

45 Chapman, G. W.

47 Roberts, W. T.

49 Gee, J. N.

51 Marshall, J.

53 Clinton, D. P.

55 Delaney, T.

57 Jackson, F.

59 Whiteside, R. E.

61 Quayle, G.

63 Myers, W.

65 Collister, R.

67 Postlethwaite, R. G.

69 Butcher, G. H.

71 Neild, T. E.

73 Tomlinson, P.

75 Barrow, J.

77 Quayle, W.

79 Askew, W.

81 King, W. H.

83 Peutherer, W. C.

85 Woods, T.

87 Dent, F.

89 Ware, H. O.

91 Kellett, M. E.

93 Pawley, F. W.

95 Chappels, J. A.

97 Cain, A. J.

99 Woolcock, J. H.

101 Allonby, R.

103 Postlethwaite, R.

105 Carter, W.

107 Standing, H.

109 Stevenson, B.

111 Walker, T.

113 Birbeck, S.

115 Townson, J. T.

117 Tyson, J.

119 Ormandy, J.

121 Robson, W. H.

123 Whittam, J.

125 Shepherd, M. A.

127 Procter, S. E.

129 Tyson, E. J.

131 Braithwaite, J. R.

133 Burns, J.

135 Bourne, J.

137 Conway, J.

139 Knight, T.

(Right Side.)

36 Chappels, S.

38 Cox, W. E.

40 Kellet, J.

42 Hanna, J. J.

44 Boulton, T.

46 Wilson, W. E.

48 Brown, A.

50 Neild, J.

52 Trelore, B. S.
54 Blamire, E.
56 Lloyd, W.
58 Chappels, R.
60 Dunkley, J.
62 Speight, I.
64 Windle, E.
66 Wilson, W. E.
68 Pearce, H. S.
70 Trelore, T. W.
72 Marshall, F. C.
78 Jackson, W. P.
80 Dent, F.
82 Peutherer, R.
84 Birbeck, H.
86 Mawson, F.
88 Butcher, J.
90 Bodley, F. M.
92 Holmes, S.
94 Hewitson, W.
96 Vinicombe, M.
98 Wood, T.
100 Cussons, A.
102 Coward, R. B.
104 Carter, J. W.
106 Rawlinson, F.
108 Jackson, F.
110 Askew, J. T.
112 Quayle, R.
114 Coward, M.

VICTORIA STREET.

(Right Side.)

1 and 3 Thompson, M., *Askam Hotel.*
5 Smith, W. G.
7 Leece, Wm.
9 Atkinson, J.

11 Walker, J. R.
13 Wallace, J.
15 Guy, G.

(Left Side.)

12 Wallace, J.
14 Brown, J. G. R.
16 Bell, W. J.
18 Finlayson, R.
20 Alexander, H.
22 Crossley, J.
24 Atkinson, Wm. B.
26 Alexander, J.
28 Jinks, T.
30 Trelore, W. A.
32 Jinks, W.
34 Yates, H.
36 Murray, J.
38 Williams, G.
40 Hartley, E. H.
42 Backhouse, J. D.
44 Backhouse, E.
Brockbank, E., *Sea View.*

WALKER STREET.

2 Constable, J.
4 Jones, G.
6 Wilson, E. A.
8 Satterthwaite, T.
10 Nanson, F. A.
12 Walker, H.
16 Long, F.
18 Robinson, E.
Scott, M., (Nurse.)
20 Walker, I.
22 Gaskell, J.

ASKAM VIEW.

1 Walker, E.

3 Butcher, T. W.

5 Johnson, J.

7 Bogie, E.

Ormandy, J., *Under Dale*.

Smith, W., *Ashley Bank*.

Walker, E. N., *Ennerdale*.

Sharpe, M. A., *Bankfield*

DALTON ROAD.

1 Relph, S.

3 Atkinson, J. P.

5 Bayliss, J. T.

7 Benson, R.

9 Noble, I. P.

11 Boardley, B. M.

13 Armstrong, E.

15 Knipe, A.

17 Walker, E.

19 Brocklebank, T. B.

21 Sunderland, J. R.

23 Stuart, E. L.

25 Dixon, T. E.

27 Fitzsimmons, H.

29 Cartmel, W.

31 Walker, W. C.

33 Foster, R.

35 Martin, J.

37 Marshall, J. T.

39 Mercer, T.

41 Leece, H. E.

DALE STREET.

(Left Side.)

1 Kitchen, F.

3 Shaw, J. T.

5 Eccles, W. R.

7 Wilson, W. H.

9 Robinson, T. F.

(Right Side.)

2 Johnson, H.

4 Hughes, T. H.

6 Barton, I.

8 Newton, D.

10 Birchall, E.

12 Mooney, A.

DUDDON VIEW.

1 Campbell, G. G.

3 Garforth, G.

4 Naylor, E. T.

5 Southward, M.

6 Beavers, J.

7 Ridley, J. M.

8 Burch, J.

9 Kitchen, M. J.

11 Askew, R.

Steel, W., *Glenwood*.

HOLLOWGATE.

4 Atkinson, F.

6 Woods, R.

8 Broome, G. E.

10 Sanderson, D.

12 Preston, M.

14 Satterthwaite, F.

16 Sanderson, J.

17 Trenwith, C. H.

19 Sanderson, H. R.

IRELETH.

Walton, M. E., *Cliffe Cottage*.

(Sharp's Cottages.)

1 Bell, W. G.

3 Chester, F.

Stables, T., *Mollycroft*.

3 Henley, G.

4 Henley, G.

5 Gilchrist, J.

6 Postlethwaite, G.

7 Venables, J.

8 Holdsworthy, A.

Chapman, R., *Garth House.*

10 Clapham, J. K.

11 Postlethwaite, D. A.

Coward, R.

Johnson, W., *Brookside Farm.*

Calderbank, A., *Brooklea.*

Jackson, E. A., *Lowbrook Farm.*

20 Long, W. E.

20a Brunt, M.

21 Pope, A.

22 Thompson, F.

23 Askew, J. C.

24 Picthall, I.

25 Eadie, A.

Kendall, T. A., *Brookfield.*

(Brook Vale.)

1 Smith, W.

2 Jackson, J.

3 Burton, A.

27 Daniell, J. B., *Anvil House.*

(Evers Cottages.)

28 Tyson, E.

29 Griffiths, J. W.

30 Brown, A.

31 Swindle, T.

Slater, W., *High Haume Farm.*

Dunlop, H., *High Haume Bungalow.*

Ireleth Schools.

Spencer, A. A., *Beulah.*

A view of Askam Police Station, Post Office, Doctors, Co-op, Shops and Train Station. (Kevin Alexander Collection)

ACKNOWLEDGEMENTS & BIBLIOGRAPHY

I am sincerely grateful for all the help I have received over the last 20 months it has taken me to bring this beast together. Above all I need to thank the team at Cumbria Archive Centre, Barrow. Especially Susan Benson and Selena Kendall for their patience and professionalism. I would like to thank my wonderful wife and brilliant lads for their patience and understanding while I spent time away from them during this endeavour.

I would like to take this opportunity to thank the following for all the help they have given me.

- Janice Cumming (Askam History Club)
- John Clegg
- Askam Village School
- George Henry
- Brenda Jefferson
- Dave Huitson
- Daniel Edwards
- Steve Alexander
- David Robinson
- William & Hilda Eccles
- Maxine & David Hughes
- Dorothy Alexander
- Jan & Pete Bigland
- Ray & Jane Alexander
- Peter Burt
- Garry Glew
- Leslie Eveson
- Ted Grayless
- Jeanette Shepherd
- Mark MacLean
- Peter Holmes
- James Collinge (Furness Brick)
- Walter Jinks
- Muriel & Dennis Wilson
- Askam Rugby Club
- Kelly Alexander

BOOKS;

ASKAM IRON, Alan Harris.

BARROW RUGBY, IN THE BEGINNING, THE UNION YEARS, Dave Huitson.

THE EARLY IRON INDUSTRY OF FURNESS AND DISTRICT, Alfred Fell.

FURNESS, PAST AND PRESENT, J. Richardson.

LOW FURNESS, PAST AND PRESENT, John Garbutt.

RED EARTH, Dave Kelly.

RED EARTH REVISITED, Brian Cubbon, Peter Sandbatch, Colin Woolard.

SCHNEIDER, A. G. Banks.

TIMESPANNER BLOG.